THE CULT OF THE WILL

The Cult of the Will

of the

Will

GERARD A. BESSON

Published by
Paria Publishing Company Limited
Second Avenue, Cascade, Trinidad, W.I.
Email: paria@trinidad.net
www.pariapublishing.com
www.content-providing.com
www.pariapublishing.blogspot.com

Printed by Lightning Source, U.S.A.

ISBN 978-976-8054-82-1

"ALL HISTORY IS CONTEMPORARY HISTORY"
BENEDETTO CROCE

IN MEMORY OF MY FATHER, JOSEPH BESSON,
TO MY SONS, ANDRE, AARON & DOMINIC;
& ALSO TO CELEBRATE THE 1000TH ANNIVERSARY
OF THE BUILDING OF THE CHURCH
AT BESSON, SITUÉE DANS LE DÉPARTEMENT DE L'ALLIER ET LA
RÉGION AUVERGNE. FRANCE,
WHICH TOOK PLACE IN 2009.

Map of the Lesser Antilles.
From "Six Months in the West Indies", Coleridge, 1825.

CONTENTS

Acknowledgements   8
Introduction   12

PART I

1 François Besson   16
2 François Moves to Trinidad   47
3 Fédon's Revolution   56
4 The Afro-French Creole Society   69
5 The End of Plantation Slavery   83
6 The 19th Century Descendants of François   100
7 The Children of Charles François Besson & Rose Honoré   119
8 The Bessons in Freemasonry   121
9 The Besson Family to the Present Day   132

PART II

Introduction to the Second Part   139
1 The Intellectual Roots of the Eric Williams Narrative   143
2 The Social Stratum of the Williams Family   163
3 The Cult of the Will   177
4 Formulation of the Political Personality   203
5 The Neurosis Manifests   212
6 The Afro-French Creole Narrative   233
7 Conclusion: The Williams Legacy   248

APPENDICES

Appendix I:
Some Wills of the Comissiong, Loreilhe & de Boissière families   255
Appendix II:
The Use of the Particle "De"   267
Appendix III:
Some Wills of the Besson Family   268
Appendix IV:
Descendants of Geraldine Carige   273

Bibliography & References   274

Index   279

Acknowledgements

This study could not have been undertaken had it not been supported, encouraged, aided and contributed to by my wife Alice. She was translator, guide and travelling companion. She, with utmost patience, listened to the several arguments, discussions and backs and forths between informants, proof readers, critics and myself over the two year period in which it was written. For all of the above and for your timely interventions and contributions and a lot more, I can only say thank you Alice.

The catalyst, however, for all of this was my friend and teacher Professor Bridget Brereton. It was she who with great generosity allowed me to read some of her research work, articles and published papers on the topic of competing narratives. She introduced me to the idea that in the equinox of the historical narratives, the point in time when one interpretation of the past gives way to another, is where the historian might explore and discover those elements in which the die of the future is cast. Thank you Dr. Brereton.

Professor Gordon Rohlehr, quite unbeknownst to himself, was of great help as he with tact and kindness in his books of essays, *My Strangled City* and *The Shape of that Hurt*, pointed out the scapegoating tendency that has entered our collective psyche. Professor Selwyn Ryan, through his books and in our conversations, rendered invaluable help and guided my thinking with particular regard to the politics of the Williams narrative. He allowed me to develop ideas in those conversations that I know he felt were speculative, but in being the *eminence grise* that he has become, quite afforded me all the rope I needed. Thank you, gentlemen.

Ronald Harford kindly gave me valuable Grenadian archival material and Michael Jessamy of St. George's Grenada, courageously undertook to search the island's ancient records for traces of our families' past. Freda Scott kindly made available her prodigious memory of things Grenadian and on many an afternoon and well into the gloaming, evoked the shades of times long past. Thanks for the memories. Thanks to Hazel Pillai née Comissiong for making available the Comissiong genealogy and the will of her ancestor Domingo Comissiong of St. George's, Grenada, thanks too for the photographs of your family, and for the careful reading of the manuscript and for lending me Beverly Steele's *Grenada - A History of its People,* Jenelle Comissiong kindly gave me permission to use her photograph. John Sellier, Gregory Wight, Vida Pocock and the Espinet sisters were very helpful in sharing their memories of those heady days that saw the end of Empire and the advent of the Williams narrative. Adrian Camps-Campins' kind words and encouragement were very timely, not to mention the visuals he let me have use of. Thank you Adrian.

There are others who are no longer with us who shaped this work even before it was actually conceived. They are my de Boissière relatives, Ralph de Boissière, whose letters from Australia were always informative and a delight to receive. Mervyn Williams, who wrote from New York, sharing his memories of growing up with his elder brother Eric. Their sister, Flora Gittens passed on to me the valuable research work undertaken by their cousin Ernest Laborde of St. Vincent on the history of the Comissiong, Smith, Hunt and Williams families, and generous with her time, gave me several insightful interviews. Thanks as well to Patricia Gittens for sharing with me her memories of her cousin Phillipa Laborde and for letting me have pictures of her uncle Dr. Eric Williams and her grandparents Thomas Henry Williams and Eliza Williams. Michael Pocock, who researched and wrote *Out of the Shadows of the Past,* a history of the de Gannes and the de Boissière families out of which came a quantity of new information, some of which is presented here. Andrea MacCarthy and Enid Hosten née Boissière let me read some of the letters and family papers, and were very helpful in recalling the way of life enjoyed by the descendants of the Free People of Colour in Trinidad at the turn of the 19th century.

The same can be said for some of my father's relatives and connections; my stepmother Clementine Besson, for passing on some of his child-hood memories; Josephine Lezama, who remembered him as a young man; Theresa (Terry) Bedford née Gantaume, who kindled my interest in doing the Besson research, as did Emanuel (Noche) Jean-Marie Lange. Pauline (Polly) Gellizeau née Sorzano, passed on to me all she knew of our history; Madeléine Léotaud née de Gannes, and Maurice and Basil de Gannes, shared their memories of my father with me. From them all came valuable documentary material, photographs, a host of memories, hospitality and some very good times, thanks so much.

The late Lionel Seemungal, S.C., Masonic historian and archivist, wrote books and papers that were of considerable help to me in writing this work; thanks to him I was able to piece together the activities of some of our more obscure ancestors. My appreciation must be expressed to French author and academic Cécile Révauger, who introduced me to the activities of the late18th century British Freemasons. Paul de la Bastide, from whose voluminous genealogical records I was able to create the fam-ily trees shown herein, and from whose collection of family photographs I was able to draw, thanks Pablo. For visuals I must say thanks to Geoffrey MacLean for letting me use some of his Michel Jean Cazabon reproduc-tions. The same must be said of the National Museum of St. George's, Grenada. To which I must add my gratitude to Vel Lewis, curator of the National Museum in Port-of-Spain, for his permission to use some of the visuals that are held there.

M. Rossignol and his circle of friends in the French Antilles were generous with their time and with their considerable knowledge of the French presence in the Caribbean during the 17th and 18th centuries, *merci beaucoup mes compères, j'espère que le goût de nôtre présence continuera et que nos descendents resembleront leurs ancêtres, particulièrement leur charme et generosité d'esprit* . . . .

Thanks go as well to the helpful staff at the Archives Nationales and the Bibliotheque Nationale in Paris. My appreciation has to be expressed to the staff of the *Mairie* of the Village of Besson in the Auvergne, France, for allowing us to look at and make use of their valuable records, books and documents. I should mention the surprise and the pleasure it was to meet *Mlles.* Mossion and Thibaudeau, our very distant relatives who we met in the medieval city of St. Saturnin de Pons in 2008. The memory of their spontaneous welcome and hospitality will stay with us for a long time.

I must thank Fr. Anthony de Verteuil who willingly shared with me some of the material gathered by him while doing research in the National Archives in Port-of-Spain for his book, *The Black Earth of South Naparima,* and for reading and remarking on some of the material that has gone into this work. I thank him also for allowing me the use of the photograph of the house on the corner of Besson Street and Piccadilly Street.

I would like to thank the staff of the National Archives, and those of the Registrar General's office in Port-of-Spain, where I was able to read the wills of several persons mentioned herein, to the ladies of the Presbytery of the Cathedral of the Immaculate Conception and to the helpful staff of Archbishop's House in Port-of-Spain for their willingness and patience. Kim Johnson was generous with his collection of images and I would like to thank him for this.

Thanks to Simon Lee this work is a little shorter. Thank you Simon for your insights and for helping me to say things that I did not know anything about. Jannine Horsford was the first proofreader, editor and commentator of this work. Her insight and clarity prompted some serious stocktaking, thank you Jannine, I am especially grateful to Mrs. Hazel Pillai née Jagassar for her careful reading and well thought-through remarks. Professor Ramesh Deosaran was generous with his time, plain speaking and with his encouragement, I was especially heartened by his remark that I ". . . have created a serious challenge to orthodoxy." Well, for any aspiring historian, who could ask for more? I am sure that there are others who have encouraged, helped, listened, given, and shared in the making of this study of our past possible—to them all I say thanks.

INTRODUCTION

This study concerns aspects of the Afro-French Creole historical narrative of Grenada and Trinidad from about the mid 18th century. It was prompted by a conversation that I had with distinguished social historian, author and university lecturer, Professor Bridget Brereton. We had been discussing the manner in which the post-colonial narrative of Trinidad and Tobago, which had come into existence with independence in 1962, had treated the18th and19th century European planters and businessmen, sometimes referred to as "the planter class," and their descendants.

I complained, somewhat naïvely perhaps, that a significant aspect of the current narrative, tends on the one hand to stereotype the European planters and their descendants as "villains" and on the other hand characterises the African slaves, and latterly their descendants, as "victims". To my mind, the idea of "inherited victimhood" was as flawed and reprehensible as the notion of "inherited guilt".

When I suggested that the colonists, in the context of the European reality of their day, were brave and adventurous, and that they possessed courage and vision, the professor responded with obvious sincerity: "Do you want to make them heroes?"

I felt at the time, that the idea of treating the colonists as the "planter class," and not attempting to understand the European pioneers in the context of their time and as individuals, each with his own circumstances, was a mistake. I instinctively objected to the apportioning of collective guilt. This notion is reflective of Marxist determinism, which categorises people morally not as individuals, but as members of a particular economic class. This view abandons the notion of individual guilt, and with it the entire Judeo-Christian ethic of personal responsibility, by denying any importance to the individual. I felt compelled to challenge this scapegoating—the result of Marxist dialectic and psychological impulse—which stigmatises a group of individuals (usually a minority) according to the conduct of some individuals belonging to that group in the distant past. This treatment is perceived by today's academic standards as fundamentally immoral—or at best as academically unsound. Somehow, in the case of the people of European descent in the Caribbean, scapegoating seems to have silently replaced rigorous academic analysis and treatment, and I decided to research this issue and to examine, if at all possible, its origins in the context of Trinidad and Tobago's postcolonial experience.

As a result of that conversation with Professor Brereton I got out the scattered notes, family trees and various pieces of information that I had gathered or that had been sent to me on the life of François Besson and his descendants and those on Dr. Eric Eustace Williams, the first Prime Minister of Trinidad and Tobago and his extended family.

What follows in part one is hopefully not a conventional genealogical history per se. It is an outline, and one hopes sufficiently delineated, to get a glimpse of the individual who founded the *branche américaine* or New World branch of my father's family. It speaks of the *plaçage* (concubinage) during the period of plantation slavery and afterwards, and discusses the long-term effects of this on the emerging society. It also tells of family members, children of the *plaçage,* set adrift on a sea of war, becoming part of the racial, social, and political revolutions that swept the Caribbean and South America during the late18th and the early 19th centuries. Revolutions that produced heros, but also fratricides; young men who were capable of murdering their own kin.

For the second part, I examined the material in my possession concerning the family of Dr. Eric Williams, who was related to my mother through the de Boissières. I will comment on the manner in which the Williams family was affected by the Afro-French Creole colonial experience. I will also remark on the outcome of their interface with the dominant British colonial system during the 19th century and the first half of the 20th, and how this may have shaped Dr. Williams' political personality.

Mixed-race people, "Free Blacks and People of Colour," [1] in Trinidad in 1834—at the end of slavery—numbered some 12,006 persons, there were also 3,993 persons of European descent and 20,656 who had been enslaved Africans. [2] A crucial issue for the People of Colour, that is mixed-race people, from the early 18th century onwards was that of gaining social recognition and advancement. The way to achieve this was to be given an education, or some form of training, and, or, to receive an inheritance from one's European relations. Just as important, was to bear the name of one's European relations and as such be able to share in that family's prestige. If this was forthcoming, the coloured individual and his immediate family would be seen by his contemporaries as a beneficiary, a victor, so to speak, of what I call the "cult of the will." His European connections could cause him to be perceived among his peers as having good breeding, coming from an acceptable family, and as such, depending on his education, grasp of European style and behaviour, as being respectable. However, if he was not included in the will or did not benefit from a bequest, he could become its victim, he may slip into poverty and suffer consequences that in a real way would be the opposite of those enjoyed by the beneficiaries.

It will also be shown that not only black and coloured people became the victims of the cult of the will, but that persons of European descent could be among those whose legacies would elude them.

In the opening decades of the 20th century, the Williams family found themselves in the unenviable situation of having fallen into indigence, although possessing the right credentials both in terms of respectability and of pedigree. This had happened because the family had been cheated of more than one legacy rightfully its own—plainly a miscarriage of justice. From this familial debacle as well as other unfortunate circumstances would emerge a charismatic political personality.

This was Dr. Eric Williams, 1911–1981. He was an historian turned

---

1   Free Blacks and People of Colour is a term used to describe the descendants of the Europeans and the slaves who were legally free and as such might enjoy certain rights and privileges, particularly those outlined in the Cedula of Population of 1783.

2   Wood, Donald, *Trinidad in Transition*, p. 44

politician. I will suggest that he, drawing on his and his family's experiences—his education, from the times in which he was living, the people who influenced him, and from being convinced of his position—was able to mount a counter discourse to the dominant narrative of the West, the British Empire's interpretation of the past with regard to the African slave trade and the reason for its ending, which, according to British historians and politicians, had been founded on the principles of "justice and humanity." I will suggest that Dr. Williams' political personality was constructed around 18th and 19th century events and that his perception of these events would eventually produce a political culture in which the role of the victim and the perpetuation of guilt were as readily embraced as they were easily politicised.

I will pose these questions: did Williams' recasting of history produce a usable past, one that could be placed in the service of conceptions and needs of the future?

Did politicising inherited victimhood result in the shedding of moral responsibility, a blurring of the difference between right and wrong, the assertion of entitlement at times unearned or undeserved, and the claiming of moral superiority over those not so victimised, in the population at large in the post-independence period? Did this allow for the psychological mechanism of scapegoating, based on the notion of inherited guilt, to become a part of the political discourse of Trinidad and Tobago? And finally, has the Williams narrative come to a close, now made irrelevant with the election of Barack Obama as the first mixed-race President of the United States of America? President Obama has, along with several American academics and thinkers, criticised the politicising of victimhood and its continued relevance to African American politics, indeed to world politics. Would this signal a new trope, perhaps a radical change in how history will be interpreted and presented and the manner in which new historical narratives will shape and guide political cultures in the future? Has the Obama narrative replaced the Williams narrative?

Gérard A. Besson
21 April, 2010

A view of St. George's, Grenada, as a French possession in the 18th century. (National Museum, Grenada)

FRANÇOIS BESSON: GRENADA
1

Eli François Xavier Besson, was born in 1734. He was, *natif de St. Saturnin de Pons, diocèse de Saintes en Saintonge, France*. He was the fourth and last child of Pierre Besson and his wife Elizabeth, née Thibaudeau. [1]

Pierre Besson was the Royal Notary [2] at Pons and either he, or an uncle also called Pierre, had been listed among the notables by Pierre d'Hozier, Royal Historiographer and Genealogist of France.

Pierre Besson's reference in d'Hozier reads: *Besson, Pierre, ecuyer, No. d'ordre de d'Hozier 970. D'azur à une croix alaissée d'argent cantonnée dont les angles de quatre bezants, de mesme et chargée de 2 anneamy ovales passés en sautoir et entravaillés de gules format 4 coeurs vides et équipoles en pairle*

---

1   Registres Paroissiaux de Gosier (Guadeloupe) and the baptismal registry of Pons.
2   The Royal Notaries or Advocates were public officials nominated by the Keeper of the Royal Seals. They were trained jurists and formed the membership of the *parlements*, or High Courts of France. They were administrative magistrates, and specialised in legal draughtsmanship with particular regard to land transactions.

et contre-pairle l'un dans l'autre brouchant un toute. [3] Pierre Besson may have been a descendant of Pierre Besson of the village of Besson in the Bourbonnais, who was, in 1338, the *Reccour Royal* at Poitou. Poitou and Saintonge in Western France are in close proximity to each other. Patents of nobility had been granted in the 14th century to the *Seigneurs de Besson* of the village of that name in the *Auvergne, diocèse de Souvigny en Bourbonnais.* [4]

François' first marriage was to Marianne Esnard (also spelt Isnard), who might have been a relative, in that his grandmother was Marguerite Esnard. François and Marianne were married in 1762. (She may have died in childbirth in Grenada in the West Indies.) They had a daughter named Marie Françoise Adelaïde Besson de Beaumanoir, born 1763.

Marianne had inherited from her parents Soubise estate, 350 acres, in Grenada. There was also a sum of 50,000 *livres*, which was stipulated in their marriage contract as "a separate estate of the intended wife and to belong exclusively to her and to the heirs of her own stock and line independent of the community formed between husband and wife as to the residue of their property…" [5] Their daughter would inherit this upon her majority.

François and his young bride Marianne Esnard may have journeyed to the Caribbean representing the extended families' attempt to create an investment there and to escape the hard times being experienced in France. Coming from a background that appears to have involved working in the French legal system, François appears to have held various administrative positions in addition to being a farmer and planter.

Michael Jessamy, Grenadian writer and researcher, who conducted research into the Grenada records for me in 2003, remarked that it would appear that "M. Eli François Xavier Besson de Beaumanoir was sent to

---

3   Registre Heralogique de d'Hozier: registres de dessins de l'Armorial de France de 1696

4   Pierre and Louis de Besson, Seigneurs de Besson, de Verneuillet: Archives Nationales Annobl. J J, No.149, VIII, 1379. 176. J J, No. 200 . 1385 (microfilm)

5   Indenture 1785. Grenada, Registry Office.

Grenada by the French government as a *Rapporteur*, [6] as he was dealing with many influential persons on the island and that he was a member of the Council prior to the British conquest of 1762."

François may have previously held the position of *Ordonnateur* [7] before 1762. Jessamy had listed the members of the French Council as MM. La Mere, *Ordonnateur*, Prudhomme, Noel, Besson de Beaumanoir, de Gannes de la Chancellerie, Molenier, and Olivier, who apparently was a some time substitute for the *procureur général du Roy*. Jessamy had the impression that François was sometimes acting as *Ordonnateur* and at times acting *procureur général du Roy*.

François, according to the *Journal of an old inhabitant of Saint Marie 1745–1765,* [8] was in Martinique in 1754. In ships' lists at the National Archives in Paris, he sailed from Marseille in 1754 for Haiti; at a later time, he is referred to as a lieutenant of artillery. [9]

"Grenada had been a French possession from the mid-17th century, when in 1665 the Count de Cerillac sold his rights to Grenada to the French West India Co. for 10,000 crowns, and it remained in the company's possession until its dissolution by Royal Edict in December 1674, when along with the company's other colonies Grenada passed under the domination of the French Crown," notes the Grenada Handbook of 1909. It continues: "For the next eighty-eight years the French colony, notwithstanding many wars and rumours of wars around it, appears to have enjoyed the blessings of peace and a measure of prosperity which

---

6   *Rapporteur*: judge who presented a summary of the evidence uncovered by the investigating magistrate to all the judges appointed to hear a case.

7   *Ordonnateur*: an agent of authority at the head of a department, a local authority, a public institution or service whod has, in addition to his duties as a director, a financial power of decision. However, according to the principle of independence between the officers and accountants, he has no jurisdiction to directly handle public funds.

8   "L'encadrement français de l'île de la Grenade en 1782" by Jacques Petitjean Roget in Cahier 15, 1985, du Centre de Généalogie et d'Histoire des Isles d'Amérique, pp. 9 and 13, d'apres "Etrennes mignonnes de la Granade pour l'an de grace 1782", possession d'un habitant de Trinidad. Philippe Cottreill, 2003

9   ibid.

is evidenced by its population growth. [This observation obviously does not apply to the enslaved population] In 1700, its European population was 257; 53 Free Blacks; 525 slaves, on 3 sugar plantations and 52 indigo estates. In 1753 there were 1,263 Europeans; 175 Free Blacks and 11,991 slaves on 83 sugar estates; 2,725,600 coffee trees; 150,300 cocoa trees, and 8,000 cotton trees."

During this period in France there was widespread poverty. Some historians, Will Durant in his *Rousseau and Revolution* for example, describe conditions as close to famine. The majority of the population was reduced to "walking skeletons" as the wars and the extravagance of the court of Louis XV took a heavy toll on the population and the country's resources. "Thousands of acres farmed in the seventeenth century were left uncultivated in 1760, and were reverting to wilderness. Livestock was depleted, fertilizer was lacking, and the soil was starved." [10] It is not surprising that an adventurous young man, the third son and fourth child, would seek his fortune in the colonies.

François' roots seem to have been in the hamlet of Tanzac, close to the medieval city of Pons in Saintonge in Western France, where his antecedents have been recorded since 1605.

The Besson family had married into the Esnard family three times since 1605 and into the Thibaudeau family twice during this period. These family names, all listed by d'Hozier, have connections with the legal profession, or the "nobility of the robe, *noblesse de robe*," as it was called in pre-revolutionary France. Other alliances through marriage, such as with Drourad, Mossion, Landon, Brousse, Fleury and Fouquet, to name a few, connect them to the land owning families of Poitou, Aunis and Saintonge.

François came from a family described as "ancient" [11] in which legal office may have become hereditary from the 12th century. Junian Besson had been a judge in the city of Limoges in 1176. [12]

---

10   Durant, *Rousseau and Revolution*, p. 76.

11   Rev. hist. de l'Ouest, Doc I, 52w

12   *Gallia Regia*, National Archives, Paris

View of the town and harbour of St. George's, Grenada, from the hill above Belmont, showing the barracks and Richmond Hill on the right and Fort George on the left. Drawn by Captain H.A. Turner, Royal Artillery. (National Museum, Grenada)

Charles the Great had created "palsgraves" in the 8th century as judges and magistrates to adjudicate over the legal system of the Franks.[13] As with many callings, professions and trades during the Middle Ages, the learning, knowledge and practice of the law were passed from father to son.

The name Besson is Gallo-Roman and is derived from the Latin Bettius, or Vettius, suggesting a Latin or Roman remnant in Gaul that might have retained, knowledge and practice of the law in a family dating from the start of the Middle Ages, circa 600 A.D. Archeological digs in the area show that the village was originally sited on a Roman *villa*. Documents kept at the town hall in Besson show that in the year 915 A.D. in the presence of the Lord of Bourbon L'Archambault, Hugo and Rotilde "Behson" donated the village to the Abbey of Cluny, [14] founded 910. Pierre Bes-

13   Durant, *The Age of Faith*, p. 463
14   Collas, Henri, *Besson–Essai de Monographie*, 1968, reference to *Le 24-4 1104 Par. Pascal*

Green: estates owned by the extended Besson family, sons in law of François Besson.
Red: estates owned by the Roume family, two of which were called St. Laurent.
Purple: De Gannes estate

Retraîte, Canteloupe estates, owned by the in-laws of François

Soubise, (LaBay) came to François' upon the death of his first wife's parents (Esnard).

Belvedere with Mount Qua Qua was owned by Rose Roume, née de Gannes. Later owned by Julien Fédon

Bellevue, Richmond and Balthazar estates owned by François Besson

Mount d'Or

St. George's estate

Point Salines owned by François Besson

Map of Grenada after the survey of Monsieur Pinel in 1763. From: "A Topographical Description of the Island of Grenada" by Lieutenant Daniel Paterson, London 1780. (Harford)

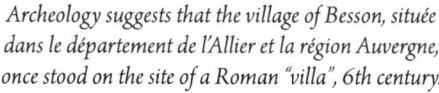

Archeology suggests that the village of Besson, située dans le département de l'Allier et la région Auvergne, once stood on the site of a Roman "villa", 6th century. (?) Evidence of its Roman past is kept in the 11th century church, where the mythological twin founders of the village are to be seen, top left. This may have been the "lares," familiars or genius loci, the household gods of the Roman family of Bettius. The name Besson is derived from the Latin Bettius, meaning two or twin.

There is documentary evidence that the village was presented to the Order of Cluny (founded 910) in the year 915 by Hugo and Rotilde "Behson" in the presence of the Lord of Bourbon L'Archambault, Aimon Meroving Bourbon, Baron de Bourbon. The church of St. Martin in Besson; was built in 1009.

The Duchy of Bourbon came into existence in about 1323 upon the marriage of Robert of France, Count of Clermont and son of Louis IX of France (Saint Louis, depicted in the church window above), to Beatrice, heiress of the Lords of Bourbon L'Archambault. Sire Everard de Besson was Seneschal of the fortress Bourbon L'Archambault in the 14th century. Right, the Romanesque doors to the one thousand year-old church; below, a medallion showing the arms of the seigneurs of Besson which were granted to Pierre Besson in 1379.

Top, left and right: Rue de la Loi (street of the law) in the city of Limoges might have been the address of Junian Besson, a judge there in 1176.
Middle: The entrance to the château in the city of Souvigny in the Bourbonnais. This was the duchy of Bourbon's administrative centre; the sires de Besson were its seigneurs intermittently from the 13th to 16th century. Left: detail of the Bourbon ducal palace in the city of Moulins, where Pierre Besson in 1343, as notary to the dukedom, made amendments to the existing land tax laws.

Top: The residence of the Notary Royal of St. Saturnin de Pons where Pierre Besson, father of Eli François, would have lived and worked in the mid-18th century.

Above left: The dungeon in Pons was built by King Richard Coeur de Lion in the 12th century. At right is the Mairie which formed part of the town's fortifications; right, a view of Pons. Below is the signature of Pierre Besson, Notary Royal, Pons, in 1728.

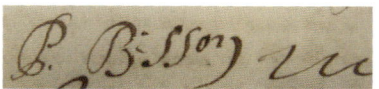

Domaine de Bellevue just outside of the village of Tanzac, diocèse de Saintes en Saintonge, France, covers several acres of vineyard and farmland and may have been a seigneury held by the Besson family in the 18th century. The antecedents of Eli François Besson are recorded as residing in Tanzac from 1604. One is encouraged to believe this might be the family's house because François would name his plantations in both Grenada and in Trinidad, Bellevue.

Above: The well-restored manor house at Bellevue was built perhaps in the 18th century. It may have been the site of an older building, as there is evidence of older structures quite close by.

Left: The gates of Bellevue open on to a driveway that leads to this charming house which may have, in its original form, been called Beaumanoir, a title carried by François in all official French and British government documents during his stay in Grenada in the 18th century. (Photos: Alice Besson)

The church of St. Saturnin in Tanzac shows well-restored stonework and vaulting with early Ro-
manesque capitals that give a sense of harmony and balance at the altar, opening to two side chapels.
The baptistry in the south chapel at the church of St. Saturnin in Tanzac shows frescoes dating from
early Christianity. The font itself, below left, is Romanesque of Gallo-Roman times. Several generations
of Bessons would have been baptised there.

In the 14th century, Oliver de Besson, écuyer, commanded a company of Knights under Oliver de
Clisson, Constable of France, 1326-1407. In Brittany, de Clisson had succeeded Bertram de Guesclin,
1320-1380, as Constable. Below: the effigy of Bertram de Guesclin, St. Denis basilica outside of Paris.

son was notary to Pierre, Duke of Bourbon in 1343 [15] and is described as drafting a tax regime for the newly created duchy.

The *noblesse de robe,* to which this branch of the Besson family belonged (others were considered to be of the *noblesse d'épée*—for example Oliver de Besson, *écuyer,* 1379, was a companion in arms of the Constable of France Bertram de Clisson [16]), acted as judicial or administrative magistrates and were members of the thirteen *parlements* that served as law courts in the greater cities of France. Phillip Besson is described as a *parlementarian* in Paris in the 16th century. [17] Their office would over time become exclusive. [18] Will Durant in his *Age of Voltaire* writes that, "by 1789 because of the impecuniosity of the *noblesse d'épée* and the wealth of the *noblesse de robe,* social barriers had collapsed … Only the Jacqueries of the revolution could overthrow its costly privileges." (p. 252)

The British, after the fall of French Canada, turned their ships south and attacked the French islands, capturing Guadeloupe in 1759 and Martinique in 1762. A squadron of British ships of the line under the command of Commodore Swanton received the surrender of the French in Grenada on 4th March, 1762. The island of Grenada after 112 years of French rule would became a British possession.

"The British, to add to the profits of victory," writes Will Durant, "sent squadrons to Africa to capture the French slave stations on the West Coast. Successful, the French trade in slaves collapsed. Nantes, its chief port in France, went into decline. The price of slaves in the West Indies rose and British slave merchants made new fortunes in supplying the demand." [19] In Grenada, the entire island was declared Crown property and

---

15   Inventaires et documents publiés par ordre L' Empéreur titres de la Maison Ducal Bourbon. Huilard-Breholles Book 1. Paris 1807.

16   Odorici, *Recherches sur Dinan et ses Environs,* 1977

17   ibid.

18   Lefebvre, "Coming of the French Revolution" p.41 in Durant, *Rousseau and Revolution,* p. 90.

19   Durant, *Rousseau and Revolution* p. 58. Nantes in fact flourished at least until 1789, based on St. Domingue sugar imports.

a comprehensive survey was undertaken by M. Pinel. In 1763 advertisements appeared in England, Barbados and Grenada, offering land for sale. The French planters were given the option to lease back their properties for a period of forty years so long as they were willing to swear loyalty to the British Crown. Failing that, they were given eighteen months to sell their estates to British subjects with the understanding that no one person would be allowed to purchase more that 500 acres. Some French estate owners preferred to leave with their slaves, having sold out their estates. There was a significant response to the availability of land, both developed and otherwise in Grenada as it was perceived as most desirable to own sugar-producing estates in the Caribbean.

Problems arose almost immediately with regard to these changes in the overall civil society and particularly in the behaviour of the slaves. The British introduced a different approach in the their dealings with them, which was seen as brutal. This caused reactions in the slave population, which prompted even sterner responses. It was generally imagined by the population that the French planters possessed a kinder and more tolerant manner in their dealings with the slaves (Steele 2003, 70). There was also the sense that the British tended to look at the French people on the island and especially the Free People of Colour, as inferior to them. Beverley Steele in her *Grenada: A History of its People* (p. 70), observes that "the newly arrived, instead of looking to see how this slave society had survived in relative peace for over one hundred years under French rule, immediately began to substitute the harsher British mode of handling slaves for the gentler, more humane conditions practised by the French planters."

It was understood that religious tolerance was to be guaranteed "as far as the laws of England permit." It was not the intention of the British to cause upheaval in, or to destroy the agricultural economy of Grenada, but they were determined to anglicise the island. This was commenced by the act of changing place names and street names and placing the administration of the Catholic church in Grenada under the administration of the Roman Catholic Bishop of London.

By the following year, on the 10th February, 1763, under the terms of the Treaty of Paris, Grenada, Tobago, St. Vincent and Dominica passed formally to the British. France, in making peace, relinquished both Canada and its Indian colonies in exchange for Martinique and Guadeloupe. Grenada would remain in British hands. It is of interest to historians that at the time of the cession, the French were allowed to remove all public documents to Martinique. As a result, there are very few public records in Grenada before that date, although there are some church records extant.

Also in 1763, François married Marie Ann Elizabeth La Prade in Guadeloupe. [20] She was the daughter of Jean Baptiste La Prade, *procureur du Roy,* and Marie Louise Blanchard, Jean Baptiste La Prade was to become a member of the *conseil supérieur* of Guadeloupe. [21] This was an important legal position, and because François would hold it as well in Grenada, some background to its origin may be of use.

César Gabriel de Choiseul, Duc de Praslin, minister of the Navy and of the Colonies, had supported the growth of French colonies in the West Indies. Grenada had benefited, especially during the 86 years of untroubled development. The Duc had added Corsica to the French Crown in 1768—sold to France after some 200 years of Genoese rule. By the end of the century, several Corsican families would make their way to the Caribbean and to Trinidad under the terms of the Cedula of Population of 1783.

De Choiseul had also sought to bring France and Spain together by the 1761 *pact de famille* between the Bourbon kings. This plan did not hold except in the minds and hopes of some West Indian colonists. He did make peace with England, some would agree on better terms than the military situation appeared to support. According to Will Durant, "He foresaw the revolt of the English colonies in America, and strengthened the French position in St. Domingue, Martinique, Guadeloupe, and French Guiana,

20   Régistres Paroissiaux de Gosier (Guadeloupe)
21   ibid.

in the hope of establishing a new colonial domain that would compensate France for the loss of Canada." [22]

René Nicholas de Maupeon became the de Choiseul's successor and to some extent continued his support for the colonists. One way in which this was achieved was by improving the manner in which justice was administered in the colonies.

The political and administrative situation in France, against the backdrop of the financial collapse in the wake of defeat in the Seven Year War, in addition to the confrontations between the Louis XV and the *parlements* was forcing, if not change, but the pursuit of fresh arrangements within the local administrative apparatus. One of these changes was the supplanting of the *parlements* with a new judicial organisation. It must be borne in mind that in France, the *parlements* were high courts and not representative bodies. At any rate, under de Maupeon's direction, and sanctioned by royal decree, a superior court (*conseil supérieur*) was set up in Paris in 1772 and in various provinces, [23] and apparently in the West Indies as well, where *conseils supérieurs* were established as appellate courts.

Notwithstanding the British conquest of the island, and the strictures imposed on the French inhabitants, François continued to live and do business there. He sold property to Anthony Malcolm and others in 1767, and among other transactions gave loans on mortgage to L.A.R. de Simon and to Pierre Bartholomew Julien. [24]

The slaves on several plantations rose in revolt in 1767. There were many causes for this uprising, not the least of which was the change in the nature of their servitude under the British. By all accounts, and the most lurid come from Père Labat, a Catholic cleric who wrote in the early 18th century, the British overseer/manager was notorious for the ill-treatment of slaves, particularly when rebellion threatened or uprisings occurred.

---

22   Durant, *Rousseau and Revolution*, p. 58. Sugar, grown with slave labour by the French West Indian planters, was perceived so precious that in 1763 France agreed to cede the vast territory of New France to the victors in exchange for keeping the minute Antillean island of Guadeloupe.

23   ibid. p. 94

24   Grenada Registry office

Beverley Steele records Labat's description of events in Barbados in the 1700s: "…The slaves who are captured are sent to prison and condemned to be passed through the cane mill, or burnt alive, or be put into iron cages that prevent any movement and in which they are hung up to branches of trees and left to die of hunger and despair." (Steele 2003, 71) The revolt was put down by troops from the garrison, and a quantity of slaves were killed. Quiet was restored, but the estate owners, managers and their families lived in fear of being burnt alive in their houses or otherwise killed in revenge, "particularly those who had laid themselves under the necessity of using violent methods," records the Abbé Raynal. [25]

François acquired Richmond estate, 217 acres, which he bought from Jean Delpèche de La Roque. He had sold Soubise estate, which he had inherited from his late wife, Marianne, in 1766 for 513,200 *livres* [26] (the equivalent of approx. £10,000 today) to a consortium comprising Rochard L'Épine, Simon de Beauford and other families. Included in this transaction were "eighty-five slaves of both sexes, particularly named in the schedule herein, also contained fifteen mules and five head of horned cattle." [27]

A daughter was born to François and Elizabeth in 1764; she was christened Marie Louise Antoinette Besson de Beaumanoir. In 1766, they had a son who was named François Étienne Besson de Beaumanoir. [28] That year, Grenada experienced a severe earthquake, which caused considerable damage to buildings and sugar works.

Other members of François' immediate family are recorded in the French islands during this time. In "The Officers of the Sovereign Council of Martinique" by Emile Hayot, a note on Louis Eli Besson says, "brother of Eli François Xavier Besson." [29] In 1765 Louis was 47, and "captain in the quarters of the deputy", the husband of Madeleine Lascarie (or Lascaris)

25   Raynal, Guillaume Thomas "Histoire philosophique et politique", in Borde, *History of Trinidad under the Spanish Government*, Vol I, iv, 1. xi. 223 et eqq.

26   ibid.

27   Indenture 12 Aug. 1766 Registry Department, Grenada

28   Régistres Paroissiaux de Gosier [Guadeloupe]

29   Martinique Historical Society, 1964

and the father of Étienne, Jean Baptiste, and Pierre Besson, born in Saint Lucia, who were 21, 20, and 18 years respectively. These and other relatives of François and his second wife Elizabeth La Prade may have gone to Trinidad in the closing years of the 18th century to escape the revolution in France or the repercussions that were felt in the French islands. Attracted by the terms of the Cedula of Population of 1783, they joined their cousins in developing plantations in the south of the island.

In 1768, it was decided by the British government to provide three seats in the Legislative Assembly of Grenada for the French inhabitants. Among those nominated was a 25-year old man by the name of Philippe Rose Roume. By 1776, he was the only French member left. "These members," records the Grenada Handbook of 1909, "who had taken the oath of allegiance to the King of England, might be elected to the House, and these were allowed upon election to refuse if they were Roman Catholic to subscribe to the 'test' [30] as the disavowal of belief in the doctrine of transubstantiation was called, a most liberal proceeding regard being had to the spirit of those times." [31]

This issue led to all sorts of upheavals in the society that was much divided by religious, cultural, racial and political differences, causing resignations from the Assembly. Roume would retire as well, his reasons unclear, and his retirement would lead to François taking a place on that body as the only Frenchman representing French planter interest.

In official documents during this time, François is described as Lieutenant of Artillery and Captain, Commandant of Grand Marquis, the Parish of St. Andrew. [32] He had bought Balthazar estate, 384 acres, from Flavigny in St. Andrew, and Point Salines estate, 339 acres, from D'Imbert in St. Georges. [33] At the time of the marriage of Marie Adelaïde, François' first daughter, to Joseph Alexander, the Count de Poullain, [34] garde de corps de

---

30 In the United Kingdom, Roman Catholics were not 'emancipated' until 1829, when the Test Acts were repealed.
31 *Grenada Handbook*, 1909, p. 26
32 Pinel, "A Topographical Description of the Island of Grenada" 1763, p. 8
33 ibid.
34 GHC number 87 pp 1795-1796.

Monsieur (Duc D'Orleans), and son of Jean and Jeanne Delpeche de La Roque, [35] François had given to them an estate of 94 acres which bounded on his own Balthazar estate. His Richmond estate was very close by. During this period, he bought 239 acres from Chatillon de Vouyours. This estate came with a water mill, a factory (old works), and 188 slaves. These lands co-joined both Richmond and Balthazar and were named Bellevue. These land holdings taken all together, virtually joining each other, added up to some 840 acres. [36] François may have owned several hundred slaves during this time in Grenada.

In addition to the difficulties experienced due to the exorbitant price of slaves, the uncertainties of war and the variations on the commodities markets in Europe, in 1770, the planters of Grenada were to suffer an attack from a small red ant that would undo years of patient husbandry. The red ant or sugar ant had made its appearance at Petit Havre (now Woodford) and rapidly spread over the island, for the next ten years severely damaging sugar cultivation, lime, lemon and orange trees. [37] This development may have caused François to buy the Point Salines plantation, as it was planted in cotton. The devastation caused by the ants, described in the most compelling language, had to be seen to be believed. Apparently, it was only relieved when a powerful hurricane destroyed almost all the island's plantations. In addition, the hurricane caused 19 Dutch ships, fully loaded with cargo, to sink at anchor. The ants, to everyone's relief, were also destroyed. [38]

In 1779, war having resumed between England and France, a French fleet under the command of the Count D'Estaing captured the island for the French Crown. [39] On the 17th of July of that year Grenada was returned to France. The Articles of Capitulation were framed in the context of what was considered to be the humiliation of the French in Grenada

---

35   Inventaire de Colonies C8 Correspondance des Gouverneurs, Martinique.

36   Pinel, "A Topographical Description of the Island of Grenada" 1763

37   *Grenada Handbook*, 1909, p. 27

38   ibid, p. 29

39   Grenada was occupied by France from 1779 to 1783, when it was returned to Great Britain.

during the British occupation. Retribution would be sought, property confiscated, and humiliations revenged. Free Blacks and People of Colour and slaves who had taken up arms against the invading French forces were enslaved or returned to slavery.

Not long after the reconquest of the island, Philippe Roume commenced negotiations with the Spanish Governor in Trinidad to permit immigration to that island. For several years there had been much discussion among the French planters as to whether migration to Georgia, Carolina and Florida would be a viable option (Steele 2003, 93), particularly bearing in mind the growing paucity of the soil in Grenada, the danger of hurricanes, ants, earthquakes, the depredations of the pirates, and the probability of religious persecution .

Of the Roume family, Michael Pocock writes in his *Out of the Shadows of the Past* (p. 13):

> "At the beginning of the 18th century, Philippe Roume had been sent to Martinique as *sub-delegue* to the Intendent, where his son, Laurent Philippe Roume, was born to his wife Francisca le Clare. In 1727 Philippe obtained the post of *conséiller à la cour royal* in Grenada, under the jurisdiction of the Governor General of Martinique, where he died in 1747. Laurent Philippe Roume married Rosa de Gannes de la Chancellerie; their first child was born in Grenada on the 13th of October 1743, he was named Philippe Rose Roume. She had two younger children, a daughter and a son, François."

Laurent Philippe Roume died in 1765, not long after the birth of his last child. He had been a planter owning several estates in the *Quartier des Sauteurs* or Parish of St. Mark; his residence and principal plantation was called St. Laurent, 225 acres.

The de Gannes family came from the ancient high *noblesse d'épée* of Britanny and Poitou, [40] and had come to the New World, settling first in Canada. Historic events had brought them to the French islands. By 1722, they were in Grenada and in possession of Waltham estate, 631 acres. Rosa de Gannes was born there in 1728, one of two daughters of the first marriage of Simon de Gannes de la Chancellerie.

---

40 L'Armorial General de France 1696

At her husband's death, Rosa came into a considerable fortune, apparently owning several large plantations: Paradise estate, 320 acres; Lataste, 262 acres; Trievia, 100 acres; Duquesne, 296 acres; and St. Laurent, 225 acres. Her principal estate and her home was Belvedere, 902 acres. She owned some 2,105 acres in all. [41] After her first husband's death she remarried Bertrand de Charras, who was an officer of the French navy.

Her eldest son, Philippe Roume, upon his maturity, took over the family's affairs. This was to prove a disastrous decision. In need of money to finance the operation of the plantations, he approached a City of London firm of moneylenders, Messrs. Bosanquet & Fatio, who had come to the island in search of the gullible. Within a few short years both Philippe and his mother were almost bankrupt, having lost the plantations and almost all of her personal possessions. [42] Philippe had mortgaged their entire asset base, all the plantations, but apparently not all the slaves, for ten years to John Fatio, partner of Samuel Bosanquet, for the sum of £97,000. [43] However, it appears that Philippe had not received full payment of the money from Fatio and as a consequence was not able to finance the operation of the estates in a manner that would allow him sufficient returns to meet his commitments to Fatio and his partner.

In 1770, François was able to come to Rosa's assistance. He effectively took over her dealings with the moneylenders, who had proven to be far cleverer than her son, and arranged for her to purchase from him the Point Salines plantation, she having lost Belvedere estate.

François' dealings with her, as preserved in the National Archives in Paris and written in Rosa's own hand in a collection of documents pertaining to her legal affairs, were thought by her to be "noble and efficient." It was also remarked that ". . . his business reputation was a sound guarantee for a reliable purchase, the sale was conducted and concluded with candour and honesty. I gave him on payment on terms all the letters of credit I had received with the exception of the last two," wrote Rosa de Gannes de Charras. [44]

---

41 Pinel, "A Topographical Description of the Island of Grenada" 1763
42 Pocock 1993, 50 – 62.
43 I may have this sum wrong.
44 National Archives, Paris

Philippe Rose Roume would be destined to play several roles in the quickly changing political scenario of the Caribbean at the end of the 18th century and early 19th century. Adopting the Royalist-style "Sire de St. Laurent", which he used while negotiating Trinidad's Cedula of Population and when he served as Ordonnateur of Tobago, he would become "Citoyen Roume" when he served the French Republic in San Domingue and in Santo Domingo as a Commissioner. (National Museum of Trinidad and Tobago)

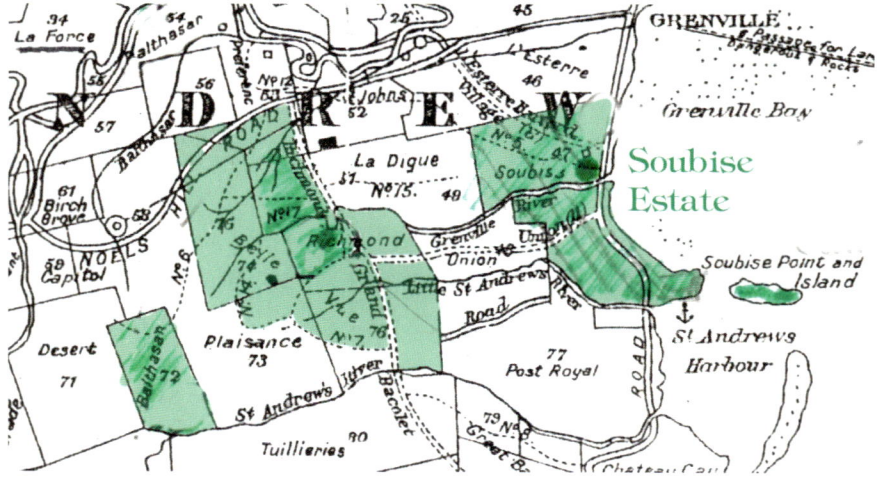

Detail of a map of Grenada showing François' plantations: Balthazar, Richmond, and Bellevue. Soubise estate had been inherited by him upon the death of his first wife. It was the site of the first massacre of the Fédon revolution carried out by Stanislas Besson and Julien Fédon in 1795. (Pinel Map 1763)

A NEGRO FESTIVAL drawn from Nature in the ISLAND of St. VINCENT.

From an Original Picture by Agostino Brunyas, in the possession of Sir William Young Bart. F.R.S.

The island of St Vincent formed a part of the French establishment in the West Indies for most of the 18th century. Commencing from 1719, French settlers cultivated coffee, tobacco, indigo, corn, and sugar on plantations worked by African slaves. St. Vincent was ceded to Britain by the Treaty of Paris (1763), restored to French rule in 1779 and regained by the British under the Treaty of Versailles (1783). François Besson, in 1783 married Marie Ann Elizabeth La Prade in Guadeloupe. She was the daughter of Jean Baptiste La Prade, procureur du Roy, and Marie Louise de Blanchard, who may have been related to Philbert Rouxel de Blanchard, commander of the French garrison in St. Vincent. Augostino Brunias ,the artist, was able to capture something of the nature of the times, the relationship between the French planters their wives, the Free Coloureds and the slaves. (Edwards; Paria)

The West Indian Slave Trade

Slavery provided labour for some of the most profitable industries in history. 70% of the slaves brought to the New World were used to produce sugar, the most labour intensive crop. The rest were employed harvesting coffee, cotton and tobacco. Slaves were also used in mining. The West Indian colonies of the European powers were some of their most important possessions, so the colonists went to extremes to protect and retain them. For example, at the end of the Seven Years War in 1763, France agreed to cede the vast territory of New France, Canada, to the victors in exchange for keeping the small Antillean island of Guadeloupe.

The slave trade profits have been the object of many discussions. Returns for the investors were not absurdly high [around 6% in France in the 18th century], but they were higher than domestic alternatives [in the same century, around 5%].

Risks, maritime and commercial, were always a concern for individual voyages. Investors always mitigated them by buying small shares in many ships at the same time. Between voyages, ship shares could be freely sold and bought. All these made the slave trade a very interesting investment.

By far the most attractive and successful West Indian colonies in 1800 belonged to the United Kingdom. After entering the sugar colony business late, British naval supremacy and control over key islands such as Jamaica, Trinidad, and Barbados and the territory of British Guiana gave it an important edge over all competitors; while many British did not make gains, some made enormous fortunes, even by upper class standards.

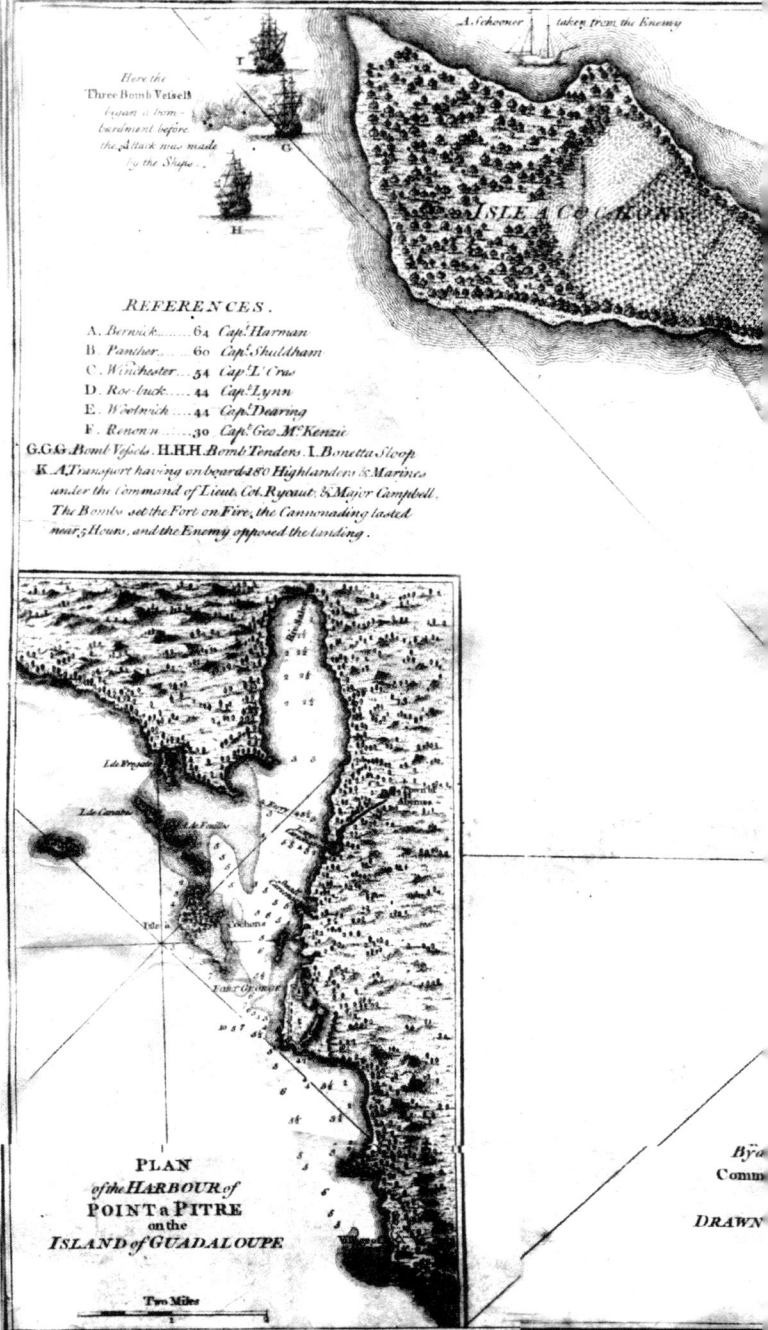

REFERENCES.

A. Berwick........64 Cap.t Harman
B. Panther........60 Cap.t Shuldham
C. Winchester....54 Cap.t L'Cras
D. Roe-buck......44 Cap.t Lynn
E. Woolwich......44 Cap.t Dearing
F. Renown........30 Cap.t Geo. M.c Kenzie
G.G.G. Bomb Vessels. H.H.H. Bomb Tenders. I. Bonetta Sloop
K. A Transport having on board 480 Highlanders & Marines
under the Command of Lieut. Col. Rycaut, & Major Campbell.
The Bombs set the Fort on Fire, the Cannonading lasted
near 5 Hours, and the Enemy opposed the landing.

PLAN
of the HARBOUR of
POINT a PITRE
on the
ISLAND of GUADALOUPE

Two Miles

This advantage was reinforced when France lost its most important colony, St. Domingue, western Hispaniola (now Haiti) to a slave revolt in 1791 and supported revolts against its rival Britain after the 1789 French Revolution in the name of liberty, but in fact selectively, as opportunities were presented.

Before 1791, British islands were producing sugar in quantity, and the British people quickly became the largest consumers of sugar. West Indian sugar became ubiquitous as an additive to China tea. (Internet)

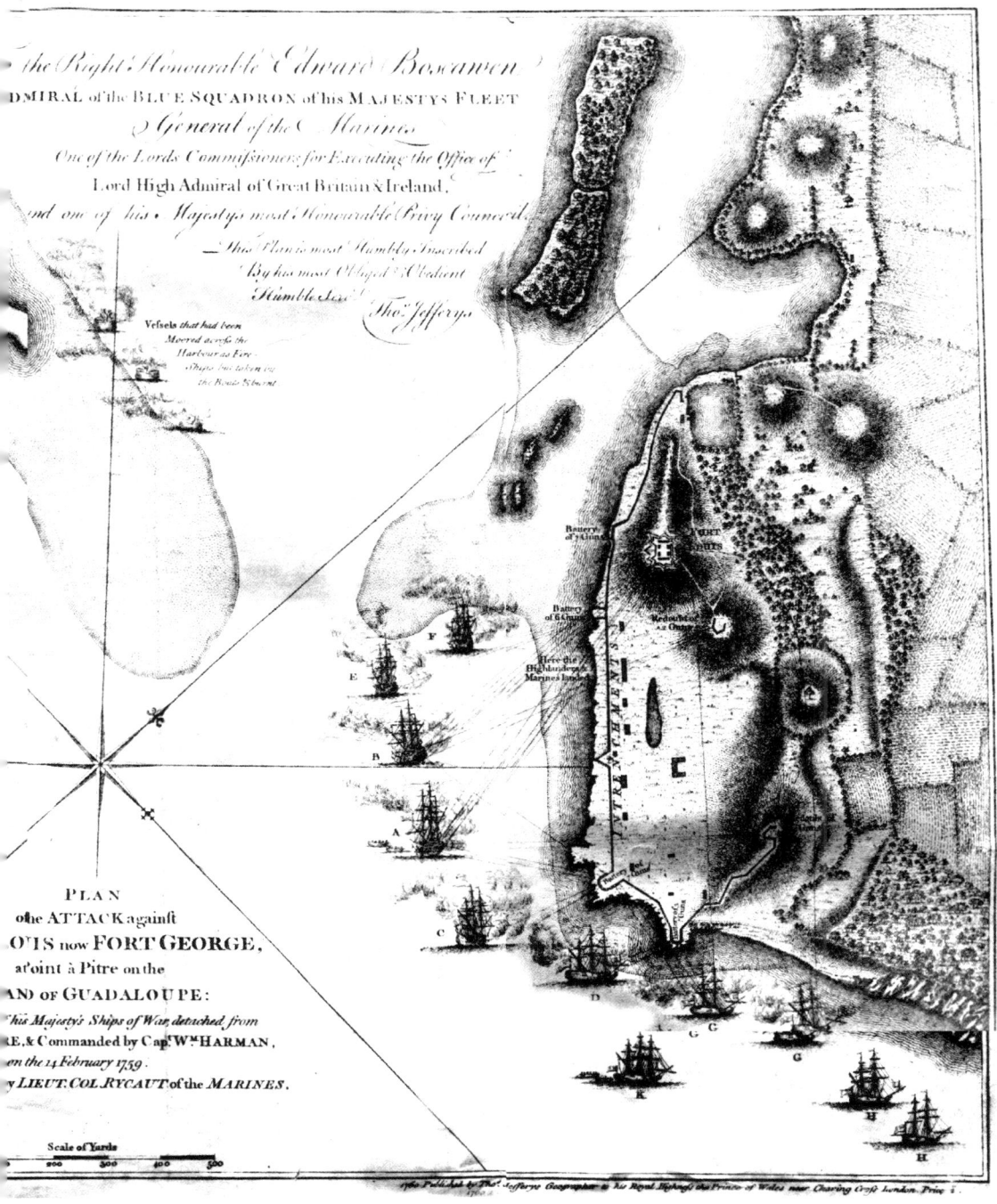

Plan of the attack against Fort Louis, now Fort George at Pointe à Pitre on the island of Guadeloupe. By a squadron of His Majesty's ships of War, detached from Commodore Moore and commanded by Captain William Harman, on the 14th February 1759. Drawn on the spot by Lieutenant Colonel Rycaut of the Marines. (Cambridge)

According to lists of passengers sailing to France, [45] François travelled in 1772. It is not clear when he returned. Five years later, in 1777, François bought back Point Salines estate from Rosa and her husband. Bertrand de Charras appears to have died, perhaps at sea not long after their marriage.

After the capture of Grenada by France in July 1779, Roume was invited to become temporary *conseil supérieur*, or chief judge, a position he held for some months before leaving for Venezuela. There were matters, however, that would have to be brought before the court over which he would not have been able to adjudicate.

"It was not until 1780 that Rosa's matters were heard before the French tribunal established on the island upon its re-conquest, and by a verdict of the 5th of August 1780, previous decisions given in her favour were upheld. Rosa had appealed to the *conseil supérieur* of Grenada and obtained a verdict in her favour. The decision was handed down on the 9th September 1780, reversing previous judgments." (Pocock 193, 59)

François had been appointed *conseiller au conseil supérieur*. [46] It is not clear whether Rosa's case was brought before François as judge of the court of appeals. Rosa's legal affairs were to drag on in both the French and British courts for several years. It is not clear whether she was ever able to recover all that was lost as the result of the encounters with the London moneylenders. One of the somewhat strange fallouts to occur was Belvedere estate, which had come into the possession of the firm of London moneylenders, falling into the hands of a young educated coloured man by the name of Julien Fédon.

Beverley Steele relates in her *Grenada: A History of its People* (p.108f):

> "Julien Fédon was the son of a Frenchman, Pierre Fédon, and a Free Black woman, Brigette, a native of Martinique. Fédon had a brother called Jean, and the names of both Julien and Jean Fédon appear on the list of property owners for1794. Fédon was married to Marie Rose Cavelan, reputed to be a person of mulatto and Amerindian ancestry. Hay says that Fédon was educated in England, but there is no other

---

45   ibid.
46   Roget, "The Superior French Staff of the Island of Grenada in 1782", after "The Precious Firsts of Grenada" Cahier 15 of CC-HIA 1986

evidence to substantiate this. As was common among the West Indian French, Fédon was baptised a Roman Catholic, and was raised in his father's house. Fédon had two daughters.

Fédon and his wife owned Lancer estate up to 1791, when they sold it. Belvedere estate was purchased by Fédon from James Campbell in May 1791. It was an estate of 450 acres and eighty slaves. Fédon also bought a house in Gouyave from Charles Nogues and his wife, Marie Louise Fédon Nogues, Julien's sister. Jean Fédon owned a coffee plantation of 139 acres in St. John. Charles Nogues, Fédon's brother-in-law, was a tailor in St George's, and previously a landowner there."

It should be noted that Rosa's son Roume, who according to Pocock received his education in Grenada, (Pocock 193, 59) was 22 when his father died in 1765, and 27 when he fell under the charm of the moneylenders. He was not alone; many others were duped. Several French planters and their families were to suffer as a result of the rapaciousness of the London moneylenders in Grenada during the 1770s.

The hardships caused by the moneylenders were also experienced by the slave population. In foreclosing on the estates, the moneylenders would sometimes sell off the slaves, who were in some cases worth more than the land. This would cause distress to the slave population by the breaking up of their families.

These setbacks at such a young age may have prompted Roume to seek his fortune, some time later in 1781, in Trinidad. He had by that time married and was starting a family. He was to purchase lands in Trinidad at Diego Martin for himself, an estate for his wife at Ariapita, and one for his mother at Maraval, which Rosa would name Champs Elysées.

The question sometimes raised is, did Roume act alone in pursuing a new establishment for the French planters of Grenada and of the wider Caribbean? It has been speculated that because of François' official position on the island, over some twenty years; his knowledge of French interest in the region, world affairs and trade; his experience in legal dealings; his involvement with the family of Rosa de Gannes with particular regard to Roume's difficulties, bearing in mind Roume's inexperience and *naïveté* in legal affairs (in Rosa's written statement, she points out on more than one occasion her son's misunderstanding of legal matters); his age etc., that François may have been the instigator behind Roume's efforts to cause a new Cedula to be distributed among the Catholics in the Caribbean area with a view to settling the sparsely populated Spanish island of Trinidad.

The correspondence alone, first to Caracas, then to the Spanish Court, would have required the work of a person who was trained to express himself in legal terms and who was accustomed to writing in a language, or languages, that would be recognised by like-minded personages in the Royal Court of Spain. Courtly language was an art in itself. Was François Besson that person behind Philippe Roume de St. Laurent? This conjecture might be worth more investigation.

François' involvement with Rosa's affairs is of interest; he seemed to have come to her aid in a very generous manner, looking after her welfare in both the short and the long term. An entry of a marriage in the Catholic Cathedral records in Port-of-Spain, Trinidad, states, "Charles Besson, legal son of François Besson and Mrs. Marie Ruim Besson, married Miss Rose Celine Darmanie, daughter of François and Mrs. Marie Ann Darmanie, on the 21st of January 1834". This is of interest because of the name Ruim—could this be how the priest spelt the name Roume? There is no other evidence of a family in Trinidad or in Grenada by the name of Ruim during the 18th or the 19th century.

This has caused me to speculate as to whether François *fils*, the son of François, who is the subject of this work, had married a member of the Roume family, a daughter of Philippe's brother François, who had married Eugenia Rose de Rignault de Rosée. Their son James Roume de St. Laurent married Marie Victorine de Rosée. James' sister, if he had one, would have been a contemporary of François *fils*, who was born in 1766.

The historian, Bryan Edwards spells the name Roume, Room. Toussaint L'Ouverture, the liberator of Haiti, spelt it Roome. In Burgundy and in parts of Germany, where the name is well known, it is spelt Rome or Röhm, and in a list of names of slaves sold by François at the purchase of the Soubise estate by the Rochard L'Épine family, a slave is recorded as Ruime.

French forces under the leadership of the Comte de Grasse in Tobago in 1781. At right, a black man, who may have served as a body guard of a French officer, comforts his fallen comrade. Philippe Roume would serve the French Government under Governor Arthur Dillon in Tobago as "Ordonnateur".
(Jardine)

A view of Bay Town, St. George's, Grenada during the 1800s. (National Museum, Grenada)

"Sunday morning in the country: The markets in the West Indies were supplied almost entirely by the Negroes of the surrounding country. As their absence from the estates on week-days would have been a great loss of work to their masters, they had been allowed to acquire a kind of prescriptive right to the Sunday morning for that purpose."
(Richard Bridgens, circa 1820, Trinidad, courtesy Adrian Camps-Campins)

At any rate, on the 23rd of November 1783, the Cedula of Population was passed into law, which would encourage immigration to Trinidad. In all some fifty-seven families would move to Trinidad from Grenada. This number would include a sizeable quantity of Free Blacks and People of Colour and with them 4,965 slaves. [47] Also, the Treaty of Versailles was signed on the 3rd of September of that year, restoring Grenada and the Grenadines to the British Crown.

Of the 33 subscribers to the publication, *A Topographical Description of the Island of Grenada surveyed by M. Pinel (1763) by Lieut. Daniel Peterson (1780)*, François Besson de Beaumanoir is the only Frenchman listed. The new British Governor, Lord Macartney, heads the list. François takes four copies. It would appear that this list represents the membership of the new House of Assembly.

The new British administration took prompt steps to re-establish the Assembly and to alter the privileges formerly granted to the French planters. It was in their interest to keep the island's economy profitable, while at

47   Gomes, Sue-Anne, *Book of Trinidad*, p. 90.

the same time, they took steps to impose obnoxious religious conditions on the French Catholic population, black, white and coloured, that, in the not too distant future, would help bring about disastrous consequences.

The island was reasonably prosperous, exporting in 1787, 175,548 cwt. of sugar; 670,390 gallons of rum; 2,716 cwt. of cocoa; 2,062,427 lbs. of cotton and 2,810 lbs. of indigo, all this worth in excess of 614,908 *livres;* and employing for its transport 188 ships of 25,764 tonnage. [48]

Without a doubt, Grenada's development at the end of the 18th century, when compared to Trinidad's, was significant. After some three hundred years of Spanish rule, there was hardly any development in the latter island. Trinidad's population figures indicate this: in 1783 there were 126 Europeans, 295 Free Coloureds, 310 slaves, and 2,032 indigenous people: a total of 2,763. [49]

Trinidad, in this period, was covered in virgin forest that was described on contemporary maps as "impenetrable". Its area is approximately 1,841 square miles with an average length of 50 miles and an average width of 37 miles. Well watered with several rivers, it enjoyed the continental climate of "The Spanish Main," sharing many of its flora and fauna, and a dwindling Amerindian population. Trinidad's Amerindian name was perhaps Iere, derived from the Arawak name for hummingbird, *ierèttê* or *yerettê*. Christopher Columbus renamed it in 1498 *"La Ysla de la Trinidad,"* "The Island of the Trinity," fulfilling a vow he had made before setting out on his third voyage of exploration and discovery.

48   *Grenada Handbook,* 1909, p. 30
49   ibid.

In 1779, the plantation known as "Champs Elysées" in the Maraval Valley, (281quarrés, or approximately 927 acres at its fullest extent) had been obtained by Monsieur Philippe Roume de St. Laurent
from the Spanish Government, on behalf of his mother, Madame de Charras, the former Rose de
Gannes de la Chancellerie. At her death, the estate passed into the hands of Thomas Maturin, * Chevalier de Gannes de la Chancellerie., by whom the property was administered, and of Louis François de
Gannes, his brother. In 1820, the estate came into the possession of Jean Valleton de Boissière and would
remain with this family for over one hundred years. (Richard Bridgens, 1820. Paria)

The Champs Elysées estate is connected to both Philippe Roume, whose mother, Madame de Charras,
made it her home, and to Dr. Eric Williams, whose ancestor, Jean Valleton de Boissière, acquired it and
lived there. Both these men, Philippe Roume and Eric Williams, were to leave an indelible mark on
the history of Trinidad and Tobago. They were both responsible for the creation of new narratives that
would define the future of this country–Roume, by causing the Cedula of Population of 1783 to be dis-
seminated, and in so doing encourage immigration to Spanish Trinidad; and Williams by creating the
political movement that would take the country to independence from Great Britain in 1962.

*Chevalier: a rank assumed only by the most noble families and the possessors of certain high dignities
in the Royal Court of France. Noblesse chevaleresque or knightly nobility: holders of patents of nobility
from before the year 1400. Members of the Orders of Chivalry had the title of Chevalier, but not the
rank of Chevalier, which can be confusing. The Royal and Military Order of Saint Louis was a military
Order of Chivalry founded on 5 April 1693 by Louis XIV and named after Saint Louis (Louis IX).
It was intended as a reward for exceptional officers. Conditions to obtain the award did not include
nobility; however, Catholic faith was mandatory, as well as at least ten years' service as a commissioned
officer in the Army or the Navy. Hereditary nobility was granted to knight's sons and grandsons. There
were twelve Chevaliers listed by P.G.L. Borde in his 'History,' five were holders of the order of St. Louis,
as known members of the military, one was the holder of the order of St. Lazarus, the others may have
inherited the honour.

François
Moves to Trinidad
2

François' decision, along with that of many other French planter families, to take advantage of the very generous terms of the Cedula of 1783 and move to Trinidad, notwithstanding the prosperity of Grenada and the inducements to stay there, may be understood against the background of the world politics of the day. Along with other considerations, some of these now may be seen, in hindsight, to be prophetic, or perhaps, informed.

France had lost what could be called the "battle for the oceans of the world." Britannia would now rule the waves. The blockade imposed during the prolonged wars between the two countries had caused great hardship to the people of France by cutting off exports and the trans-shipment of goods to other European countries. The English were despised and no doubt, some strong personal anti-British feelings were held by many French families in Grenada and in the other French islands. Further, there was the *pact de famille*, which meant that Kings of the House of Bourbon ruled both France and Spain—not that that was a political reality, really. There were encouraging economic reasons as spelt out in the terms of the Cedula. It was also believed that French families would be better off in a Catholic country with other Catholics—it should be remembered that religious feelings were very strong, and dictated most, if not all, choices made by people in those days, and under the terms of the Cedula, only Catholics were to be allowed into Trinidad.

Beyond all this, it was understood that Trinidad lay outside of the hurricane belt and was not visited by terrible and extremely destructive storms that could occur, sometimes annually. There was also the fact that the soil on the estates in the long-settled islands had been worn out over a century and a half or more by cultivation. And then there were the red ants. There were none in Trinidad. The Cedula's terms, which included the provision of land grants proportionate to the number of slaves brought in by the

colonists and their families, [50] along with generous tax concessions, offered a fresh start, and an escape from all sorts of humbug, especially of
the type inspired by the money-lending gentlemen of the City of London.
A sparsely populated, secure, fertile, well-watered island with accommo-
dating Spanish laws that favoured the debtor, offered a new beginning.

   François and his immediate family, that is his wife, his son François *fils*,
his wife and their young family, would make the move to Trinidad over
the next few years. Point Salines estate would be sold to François la Barrie;
Richmond to the firm of Simon & Hankey; and Balthazar, to the heirs of
Noel (these in turn would sell Balthazar to the Cassar family). [51] François' grandchildren (François *fils* and his wife Marie Ruim's sons), François born 1795, Jean born 1796, and Pierre Jean born 1805, were all born
in Grenada [52] but would grow up in Trinidad. François, more than likely,
would have brought with him to Trinidad most, if not all, his slaves, both
domestic and praedial.

   In Trinidad, François acquired the Spanish grant originally given to
Honoré Tardieu of 80 quarrées [53] (256 acres) in South Naparima,[54] in
1788. He would, over the next two or three years, buy La Romaine estate
of 236 acres with its 45 slaves in South Naparima; La Fortunée estate, and
an estate that he would name Bellevue of 342 acres at Guapo, in close

---

50   Article III of the Cedula states: "To each white person, either sex, shall be granted four
     fanegas and two sevenths of land [equal to ten quarrées French measure, or thirty-
     two acres English measure] and half the above quantity for every Negro or mulatto
     slave that such white person or persons shall import with them. . ." Article IV states,
     "The free Negroes and mulattoes. . . shall have half the quantity of land granted to
     Europeans, and if they bring with them slaves,. . . the quantity of land granted to them
     shall be increased in proportion to the number of slaves, and to the land granted to
     them, that is, one half of the quantity granted to the slaves of Europeans."
51   The de la Mothe family had owned Balthazar estate through Angelina Cassar, daugh-
     ter of Salvo Cassar of Malta. She had married Alfred de la Mothe. Angelina appears to
     have married at age thirteen! (Freda Scott)
52   Births, Deaths and Record of Property, July 1772–August 1809, Supreme Court
     Registry, St. George's.
53   A quarrée is three and one-fifth English acres, Joseph, E.L. *History of Trinidad*, p. 251.
54   Lists of Spanish grants given under Don Chacón, Spanish Governor of Trinidad,
     Public Record Office, Kew Gardens, England

Port-of-Spain: "On entering the Gulf, the mind is imbued with intense emotions, on beholding one of the most magnificent panoramas nature ever formed. To the east, the waves of the mighty Orinoco dispute for mastery with the contending billows of the ocean, and the lofty mountains of Cumana rise with stupendous majesty. To the west, appear the mountains, hills, valleys, and the plains of Trinidad." (Richard Bridgens, circa 1820, Trinidad, courtesy Adrian Camps-Campins)

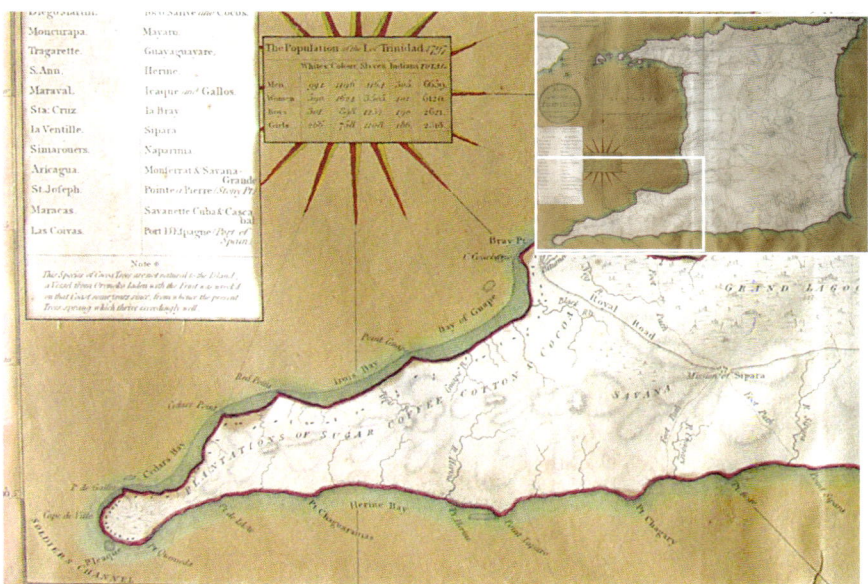

Detail of the Whittle map of 1797, showing the south-western peninsula of Trinidad from La Brea to Cedros, and the number of estates that had been established there from the 1780s. The tiny black squares are meant to be houses, "habitations", as they would have been called. The habitations towards the eastern side of Guapo Bay may have been those of François and his sons and grandsons. (Paria)

proximity to the famous Pitch Lake. If we are to judge from the compensation payments of 1835, François and his wife and their family may have lived at Bellevue estate, which he could have named like his other estate in Grenada for the Domaine of Bellevue just outside the village of Tanzac in France, where his parents may have lived and he may have been born. Over the next fifty years, his sons, his nephews and his grandsons would own or control at one time or another several plantations in the South Naparimas and in the Guapo area of South Trinidad.

In the index to *The Spanish Protocol of Deeds* [55] François is recorded as first renting half of a house and then buying Port-of-Spain properties on Henry Street, and purchasing slaves from Jacob Berio and Boue-John. The Town Book of 1810 shows properties owned by François Besson at 1a Henry Street and 3 and 4 Marine Square. The latter, he bought from Marclina Robles. This parcel of land, 20 years or so later, may have become 1 St. Joseph Road, and later 1 Besson Street, where his descendants would live up to the 1920s.

François may have received the very disturbing news from France that in October of 1789 serious rioting had broken out in Paris and that an angry populace had marched on the royal palace at Versailles. And later that the populace of Paris had taken charge of the revolution by forcing the King's hand. Now, subject to his subjects, the King accepted the Declaration of the Rights of Man as a *fait accompli,* and that a great many people were leaving France for neighbouring countries and for the Caribbean.

A malignant fever was brought to Grenada in February of 1788 from the island of Bulam on the West Coast of Africa, by passengers aboard the ship "Hankey". This disease, which was called Bulam fever, appeared to be similar to what is known in Africa as black water fever.

This fever, which could be deadly, raged in Grenada for five years. [56] François' second wife Elizabeth died during this early period of the move to Trinidad; she may have been a victim of this fever and may have been buried in Grenada, as there is no record of her death in Trinidad. 62 years

---

55   This index is kept at the National Archives, Port-of-Spain, Trinidad.
56   *Grenada Handbook,* 1909, p. 41

old, François remarried for a third time. His new wife's name was Reine Martineau.[57] Two sons were born to the couple: Vincent born 1796, and Frederick born 1800.

As war and revolution flared in the Caribbean, Trinidad, escaping the tragic results, was the recipient of the refugees and of the politics of the time. The Spanish government could actually do little to stop this; hundreds of refugees made their way to this the last island of the Caribbean chain. There was no shortage of slaves. The trade, originating on the West Coast of Africa, now firmly under English control, was remunerative to the African rulers who sold the slaves and to the shippers and the dealers who bought them. The colonists were encouraged to buy as many slaves as could be afforded, the apportioning of land to Europeans and to the Free Blacks and People of Colour being the incentive.

There was an element of uncertainty in the outcome of shipping one's produce across seas dominated by the warring fleets, and the ever present danger of slave revolt or invasion, but, notwithstanding, the process for the creation of Trinidad's society was put into place in those years. The growing economy was driven by the urgent requirements of the newly-arrived colonists. Their challenge at hand was to construct a productive economic base, hewn from the forest, which would support trade. There was as well, the need to rebuild their lives in the context of an altogether new reality. For several of them, familial and financial connections with France would become increasingly tenuous as the old régime, to which they were so intricately connected, was swept away. Gone as well for many, European, Free Black and People of Colour, were their previous establishments and connections in the former French islands.

The French colonists, in the majority, who had been encouraged by the generous provisions of the Cedula to relocate to Trinidad, were soon to become an important influence in an English colony. There had been a French and an African presence in Spanish Trinidad from the 1770s. A

---

57   On his death registration in the Catholic Cathedral it reads "Married to R. Martineau natural de Rousac." Roussac Haute-Vienne is a department in the Limousin region in west-central France . Contrary to what is written by de Verteuil in his *The Black Earth of South Naparima,* p.142 she may have been of European descent.

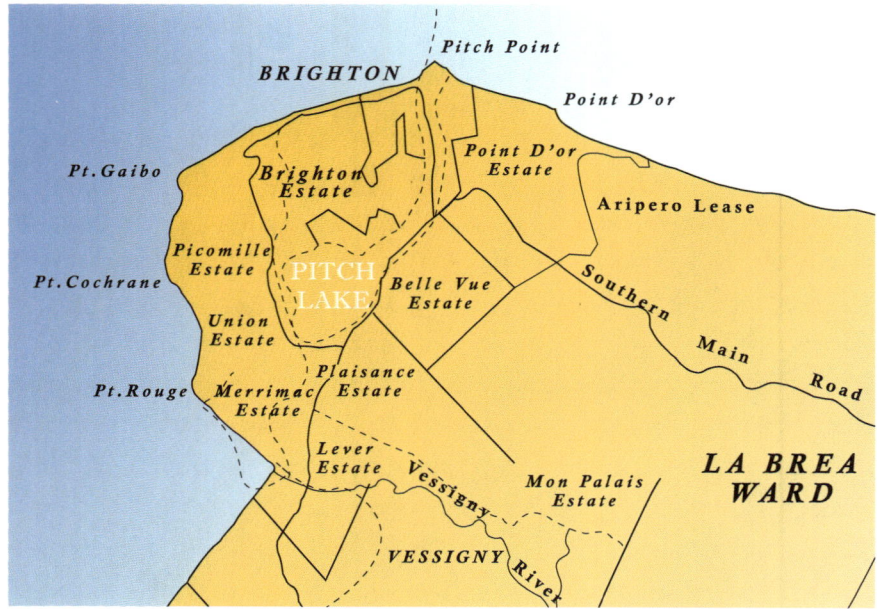

Map of the Pitch Lake area showing Bellevue estate where in 1910
the Guapo Oil Exploration Company had oil exploration rights. (after Higgins, p. 93)

The Pitch Lake formed the north western boundary of Bellevue estate. A visitor to the area in 1807,
Dr. Nicholas Nugent, wrote: "We ascended the hill … to a plantation [Bellevue?], then we procured a
Negro guide who accompanied us through a wood about three quarters of a mile. We now perceived a
strong sulphurous and pitchy smell, like that of burning coal, and soon after a view of the lake, which at
first sight appears to be an expanse of still water frequently interrupted by clumps of dwarf trees or islets
of rushes and shrubs; but on nearer approach we found it to be in reality an extensive plain of mineral
pitch, with frequent crevices and chasms filled with water." The above view of the Pitch Lake was painted
by Richard Bridgens in 1820. François would have owned Bellevue at the time of Dr. Nugent's visit and
when Bridgens had painted it. (courtesy Adrian Camps-Campins)

census that was taken in 1784 had shown that there were 335 Spaniards and 384 French colonists. Those of mixed race, who were free, numbered 633 French-speakers, and 765 who spoke Spanish. There were 260 "Spanish slaves" and 2,027 "French slaves".

The slave population would grow dramatically over the next ten years, from just over 6,000 in 1787 to more than 10,000 in 1797, and be twice that number when Emancipation was declared in 1834.

I find it necessary at this point to comment on the issue of African new World slavery in the context of this book. This period in the island's history was formative for all involved and would shape the future socially, culturally and in the long term, politically. For it would be African slave labour that would physically lay the foundation for its first agricultural economy, tragically achieved with great agony. It would be the French-speaking colonists (European and coloured) who were in the majority amongst the slave and plantation owners, who would have the dubious distinction of introducing this odious institution to Trinidad on such a scale, albeit within the laws and customs of the time, and in so doing, be made to bear the stigma of its consequences in another age, under different circumstances.

In the centuries after the entry of the Europeans into the New World, African chattel slavery would prove to be a cruel travesty of the human condition, degrading to all concerned.

The enslaved, in spite of coming from countries in Africa where slavery was an accepted aspect of those societies, experienced in the New World a form of slavery on a scale and in a manner that far exceeded what they could bear, leading to resistance, revolts and slave uprisings, and inevitably to cruel reprisals. In succeeding generations, deep psychological scars would emerge, having to do with both guilt and victimhood, to be discussed in part 2 of this book.

African slavery and European immigration would shape the essential characteristics of the New World, defining aspects of its narratives, the interpretations of its history, at different stages over time. The African presence in the Americas, as enslaved or as free people, would differentiate the entire hemisphere from the rest of the world, severely challenging the veracity of the ethical and moral foundation of its institutions, particularly in the implementation of the spirit of its laws and statutes.

The issues presented in this study are not about minimising African chattel slavery in terms of moral absolutes, but about the condemnation of what in my view, amounts to the corrupting of the scientific methodology of history for the popularisation of nationalistic politics in the mid-20th century. Those issues will be further explored in the second part of this study.

François, during his lifetime, owned many slaves. I have no empirical evidence to show that he was particularly cruel or unjust, but I would imagine that he was, as all slave owners of his time, violent, cruel, and terrible; as terrible as he could afford to be with his very expensive chattels, who, it must be remembered, were worth more alive, productive, and in good health.

Within three or four years of François' acquiring the South Naparima and Guapo properties, news arrived that the revolution that had broken out in France, had reached a stage where the King had been dethroned, and that massacres were taking place in Paris and in other parts of the country, precipitating a series of events that would alter the way of life for the French in the Caribbean. There was even news that there was a revolution against the revolution. This had broken out in far separate regions of France- the Vendée and Dauphine; and Paris itself harboured thousands of people who sympathised with the fallen King. François would have felt profoundly moved by these events, for he was no doubt a Royalist and had been a servant of the Crown, and for more than eight hundred years his family had held an allegiance to the house of Bourbon. François, no doubt, would have agreed with Goethe who remarked "From today and from this place (Valmy, 1792) begins a new epoch in the history of the world."

The revolution would serve to sever various connections of the West Indian colonists with family and friends in France. François' sister, Elizabeth, who had married financier Jean Paris, had died in 1775. A brother Pierre, born 1732, might have come to Trinidad in 1797 so as to escape the revolution and its terrors, as there is a record of a Pierre Besson sailing from Marseilles "destination unknown" in 1797.[58] He does not appear to have married or to have had children in Trinidad and there is no record of his death in France or in Trinidad that I could find, but there is a Pierre Besson unaccounted for, whose name turns up in some documents.[59]

In the colony of Saint Domingue, the French revolution found expression in 1791 in an uprising of the coloured people and slaves under the leadership of Toussaint L'Ouverture who was by the year 1793 in effective possession of that colony. This had sounded a note of awakening to their fellows throughout the Caribbean: with the cry of "*Liberté, égalité, fraternité!*"

One can only guess at the reaction to the news of the revolution its mass executions and the deaths of the King and Queen on those living in the West Indies who were loyal to the French Crown and to what was to become known in history as the *ancien régime*. Dozens of families, individuals, Royalists and Republican, sought to take advantage of the terms of the Cedula of Population and made their way to Trinidad. Within a relatively short period, ten to twelve years, despite the troubled times, a growing— perhaps thriving—plantation economy began to emerge there by the late 1790s. In 1793, hostilities broke out once again between Great Britain and France. In Grenada, the government tried to prevent the influx of people from the French and other islands, without much success. This was to have unfortunate results.

At this point, I will digress in some detail into events in Grenada that were known as Fédon's revolution. This uprising is of special relevance to Trinidad, because of the significant movement of people between the two islands that were occasioned by the Cedular of Population of 1783. As will be explained later, all this had particular bearing on François Besson, and possibly his descendants.

---

58   Archives Nationales, Fichier de Recherches, F 5 B Passengers.
59   François' nephew Pierre Louis Besson may have had a 'natural son', Pierre, by Rose (?) in 1838 Pierre L. Besson is the godfather. In 1846, Pierre L. Besson's will was probated. His widow, named as his executrix, was Françoise Louise Regous.

FÉDON'S REVOLUTION
3

Several explanations have been offered with regard to the events that led up to "Fédon's revolution," as it is called by some in Grenada, which took place from 2nd March 1795 to 19th June 1796. It was a political and a military conflict that was led by Julien Fédon, a free coloured man, and his compatriots in alliance with thousands of slaves who had declared themselves free. Fédon had the loyalty of perhaps hundreds of free coloured men and women and also elements of the French republican-minded and other Europeans who supported the cause. His band of fighters would be joined over time by elements of the French Republican army and other adventurers. As such, it was also to acquire an aspect of what has been described as the 'Brigands' War' that was a part of the French revolutionary war in the Caribbean, which involved uprisings in St. Lucia, Guadeloupe, Dominica and St. Vincent.

Carl Campbell writes in his *Cedulants and Capitulants* concerning the revolts of the coloureds throughout the Caribbean (p. 31):

> "The fighting by the coloureds at this time was not a Free Coloured revolt simply for Free Coloured objectives. The same is true of the Fédon Rebellion in Grenada in 1795. The leader Julien Fédon was a Free Coloured slave holder with significant landed property, who acted with slaves and white oppressed Frenchmen allegedly under the orders of Victor Hugues. The revolt had the appearance of a French Republican uprising against the English as well as a coloured rebellion against the Europeans. According to Cox, Fédon and his associates tried to 'turn the island over to French rule,' extend the privileges of the Free Coloureds and emancipate the slaves."

Taken from this perspective, Julien Fédon was not staging a rebellion nor was he involved in a revolt as such, but was acting as a Republican revolutionary attempting to bestow a legacy of freedom to all.

The seeds of revolt had been sown and had taken root long before, in the manner in which organised resistance to slavery had taken form from almost its inception, more than one hundred and fifty years before. Then there were the conditions on the island that had been altered by events in the recent past, when the arriving British administrators did not honour the terms of surrender made with the resident Roman Catholics, French born, Creoles, and Free Blacks and Free People of Colour during their rule, first between 1762 and 1779, and then later from 1784 to 1795, when the rebellion began. The French Catholic population in Grenada had made repeated appeals to the government in London, denouncing the outrages that were mounted against their religion. There was, however, little or no response. This failure to respond contributed to an overall discontentment, which was expressed by a sense of insecurity, fear and growing anger, likely to have been experienced by all in the community, and probably not excluding some of the slaves.

There was also the matter of how the British residents had been treated by the French during the period when the French had temporarily returned. Upon the return of the British to Grenada, reprisals were to become increasingly evident. Amongst a quantity of indignities, "The British colonists used their dominance of the legislature to seize the Roman Catholic Church buildings, lands, and properties, and then rendered all Roman Catholic marriages, baptisms and burial illegal unless they were solemnised before Protestant Anglican clergymen." [60] These very provocative moves against the Catholics, and the Church itself, had struck at the root of the French Roman Catholic faith and the culture of the people, driving a sense of alienation, stirring age-old animosities, and very likely, evoking memories of the wars of religion of a previous century in Europe.

Religion, Roman Catholicism, was central to the lives of the French colonial pioneers and the *gens de couleur*. For over the two centuries of French colonisation in the Caribbean, it had sustained their way of life. Catholicism had also formed the backdrop, so to speak, against which syncretic movements had taken place within the Creole, coloured and slave populations. A particular Creole way of life that was expressed in a

---

60   Rodriguez, Junius P. *Encyclopedia of Slave Resistance and Rebellion*, 2007, p.1925

culture that was still in its nascent stages, but already sufficiently vibrant to produce unique syncretic belief systems, peculiar to these islands, influencing almost the entire hemisphere from the Mississippi delta in Louisiana to the jungles of Brazil: *Voodoo* and *Shango* of the Caribbean, *Santería* in Cuba and on the Main, and the *Candomblé* of Brazil. These thrived in the superstitious atmosphere of Catholicism, and were accommodated by its plethora of saints. These religious movements, created in the barrack rooms of slavery, conveyed meaning and focus and brought a new interpretation of deity to those who were now deprived of virtually everything, except their imagination. These New World cults acted as bridge and conduit between the African descended and the coloureds of all conditions. Perhaps, it offered hope and purpose, bringing the enslaved together with the free in the new, hoped-for dispensation, giving to them the strength to face the wars of liberation.

The emotions of all may well be imagined when the island was finally restored to Britain by the Treaty of Versailles in 1783—the very year in which the Cedula of Population, which was meant to create a new population for Trinidad, came into effect. French families left Grenada for Trinidad. Free Blacks and Free People of Colour, those with means and those who owned slaves, also pursued the benefits being offered. Unfortunately, many poorer Free People of Colour were simply left behind.

As more and yet more families, both French and Free Coloured, left Grenada for Trinidad, taking advantage of the Cedula of Population, the remaining coloured people became the majority of "free" persons on the island. This occurred against an increased restiveness in the enslaved population, as uncertainties grew as to who among them would be taken to Trinidad, who would be left behind, and what would be their circumstances.

News of a revolt of mulattoes in Saint Domingue, that did not include the slaves, which took place from October to December 1790 at Cap-Français the colony's main city, and its subsequent suppression, and the death by torture of its leader Vincent Ogé, must have agitated the people of colour even further. The knowledge that the Ogé revolt had served to trigger the massive slave uprising of August, the following year, 1791, that commenced the revolution in Saint Domingue, would serve as an object lesson for those who would lead revolutions in the Caribbean in the near future.

Meanwhile in Grenada, various forms of alliances took shape between the now two principle populations, the black enslaved and the coloureds, both free and enslaved. The European population had become outnumbered, by some estimates, by as much as fifty to one.

News arrived in the French Antilles of the proclamation in France of 4th April 1792 that the *gens de couleur* and free Negroes in the Caribbean ought to enjoy an equality of political rights with the Europeans. This, together with the possibility of the abolition of slavery, meant a greater likelihood for a violent upheaval, in fact, it became the inevitable consequence. French slavery would be abolished by the Convention in Paris in 1794, following Commissioner Léger-Félicité Sonthonax and Etienne Polverel's abolition of slavery in Saint Domingue in 1793.

What served to exacerbate matters in Grenada was the appointment to the island, in 1793, of Lieutenant Governor Ninian Home. Home, described as an ultra-Protestant, who, ". . . completed the alienation of the French from Britain and precipitated revolution." (Rodriguez 2007, 183) This coincided with the removal of most of the British garrison to other stations in the French Antilles, as Britain had, by this time, fully entered the French revolutionary war. These changes coincided with the arrival in the Caribbean, from France, of Victor Hugues (1761-1826) in June of 1794. His purpose was to implement the "'Decree of 16 Pluviöse,' the National Convention's unconditional abolition of slavery and provision of citizenship in the French Republic to anyone domiciled in France's colonies." (ibid.) The Grenada uprising was now inevitable.

The French revolution, through the medium of Hugues, brought violent upheavals to the Caribbean. Hugues was born in Marseilles and lived in Saint Domingue in the late 1780s and early 1790s. He has been portrayed as a person of colour, but this has never been actually ascertained. Hugues had returned to France at the time of the revolution, to La Rochelle, and became an official, active in the local Jacobin Club. Hugues then was named Civil Commissioner for Guadeloupe in 1794 and with

François-Dominique Toussaint L'Ouverture, was a leader of the Haitian Revolution. Toussaint led enslaved Africans to victory over Europeans, abolished slavery, and secured native control over the colony in 1797 while being nominally governor of the colony.

the help of the slaves, the *gens de couleur* and French revolutionaries, purged the island of royalists and other counterrevolutionary movements, using the guillotine as an instrument of terror. He would have a profound effect on the minds of a great many people in the region, inspiring them with revolutionary ideas.

Hugues captured Martinique, Guadeloupe and St. Lucia in a series of bloody engagements with the British and perpetrated massacres of French royalists on these islands.

The *Grenada Handbook* of 1909 places on record the events. I quote some highlights:

> "The forces at his, Hugues', disposal being insufficient for him to do more than hold Guadeloupe against the British, he determined to attempt the capture of the British islands by stirring up insurrections.

> His first intrigues were against Grenada, and in 1795 his emissaries, finding, as has been seen, good ground on which to sow the seeds of treason amongst the Republican-minded Free Blacks and People of Colour, succeeded by a promise of assistance in the shape of arms, ammunition and an armed force, and, in some cases by threats, in inciting the French colonists to rise in arms against British rule."

The proclamation of Victor Hugues to the Grenadian insurgents commenced "Time and the defeat of the English forces in Guadeloupe had dimmed the memory of the heinous crimes by which the vile satellites of George had sullied the Windward Islands . . ." (Pocock 1993, p. 545.) In Edward Cox's, *Fédon's Rebellion*, we read: "In February 1795 Charles

Vincent Ogé (c.1755 - 1791) was a free
man of colour and the instigator of a revolt
against white colonial authority in French
Saint-Domingue that lasted from October
to December 1790 in the area outside Cap-
Français, the colony's main city. The Ogé revolt
of 1790 foretold the massive slave uprising of
August 1791 that began the Haitian Revolution. Ogé had been influenced by Robespierre
and other revolutionaries to start the uprising.
In the second part of this study, a similar-
ity of relationship is suggested between the
circumstances of Maximilien Robespierre and
Vincent Ogé, and C.L.R. James and Dr. Eric
Williams.

Detail of "The landing at Jacmel in St. Domingue"
(1790s). The Fédon rebels would have appeared in this
manner, wearing elements of European military uniforms.
(Mansell Collection)

Henri Christophe (1767 – 1820)
was said to have been born in Grenada
(some claim St. Kitts) and had travelled
to Saint Domingue as a youth. Joining
Toussaint L'Ouverture, he took part in
the Haitian revolution and later was to
declare himself King of Haiti. Prior to
stowing away to Haiti, he was a slave on
the Sans Souci estate in Grenada (Information: George Brizan "St. George's —
The Prettiest Town in the West Indies".
Picture: Mansell Collection)

Nogues and Pierre La Valette, having been appointed Captains, returned from Guadeloupe, bearing commissions naming Julien Fédon Commander-in-chief of the rebels in Grenada". [61] The *Grenada Handbook* continues (pp. 33ff): "As a leader of the insurgents, a coloured planter named Julien Fédon, who owned the Belvedere estate on the heights of St. John, was selected and a commission given to him as General Commandant under the French Republic."

Edward Cox lists those coloured men commissioned as officers of the French army as Stanislas Besson, Charles Nogues, Joachim Philippe, [62] and Jean Pierre La Valette. [63] Stanislas Besson is described by Joseph Marryat [64] as a silversmith from La Bay (Soubise estate) and second in command to Julien Fédon. Marryat writes that Hugues, "had given to them a flag, on which the words *Liberté, Egalité ou La Mort*, were written in large letters." Hugues urged Julien Fédon and Stanislas Besson as well as other revolutionaries, to rise up and overthrow the British and kill all French royalists on the island, as a new dispensation was at hand and a new page in world history was being written. As the appointed time drew near to commence the planned revolt, all free coloured leaders in the Julien Fédon movement freed their slaves. These joined other slaves who had emancipated themselves.

We find in *French Revolution in Grenada* by Arnauld Vendryes: "The rebellion broke out on the night of the 1st and 2nd of March 1795. Fédon and Besson, with 100 slaves and coloureds, took the Marquis [St. Andrew district] and the town of Grenville (La Bay) by storm". Taken by surprise the residents of the town, some fourteen British planters and their families, were roused from their beds and brought into the streets where they were shot and their bodies chopped and mangled by the cutlass-wielding attackers. The houses of the town were plundered as the attackers searched

---

61   Devas, Raymond P. "A History of the island of Grenada", 1498-1796.

62   McDaniel, Lorna. In a paper, "Madame Philip-O", she refers to Joachim Philippe "This was the son of Jeanette Philippe who, during the Grenada rebellion of 1795, acted as the chief emissary and prime military force of the leader, Fédon."

63   Cox, "Fédon's Rebellion 1795-96; Causes and Consequences", in: *The Journal of Negro History*, Vol. LXVII, No. 1 Spring 1982, pp. 7-19.

64   Marryat, Joseph. *Thoughts on the Abolition of the Slave Trade*, 1813.

In St. Domingue, the guerillas of Toussaint L'Ouverture would set the benchmark for slave resistance throughout the Caribbean. In this engraving, they stage a guerilla-styled ambush on French troops (circa 1790). One could imagine the storming of Julien Fédon's last stronghold on Belvedere estate, Mount Qua Qua, as resembling the scene depicted here. (Mary Evans Picture Library)

for survivors. We are told that three English persons were able to escape. The rebels then withdrew to Balthazar estate where they took a Mr. Ross prisoner and where the Abbé Peissonier was shot and killed by La Valette. With the leaders of the rebellion now blooded and committed, they withdrew to Fédon's estate at Belvedere. Simultaneously, there had been an attack at Gouyave, on the opposite side of the island; there, the rebels, who were led by Etienne Ventour and Joachim Philippe, had met with some resistance. These events were soon followed by the taking as prisoners, the Lieutenant Governor and some members of his government. Fédon then demanded the surrender of St. George's, and when the authorities there refused to entertain his offer, a full scale war ensued.

From all over the island "the Negroes flocked to Fédon's standard in hundreds, no fewer than four thousand joining him in the month of March alone. Moreover, these were not only Negroes, but also Frenchmen of all classes and colours in Grenada." (Steele 2003, 119). Over time,

Chatoyer the chief of the Black Caribs in St. Vincent, with his five wives. The Black Caribs' oral history of their migration from South America's Orinoco region relates that these Arawak-speaking people of the Orinoco came to St. Vincent long before the arrival of Europeans to the New World. At some point, two Hispanic ships carrying enslaved West Africans on their way to the Americas arrived on the island. The Africans, in a minority compared to the overall population, eventually integrated into the Caribs, adding an African element to the culture.

When the British took over Saint Vincent after the Treaty of Paris in 1763, they were opposed by French settlers and their Carib allies. After a series of Carib Wars, and the death of their leader Satuye (Chatoyer), they surrendered to the British in 1796. The British considered the Black Caribs enemies and deported them to Roatán, an island off the coast of Honduras. In the process, the British separated the more African-looking Caribs from the more Amerindian-looking ones. They decided that the former were enemies who had to be deported, while the latter were merely "misled" and were allowed to remain.

A distant ancestress of Dr Eric Williams comes from this heritage. (Edwards; Paria)

some 7,000 would join Fédon in the mountain stronghold and there withstand repeated assaults to capture it.

One of the decisive events to take place was the massacre of prisoners at the Fédon camp. This may have been triggered by news of the death of Fédon's brother, Jean, and an assault on the camp by British forces. Perhaps over fifty prisoners, including the governor, were killed. At first shot, they were then hacked with cutlasses, their bodies left where they had fallen to be trod on in the mud, the gore and blood covering the encampment. This brought a sharp reaction from French Republican leaders who had hoped to take the prisoners off the island, perhaps to be used as bargaining chips in the future. From this point onwards, a division was created in the running of the revolution with the French Republicans seeking to take control. Notwithstanding, Hugues would call for discipline in the struggle and the need to stand fast in the face of what was to become insupportable odds, for the love of the Republic. Hugues would write in 1796 to Julien Fédon and Stanislas Besson, and the other insurgent commanders:

> "We are pained to see how divided you are; the enemy will hear of it, and will take advantage of it to fall upon you and defeat you. Let ambition give way to love of the Republic. It is impossible for all of you to be in charge; obey those who command you and do not force us to use harsh measures against you. Listen to our appeals, they are for your own good."

Towards the end of the revolt Hugues wrote to his commanders, [65]

> "For some time now all the help and ammunition you received has been shipped from St. Lucia, because of the proximity and ease of communication between that island and yours. The English have just captured Morne Fortuné, and we hasten to send powder and cartridges to you by the 'Modeste', so you will have means to repel the enemy, should they attack.

65   Vendryes, Arnauld: "French revolution in Grenada", translated by David Watson and Ernest Wiltshire (the information is abstracted from "A History of the island of Grenada 1498-1796" by Raymand Devas as well as from the Centre d'accueil et de recherche des Archives nationales (CARAN), series: Colonies C/10A/4)

It was only after the most vigorous resistance, and considerable losses sustained in the various battles, combined with lack of ammunition, that they were able to seize the fort. A number of republicans who had been defending it left before the surrender, taking their weapons with them, and joined troops scattered throughout the island and 500 French deserters; so the war in this country will become more intense than ever.

We hope that this failure, far from vanquishing your courage, will give new strength, and although the efforts of the defenders of St. Lucia were not crowned with success, that you will still use every means at our disposal to achieve victory for your selves. You must be on your guard: the enemy will very soon have to move forces to Grenada. Try to obtain from Spanish Trinidad the help that island can provide... To speak to you of zeal, of action would be to insult you. Your devotion is well known to us, and we are certain that you will be faithful to the oath of the Republic: Victory or death."

Signed: Victor Hugues. (*23 prairial IV, 11-06-1796*)

The rebellion would sweep over the entire island and continue for more than a year. There was war and destruction on a terrible scale. Stanislas Besson may have died with what remained of Fédon's troops when they were surrounded on Mount Qua Qua, Morne Fédon, Belvedere estate [66] by British forces, where they massacred their prisoners before surrendering.

The series "Colonies C/10A/4" lists from the CARAN archives, Paris, provides the names of some 81 French citizens murdered between 6th and 8th June 1796:

"Barberrousse, aged 60, Batarelle, woman & 4 children, Beau, Pierre, Bontems, Baucaud aged 60, woman & 3 children, Charpentier, aged 60, Chautenel, Clovis coloured, Clauzier, Sainte-Marie, woman & 6 children, Darcoeuil-Clauzier, aged 80, Delisle, Desouze, aged 75, & 6 children, Dolabaille, Alexandre, woman & 5 children, Doudun, Droust,

---

66   In E. Cox "Fédon's Rebellion 1795-1796: Causes and Consequences", in *Journal of Negro History* Vol. LXVII, pp. 7-9 "Fédon had a property of 360 acres with 96 slaves". I have found no estate in Grenada with that exact acreage.

woman & 2 children, Dumont, Gerbert, woman & 4 children, Four-
teau, Jean, woman & 4 children, Furgerie, Charles, coloured, Houl-
ingue, woman & 4 children, Hypolite, coloured, La Bastide, woman &
3 children, Labatte, Lorency, woman & 5 children, Marasse de Farotte,
woman & 5 children, Morillon, woman & 5 children, Father Pascal,
priest of Gouyave, Ralph, Pierre, Rapierre, Edmond, coloured, Sibi-
laque, woman, Villar."

Despite material aid and appeals for solidarity the revolution faltered
and eventually failed in Grenada.

Fédon himself disappeared [67] and the surrender was signed by Jossee
on 10th June 1796. The *Grenada Handbook* of 1909 relates (pp. 33ff):

"Nearly all the leading men concerned in the uprising fell into the hands
of the victors either immediately or shortly after, the only notable exception being Fédon himself, who, after hiding for some time in the
woods, was completely lost sight of and nothing is known of his fate,
although it is conjectured that he was drowned while seeking to escape
in a small canoe to Trinidad. A special court of *Oyer and Terminer* was
at once appointed to try the rebels who, it should be mentioned, came
within the purview of an Act passed in 1795 accusing them of high
treason, and confiscating their lands. Forty-seven of them were con-
victed by this court on the afternoon of June 30th, and sentenced to
death on the following morning, the court not allowing them to plead
anything in their defense but convicting them upon proof of identity and telling them that any such representation should be made to
the Crown."

The following list of prisoners were condemned to the gallows:-

Jean Baptiste Ollivier, René Pasee, Edward Duffant, Jean Pierre Gou-

---

67   E.L. Joseph notes in his *History of Trinidad* p. 186: ."..many of the rebels escaped to
Trinidad. (Was Stanislas Besson amongst them?) I have heard from authority which
I cannot doubt, that the Infamous Fédon, the chief of the Grenada insurrection, escaped to this island (Trinidad) and was here at the time of its capture. The story of
his having been drowned, coming from Grenada, was a mere fabrication."   Pocock
1993 p. 544 notes: "He (Dominic Dert) sympathised with the French insurgents in
Grenada during their bloody revolt against the British ... In that year he assisted one
of these by lending him a canoe at Carenage (in Trinidad).

lard, François Cazeneuve, Joseph Verdet, Elie Sarlande, Nivel Blackfort, Etienne Babot, Louis Benoît Rouget, Pierre Rouse, François Seaux, Jacques Eloin, Joseph Covel, Pierre Marucheau, Joseph Rechou, Joseph Colombert, John Porteus, Baptiste Goodrish, Baptiste Grenoir, Roubrn Rocquevert. [68]

The Fédon revolution of 1795 appears to hold manifold connections between François Besson and some of its principle characters, one of them, Stanislas Besson, being possible his son, and links them to some locations, Soubise, Belvedere and Balthazar estates where terrible events occurred.

It would be difficult to imagine the distress felt by François and his family in Trinidad during the rebellion. It is not clear whether François' son, François *fils*, and his family were still in Grenada when the news arrived that at midnight on 2nd March, 1795, a body of insurgents under Julien Fédon, a person he surely knew, who, in the company of Stanislas Besson who was his second in command had surrounded the town of Grenville, on Soubise estate that had previously belonged to him, where a horrible massacre of European and coloured persons, both British and French, had occurred, neither age nor sex proving a bar to their murders. The town had been burnt after being looted and the insurgents had fallen back to Balthazar estate. François had been the Commandant of the *Marquis*, St Andrew's district; his principal estates for some 20 years had been located there. This would have been compounded when the ghastly news of the massacre of the women and children at Belvedere estate would have come to hand, again, very likely involving his son, Stanislas, who, as a boy François must have cared for, certainly enough to educate. This news would have hurt him deeply. Among those killed one comes across the names de la Bastide, de l'Isle, Darceuil—families into which François' descendants would marry within the next generation in Trinidad. Freda Scott née Harford recalls that in her childhood in Grenada, close upon one hundred years ago the name Fédon was never mentioned in the presence of the servants.

---

68   Grenada 30th June, 1796. Alexander Houstons; from G. Brizan, *St George's The Prettiest Town in the West Indies.* 2004, p. 49

Carting Sugar: "The conveyance of the sugar from the various estates to Port-of-Spain for shipment is attended with considerable difficulty, and often with much risk. The general want of bridges and the rapid rise of the rivers after the rain rendering the fords impassable, are the causes of what otherwise appear so extraordinary to those who have spent their lives in England."
(Detail, Richard Bridgens, circa 1820, Trinidad, courtesy Adrian Camps-Campins)

THE AFRO-FRENCH CREOLE SOCIETY
4

The mulatto, or coloured, society of Grenada, in fact of the New World, had not suddenly arrived in the late 18th century; it had taken several generations to create it. Because the products of mixed-race unions are to be examined in part 2 of this book, we will spare a short discussion on this important aspect of life in the Caribbean during and after the period of slavery.

From the earliest times of colonisation, the customs and practices of the slave society had given to all European men the right to possess and to violate black women. The Abbé Raynal, who wrote in the mid 18th century, gave his impressions, which may appear to some as racists, of the nature of inter-racial relationships in the period of plantation slavery, as it would have been perceived by a person of his time. He is quoted by P.G.L. Borde in *History of Trinidad under the Spanish Government* (first part):

"Those who have sought the causes of this taste for the Negroes, which seems so depraved in Europeans, have found the source of it in the nature of the climate, which in the torrid zone leads irresistibly to love; in the ease of satisfying without constraint and attention this uncontrollable inclination; in a certain piquancy of beauty which is soon found in the Negress when one has got accustomed to their colour; above all in a warmth of temperament which gives them the power to inspire and feel the most ardent of transports.

Also they took revenge, as it were, for the humiliating dependence of their condition by the dissolute passions, which they excited in their masters, and our courtesans in Europe did not know more about the art of squandering and ruining great fortunes than the enslaved Negresses. But the African woman surpassed the European woman in the trueness of the love, which they bore for the men who bought them. It is to the fidelity of their love that their masters more than once owed the good fortune of having discovered and prevented conspiracies which would have made the owners easy victims of their slaves."

Lewis and Maingot, dealing with this period in their paper *Main Currents in Caribbean Thought*, wrote (p. 232):

"In a very real sense, the history of the Caribbean slave regime is the history of the sexual exploitation of black women. Much pro-planter ideology was rooted in racial fears, and racial fears in turn are commonly rooted in sexual obsessions. In the Caribbean, of course, these obsessions had their own peculiar history. A number of factors facilitated inter-racial sex: the massive preponderance of Africans as compared to Europeans, the serious shortage of women both black and white in the total demographic picture, the failure of the West Indian colonists unlike the New England colonists to successfully transplant the values of the mother country to the new local society. The resultant widespread miscegenation, despite all legislative efforts to prohibit it, created the new group of mulatto Antillean people."

The colonisation of the islands in the Caribbean Sea saw the exploitation of women in several forms. The obvious example was the treatment of slave women who endured various forms of torture and punishments arising out of their supposed aggressive and violent natures. [69]

---

69   Kein (ed.), *In Creole*, 2000

Over time, this was compounded by a desire for survival and power amongst the ablest and most attractive women in the slave and the Free Coloured population; this too contributed to cohabitation and at times long-term relationships and procreation. Hearn comments in his *Two Years in the French West Indies* (p. 349):

> "Travellers of the 18th century were confounded by the luxury of dress and jewelry displayed by the swarthy beauties of St. Pierre. It was a public scandal to European eyes. But the creole Negress or mulatress, beginning to understand her power, sought for higher favours and privileges than silken robes and necklaces of gold beads: she sought to obtain, not merely liberty for herself but for her parents, brothers, sisters, even friends."

Quoting General Romanet, in *Voyage à la Martinique*, Hearn continues,

> "*La Fille de Couleur,* beautiful, beguiling as one writer said, they know how to please, they have those rights and privileges which the whole world allows to their sex, they know how to make the fetters of slavery serve them for ornaments. They may be seen placing upon their proud tyrants, the same chains worn by themselves and making them kiss the marks left, thereby the master becomes the slave, and purchases another's liberty only to lose his own."

Social pressures made a taboo of many aspects of social contacts between the Europeans and the coloureds. This was based on the notion of the "purity of the blood," a Spanish ideology founded at the time of the reconquest of Spain in the 1490s which was directed at the Muslims and the Jews and was exported over time to the New World. To offend someone, one simply had to imply that he might have "cousins on the (Guinea) coast." White-appearing persons, products of a *mustee* (offspring of an octoroon and a European) and a white man, for example, were "white in the eyes of the law, (but) under the ban of custom and prejudice". (Craig-James 2008, 37)

In Tobago, for example, "the wisest as well as the most politic planters were in favour of the public relaxing the shade distinctions, but . . . deferred instead to the opinions of white women" (ibid) — the latter no doubt motivated by jealousy.

An oil painting of what may be an African slave woman, dating from the early 19th century, displays the sensitivity of the artist in capturing the personality of the subject. (Unknown artist, Paria)

In the white male-dominated plantation slave society in the Caribbean, European women appeared to have been capable of defining the social mores of racial groupings. Susan Craig-James describes that free coloured women in Tobago during the 1830s, who had wealthy fathers or who had been educated at boarding schools in Britain or Barbados, "were accomplished in music, dancing and fashionable dressing." She goes on to say, "The predominant orientation among the coloureds was to be culturally, socially and politically accepted by the whites." (Craig-James 2008, 47) The situation of the Free Coloureds in the Caribbean on the whole, may be regarded as similar.

As a result of its history, the New Wold produced the People of Colour, the products of unions between master and slave, European and the "half-caste." They were born with gradations of skin tones that ranged from the brown of the *mulatto*, who was half European and half African; to the fair-skinned, blue or green-eyed *octoroon*, the product of a European and a *quadroon*, the quadroon being the child of the mulatto and a European.

The all pervasive but essentially flawed ideology of the racial superiority of the European and the idea of an inherent inferiority, equally flawed, of all who were descended from the African, notwithstanding the degree

La Fille de Couleur. The Creole belles of the 19th century were reputed to be the most beautiful women of their generation in the French Antilles. (M.J. Cazabon, National Museum of Trinidad and Tobago)

of European blood, emphasized separation by racial and shade distinctions as a formal principle. These prejudices were peculiar to the New World, and still basically are, and were contrived by the colonists to maintain ideas of racial superiority, resulting in the creation of 'an aristocracy of skin.'

Some coloureds were slaves on estates, others had been manumitted or had been born free and had taken an active part in the affairs of their extended families, be these European or otherwise. Many had received some education, others had been trained in skills and worked in trades, and some owned property and slaves. A great many were poor. These progeny of miscegenation, being neither one nor the other, sometimes existed in the half-light of unrealised hopes. They were often the bearers of the burden of envy, and in turn were tortured by jealousy. They could carry yet another burden, that of rejection and abandonment. The very parent that had engendered them was sometimes the person who despised them most. [70] On the other hand, this person of mixed race could

70   "The word "mulatre" from the Spanish *mulato*, scientifically means mule or hybrid; similarly the word "metis" comes from the Spanish *mestizo* that is, product issued

"Cutting canes in general commences in January: it is performed in this manner: The Negro seizes the cane by the top, cuts off the upper joints to plant for the next crop; he then cuts down the remaining stem close to the ground. When a sufficient number are cut, another Negro carries them to the cart, which is always in waiting to convey them to the mill."
(Richard Bridgens, circa 1820, Trinidad, courtesy Adrian Camps-Campins)

Carting canes: "From the field the canes are immediately carried in carts drawn by mules or oxen to the mill. Here the saccharine juice is pressed out by three horizontal, or more frequently vertical rollers, which are made to revolve at a moderate rate by machinery, of which the prime mover is two or sometimes three pairs of mules attached to the mill-swoop. A Negress, called the 'feeder,' stationed at a convenient place, introduces the fresh canes between the two first rollers." The mill and outbuildings at Champs Elysées estate would have been well established by the 1790s. (Richard Bridgens, circa 1820, Trinidad, courtesy Adrian Camps-Campins).

be the loved and cherished child of a plantation household. He could be the bearer of an aristocratic name, be presented at a European Court, and serve as a page. [71] In some rare cases, he would be university-trained and practise a profession, owning property and slaves, acquiring a fortune and passing it on to his children. [72]

In the relatively small society of Grenada, where the possession of European physiognomy, subtle shades of colour and hair texture inferred

---

of individuals, not of races, but of different kinds. The first term was more particularly used to designate the product of a European man with an African woman, and the second was more generally related to that of an European with an Indian [tribal people] woman. It is surprising that, during centuries of faith, the Spaniards, who were so religious, gave to these products the names which implied the negation of the Christian dogma of the unity of the cradle of mankind." Borde, *The History of Trinidad*, Vol I, p. 225.

71   Lebeau, *De la Condition des Gens de Couleur Libres sous l'Ancien Regime*. Cited in James, C.L.R.. *The Black Jacobins*, p. 40.

72   In the case of some members of the de Boissière family, the union between the African woman Zuzule and Jean de Boissière produced two sons. Joseph and August Boissière were both born in slavery, and although they were never manumitted, they were educated in France. Both owned property and businesses in Port-of-Spain and by the next generation, their children were wealthy.

status, recognition and acceptance, or not, there existed complicated kinship ties between the Europeans, the coloureds and the slaves. A great many Free Black and Coloured People were related to one another, to the enslaved, and to the resident Europeans, and would have been known to one another, at least by name or condition.

Both during the time of slavery and after emancipation, some coloured people were the products of an institution peculiar to the New World known as *plaçage*. Joan Martin in *Plaçage and Louisiana Gens de Couleur Libre,* comments on an aspect of the exploiting of women:

> "The plaçage system grew out of a shortage of accessible white women. France needed wives for the men it had sent overseas. Persuading women to follow the men was not easy. First willing farm and city-dwelling women, known as cassette or casket girls, because they brought all their possessions to the colonies in a small trunk or casket. Later felons were deported, (*filles du roi*) notwithstanding interracial relationships occurred almost the moment Europeans set foot in the New World, and that some Creole families who today consider themselves white actually began with mixed-race or African forebears." [73]

Plaçage was recognised as an extralegal system in which European men maintained common-law relationships with African, mixed race, free or enslaved women. This term also included relationships with Amerindian (Carib) and white Creoles.

Plaçage comes from the French *placer*: to place with. [74] Women in these relationships were known as *placées*. In the context of the Free Coloured society of Grenada, Tobago and Trinidad, these relationships were perceived as *mariages de la main gauche*, or left-handed marriages. Legal marriage in the free coloured society was rare in the first decades of the 19th century. Coloured men seldom married, and a coloured woman could be criticised for marrying a coloured man (Craig-James 2008, 47). Instances of European men marrying Free Coloured women were exceptional. The

73   Kein (ed.), *In Creole*, 2000

74   *Chained to the rock of Adversity, To be free, black and female in the old south*, edited by Virginia Meacham Gould, The University of Georgia Press, 1998, no page number. (This comes off the internet.)

practice of *plaçage* peaked from between the mid-18th century and the first decades of the 19th. [75] Often, these relationships continued for the lifetime of the partners. Lafcadio Hearn, who wrote in the 1890s, points out that: "Local custom permitted a sort of polygamy, the rich man naturally felt himself bound in honour to secure the freedom of his own blood." (Hearn, 341.) Parallel families grew up within sight of each other, and on occasion with the children of the *plaçage* joining the European family.

As we shall see in the accounts of both the de Boissière and Besson families, "It was not a rare thing to see legitimate wives taking care of the natural children of their husbands—becoming their godmothers (*s'en faire les marraines*)." (Hearn, 341.) This arrangement, uncommon in any other period in history, did produce, when it worked in the favour of the illegitimate offspring, some remarkable individuals.

The real issue, of course, must be the children of these unions. Unfortunately, I have not come across any records left by either slave or free women of colour that would give a critical view from their own perspective of their lives lived with European men during and immediately after the period of slavery. There is only circumstantial evidence left behind in the manner in which their progeny, the offspring of some of these unions, were provided for and how they conducted their lives.

To get recognition, which usually meant permission to use the European father's last name, share in its prestige, be mentioned in his last will and testament and be given an education, was vital and would make all the difference to the future of those children. They would be victors of the "cult of the will." To be forgotten or abandoned would condemn them to poverty and all that state would imply. [76]

The *plaçage* also had as a result an added disadvantage for adult African males. Hearn notes that in a list of slaves to whom liberty was given in

---

75 In Trinidad a mulatto woman by the name of Emma Clark maintained a boarding house on Broadway in Port-of-Spain in the 1860s. She would hold *mulatto* dances, "Quadroon Balls" to which she would invite wealthy young European men and coloured women known for their beauty and distinguished pedigree. (Conversations with Olga Mavrogordato)

76 The wills listed in the appendices give further evidence of the treatment of the children and women of the *plaçage*.

Martinique in the late 18th century, of the 69 mentioned, only two male adults were to be found. The coloured men are described as possessed

> ". . . of much vivacity, but are given to their pleasures, fickle, proud, deceitful, wicked and capable of the greatest crimes. . . The history of the *hommes de couleur* in all the French colonies has been the same;- distrusted by the Europeans, who feared their aspirations to social equality, distrusted even more by the Africans, the mulattoes became an Ishmaelitish clan, inimical to both races, and dreaded by both." (pp. 348-351)

To what extent this view would impact on the mixed-race male psyche in the New World is well worth investigating, as the terms "Red man complex," "Mulatto's complex," and "Chip on the shoulder" have great currency even today.

Generally, in European society at that time, any sexual relation outside of marriage (with the possible exception of the last vestiges of the aristocratic *droit du seigneur*) was deemed, strictly speaking, as immoral and socially unacceptable, possibly more so if the union was interracial. Illegitimacy carried with it an age-old curse. When combined with the notion of "black blood" in the context of the New World, it was seen as a disgrace.

A bastard child was a social liability, and even more so if the illegitimacy was immediately physically visible in a person. The European planter was not always automatically applauded for engaging in sexual relations with enslaved African women or even free women of colour. He was seen by the Church as taking advantage of the lax morality in the society and producing offspring, and, in the eyes of the law, as possibly affecting the financial position of his investors and of his family.

Besides illegitimacy, miscegenation posed a potential threat to the stability of the society in various ways. Among these were, at times, the legal limbo of the coloured offspring (for example, whether or not they were to be free or enslaved) and the upheavals in the slave population itself, where intimate association between a slave woman and her master could produce various complications, perhaps jealousy and victimisation, divisions and discord, which could lead to public dramas of passion and revenge in the slave population on an estate. Not the least of these complications, were the cases of genuine love between the European man and an African woman[77] or a woman of colour, which sometimes led to the averting of conspiratorial plots among the slave population against the Europeans.

Whichever the reasons were for miscegenation, whether rape and violence, opportunity and the pursuit of diversion, or the actual falling in love and entering into a life-long relationship; the fate of the many children of European men and women of African descent and their descendants was dependent on what children always depend upon: their family.

Coming back to François, it would not have been out of the ordinary if he had had one or several children with either slave women on his estates or Free Coloured women of the island's coloured society, as was the custom of the times throughout the islands of the Caribbean Sea. It is very possible that Stanislas Besson, described in the previous chapter, was François' son. Another Besson man of the period, who may have been François' grandson, was Julien Besson, who in the first decade of the 19th century joined the revolutionaries of Simón Bolívar, becoming one of the "Immortal 45," a party of insurgents, who, sailing from the island of Chacachacare, off the coast of Trinidad, took the town of Guiria on the mainland, and in so doing, it is claimed, triggered the second phase of that revolutionary war. [78] It is of interest that he was named Julien, like Julien Fédon. Perhaps he might have been Stanislas' son, and Julien Fédon was his godfather.

---

77   McDaniel, Lorna, in her paper "Jeanette Free Negro Woman", described the instance of a slave woman, Jeanette, who lived in concubinage with a Frenchman, Philippe, in Grenada in the 18th century. She and her several children were left substantial wealth: town properties, the island of Petit Martinique, plantations in Grenada and on the island of Carriacou. She and her children were manumitted. They moved to Trinidad and under the terms of the Cedula of 1783 became the most well-off Free Coloureds on the island. With the money earned from plantations worked by slave labour, two sons were educated in Britain as doctors: one of them was the well known petitioner J.B. Philippe; another descendant was the famous legal luminary, Crown Solicitor and Mayor of Port-of-Spain of the late 19th century, Maxwell Philip.

78   Mijares, *The Liberator*, p. 240.

*Naparima Hill, Trinidad, circa the 1820s. Porcelain lid (National
Museum of Trinidad and Tobago)*

*Hogsheads, very large barrels, would be used to ship out the estate's produce: rum, molas-
ses and sugar. Above, a hogshead has been grappled and is about to be taken from a long
boat onto the vessel that would take it to Europe.
(from: C. W. Day, "Five Years in the West Indies")*

In Julien Besson's [79] case, he may have entered Caracas with a remnant of the "Immortal 45" on 6th August 1813, at the end of the "Admirable Campaign." [80] Julien Besson may have gone to Trinidad with François in 1788 or before, as it is not clear when François first went to Trinidad. With regard to the paternity of these young men, Stanislas and Julien Besson, all this is conjecture, as there is no evidence to show who their fathers were, except that François was the only recorded adult male by that name in Grenada during those years when Julien and Stanislas might have been born. I found a baptismal record in the Cathedral of the Immaculate Conception in Port-of-Spain of a daughter of a Julien Besson in 1830.

They both may have been born at Soubise estate, also called La Bay, where Stanislas Besson, who had been trained as a silversmith (obviously his Besson father invested in his education and allowed him to carry his name), had come from and may have grown up. François and his first wife Marianne had lived there in 1762-63; Marie Françoise Adelaïde Besson de Beaumanoir, their daughter, was born there 1763. After his wife Marianne's death, François had continued to live there until 1766, when he sold the estate to Rochard L'Épine and his brothers in 1766.

It is of interest that Philippe Rose Roume, after divorcing his wife, Fanny Lambert, had married Marianne Elizabeth Rochard, a coloured woman, while acting as French Agent and Commissioner in Spanish Santo Domingo, in a ceremony in Port Republicain, now Port-au-Prince, in 1799, in the presence of Toussaint L'Ouverture, Louis Beauvais, the Divisional General commanding the forces in French Saint Domingue, and Paul L'Ouverture. Marianne Rochard was the natural daughter of Thomas Daniel Rochard L'Epine, and of a Free Coloured woman, Geneviève Katronice. [81] A daughter had been born to them in Scarborough, Tobago, in 1788, while Roume had served there as *Ordonnateur* during the French

---

79 In 1813, Santiago Mariño had liberated the East Coast of Venezuela and felt entitled to govern that part of the national territory. He confronted Bolívar on the issue. Mijares, *The Liberator*. p. 304.

80 Fernandez, *Historia del Estado Bolivar*, p. 91-97.

81 Pocock 1993, 35

A view of Marine Square looking east. The row of buildings at left are from the foot of Frederick Street on to Henry Street. François fils would have lived in one of these buildings in the 1840s. (M.J. Cazabon, courtesy Geoffrey MacLean)

occupation of that island. She had been named Rosette Roume, after Roume's mother. [82]

The fortunes of the Free Coloured people of these islands would vary depending on their circumstances. Dr. John Hay, in *A Narrative of the Insurrection in the Island of Grenada,* wrote of Stanislas Besson, "Field Commander, … as a Free Coloured man, scion of a class that could have gone to Paris and escaped the petty prejudices of parochial English planters." Take for instance, the Philippe family of Grenada, Carriacou and Trinidad, who enjoyed recognition, endowment, education and social and professional advancement from the 18th well into the 20th century. [83]

The examples of Stanislas Besson and Julien Fédon exemplify the worst fears of the Europeans in these islands in the 18th century with regard to the coloured male: that mixed-race unions in an environment under circumstances unknown to us today, did produce compassionless young men, capable of slaying their fellow Free People of Colour, old European men and women, small children, some of whom may have been their own relatives, and religious persons, notwithstanding the "state of war" existing at the time. Such was the fate of these two revolutionaries by the name of Besson.

---

82   ibid.

83   It is not without interest that we note that the Philippe family also produced a Republican revolutionary in the Fédon uprising, Joachim Philippe.

THE END OF PLANTATION SLAVERY
5

At the time of the uprising, François, who still had various ties to Grenada and whose grandchildren, his daughters' children, were still living there, must have had some very troubling times. He had spent some 25 years working in Grenada. It had been his home; he had been part of its government and had contributed to its growth and its prosperity.

Trinidad at the time was no paradise either. War between Spain and England had broken out, and in Trinidad, anarchy was the order of the day. The Spanish Governor, Don José Maria Chacón, was hardly in control. He feared an attack or an insurrection of the type experienced in Grenada. There were at hand all the similar components, highly combustible, waiting to explode. A year after the insurrection in Grenada had been crushed, on the 18th February 1797, the British would take the island of Trinidad from Spain.

The conquest of Spanish Trinidad by the British in 1797 was welcomed by many of the French inhabitants (the alternative would have been the republicans under Victor Hugues). In this entirely new environment they would rely on their own experience, but ultimately depend upon the interpretation by the English officials, of the Spanish laws, under which they had come, and were to be governed. The British left the Spanish laws extant. These tended to support the debtor; they would remain in place until the 1840s. The British, in a manner similar to the way in which they had dealt with the French planters in Grenada in 1763, did all that was needed to keep the plantation economy going—for the time being.

Of historic importance is that they accepted in the terms of surrender most of the Articles contained in the Cedula of Population of 1783. This was especially important to the Free Blacks and People of Colour, as it helped to maintain their situation in the colony—for the time being.

The French colonists in Trinidad who had come from Grenada and the other islands were, to some degree, back to where they had been fourteen years before. Britain would, however, be the guarantor of "order" and the main supplier of slaves until the slave trade ended in 1807.

To give an idea of the scale and pace of the agricultural development taking place in this previously almost undeveloped island, one has only to look at the population growth. In Trinidad in 1797, there were 2,086 Europeans (the majority of whom were French); 4,466 Free Coloureds (again, the majority were French-speaking); and 10,009 slaves. By 1802, the European population had climbed to 2,222 and 5,275 Free Coloureds, and the slaves to 19,709. Five years later, the European population had grown to 2,434 and 5,801 Free Coloureds, and the slave population stood at 20,100. [84]

François *fils* (son of François and his wife Elizabeth La Prade) and his wife, presumably Marie Roume, lived on Henry Street, in Port-of-Spain—perhaps in a rented house. This is unclear. The work, however, of the family was at Guapo and in the South Naparimas, in the development of the sugar plantations. The hard, dangerous, and difficult work of getting the Guapo and South Naparima estates operational, comprised mostly the clearing of gigantic trees, their felling, hewing and burning; the preparation of the fields; the planting of cane, cotton, cocoa [85] and food crops; the setting up of a home farm to feed the family and the slaves; plus the setting up of a factory for the refining of cane juice into sugar, molasses and rum as well as other produce for export. There was also the managing of hundreds of slaves; organising their work and enforcing strict discipline on the estates. This was a major and vastly expensive undertaking for a father and son. François was in his late sixties, and François *fils* was in his thirties. There are reasons to believe that they were joined by François' nephews, Jean Baptiste [86] and Pierre Louis Besson, as their names appear on various documents of the period. [87]

84   L.M.Fraser, *History of Trinidad*, Vol. 1, p. 289

85   The Whittle map of 1797 shows the nature of the cultivation at Guapo.

86   Jean Baptiste Besson was made a Mason at Les Frères Unis 251 S.C. in 1823.

87   Because they all have the same names—Jean, Pierre, François—it is sometimes unclear which ones are being referred to in the Trinidad slave registers. (Slave reg-

The house that they would have lived in on Bellevue estate, which bounded on the Pitch Lake, would have been a simple affair built of wood, thatched or shingled, and raised high off the ground—somewhat different from the long-established habitations of Grenada. Wooden plank floors and partitions and large, airy rooms with wide verandahs, possibly unpainted, stood out in contrast against the few pieces of fine furniture brought from Grenada that may have originated in France. There would have been many domestic slaves to look after the growing household, which by 1805 would have comprised three boys: François, Jean and Pierre Jean (sons of François *fils* born between 1796 and 1805); François, his third wife Reine, and their two sons, Vincent and Frederick, who were the same ages as his grandsons; as well as François' two nephews and possibly their families.

Michael Pocock in his *Out of the Shadows of the Past* has given a description of Rosa de Gannes de Charras' establishment at Maraval, in Trinidad, in those years (p. 67):

> "It was a large wooden house, roofed with shingles, measuring 72 x 40 feet. It was probably modelled on the estate houses that she had known in Grenada, and may well have been the prototype for the modest, but spacious and well ventilated, country dwellings that proprietors in Trinidad were to favour on their plantations. It was built on the site of the present building, to which she laid down the carriage way from the Long Circular Road, placing the grand stone gateposts at the entrance, which remain to this day. Some distance away from the house she erected the subsidiary buildings, necessary for the operation of the estate. There was a structure 70 x 50 feet, of local wood, to accommodate the slaves, of which she had about 80, a sugar usine also of local wood, 54 x 27 feet, roofed with 'texamani from the North', which housed four coppers and four spare ones, with their 'limandas' and scum removers, and all the utensils and instruments for the manufacture of sugar, a mill with iron wheels and drums, a building 27 x 27 feet for the boiler,

istration & compensation records [microform] of slaves in Trinidad and Barbados, 1813-1834. In the Public Record Office T71/939.)

which had a capacity of 300 gallons, a storehouse for coffee, with a mill
to extract the 'cereza' from the coffee, a store for bagasse and stables
for the mules, cattle and sheep. There were two kitchens, each with an
oven, and a bread oven, and also two kitchen gardens".

François' establishment would have been very similar to Rosa's.

The estate's produce, packed in hogsheads – massive barrels, had to be
shipped to Port-of-Spain by sail boat from the South of the island. This
in itself was an undertaking as each hogshead took up the entire space
in a ship's boat. Then the hogsheads would have to be sold through an
agent in England. All business was transacted by letters of credit and bills
of exchange. Little money actually changed hands. What was required for
the work of the estate and household necessities (clothes, furniture, boilers, ploughs) was shipped from England to Port-of-Spain, and then to the
estates in the South of the island. It was a hard and an amazing life; it was
life on the frontier of the New World in the early 1800s.

In 1807, the British halted the transatlantic trade in slaves. This law,
when enacted posed a serious problem for the planters, European, Free
Black and Coloured, as mortality was high on the plantations and the
lifespan of slaves short. A shortage of labour would cripple the production
on the estates. The planters in Trinidad were afraid that they would not
have sufficient time to recoup their investments before the emancipation
of the slaves, which now seemed inevitable, took place.

The children in François extended family would have been educated
at home, and then, more than likely, would have been sent abroad for a
more formal education. Many French planters and some Free Coloured
families sent their sons to France. A European education was considered
a necessity. One of the great dangers of the time was to "go local," become
too much of a colonial, a country bumpkin. The retention of French culture and social mores, manners and behaviour were vitally important to
keep one's status in the Caribbean, especially in view of the fact that links
to the "old country" were not completely severed.

Despite the uncertainties and dangers of the time, François would
have received and exchanged news from his and his wives' relatives back
in France.

The family's fortunes in France during this period (1800-1820) are of interest, François' mother, Elizabeth Thibaudeau, may have had a relative who was a renowned jurist and who had risen to a very senior position on the Council of State in post-revolutionary France. Durant describes Antoine Thibaudeau and his colleagues as "men of high calibre, not to be dictated to." (ibid. p. 162) The others on the Council were Jean-Étienne-Marie Portalis and Comte Pierre-Louis Roederer. They were the creators of The Code Napoleon. The some 2,281 articles of the Code—officially the *Code Civil de France*—became the law of France.

Thibaudeau, Portalis and Roederer comprised the Legislative Committee of that body, which, apart from accepting the basic principles of the revolution, would create the legal framework that would open the way for Napoleon Bonaparte to become Emperor of the French. It also tried to restore slavery in the French colonies— unsuccessfully in Saint Domingue but successfully in Guadeloupe and St. Lucia in 1802. François' eldest brother, Jean died in 1806 at St. Genis de Saintonge, France.[88]

In 1817, François' second daughter, Marie Louise Antoinette, the eldest child of his second marriage, married Jean Joseph Marie de Plenet. Upon her husband's death, she remarried Jean Chrysotome Le Brun de Rabot.[89] The de Rabot family was long established in Grenada and had been in possession of St. George's estate, 38 acres, overlooking the town and harbour. When the British took the island in 1762, the Hon. William Lucas acquired it. The *Grenada Handbook* relates that immediately upon the reconquest of the island by the French in 1779, the government bought this land, and Fort Frederick was erected on that site. (p. 30) The Canteloupe de Bourdieu family owned Retraîte estate, 704 acres, for almost 100 years. Jules Édouard de Poullain, son of Marie Adelaïde, François' eldest daughter, married Louise Charlotte de Canteloupe de Bourdieu. Mount D'Or estate, 48 acres, was owned by Joseph de Poullain, François' son in law, and so too was Spring estate, 106 acres.

---

88   Information from Paul de la Bastide.
89   GHC number 87 pp 1795-1796.

The Pitch Lake Palm was illustrated by Richard Bridgens, engineer in Trinidad, at the turn of the 19th century. This palm was indigenous to that area of Trinidad. Guapo Bay is in background. The hut in the foreground would have been the sort of dwelling used by slaves during this period. (Richard Bridgens, circa 1820, Trinidad, courtesy Adrian Camps-Campins)

The extended family of François (his son François, the husbands of his two daughters, and their sons) possessed all together towards the end of the 18th century in Grenada some 1,798 acres of land under cultivation. (see map on p. 21) Some members of the family stayed on in Grenada after the island passed to Britain; the majority returned to France. Only François and his son François *fils* would go to Trinidad under the terms of the Cedula of 1783.

The early 1820s saw an interesting personage arrive in Trinidad: the Abbé Besson. [90] He was referred to Bishop Poynter by Bishop Buckley as "...a great mathematician and formerly a teacher at the École Polytechnique at Paris. [91] He is not likely to have stayed long because he was too eager to fill his pockets by overcharging his parishioners. He was an authority in his field,

---

90 Perhaps a pseudonym? as we find in the National Archives in Paris: François Bacquiat, *dit* ("said") Besson, Abbé Besson, Ref.T1608 (series T etc.) years 1784-1826. A François Bacquiat appears on a list of French officers serving in the Caribbean in the end of the 18th century. (The Internet)

91 Leahy, *Catholic Church in Trinidad 1820-1828* (p. 23). Durant, *The Age of Napoleon* (p. 323). The Abbé Besson, if he was who he claimed to be, may have been a colleague of Gaspard Monge, a leading mathematician in France (1746-1818). Monge was Professor of Mathematics at the École Polytechnique He is regarded as the father of Descriptive Geometry. He was one of the savants who accompanied Napoleon to Egypt, presumably to measure ancient monuments. Another colleague, Jean-Victor Poncelet, formulated the basic theorems of projective geometry.

it would appear. The Abbé Besson would stay in Trinidad for a few years, perhaps two or three, during which time he would fall foul of the church officials, supposedly for charging exorbitant prices for the performance of his priestly duties. He was eventually encouraged to leave the island. His relationship to the family is unknown.

François died in 1819, he was 85 years old. According to the index of the "Spanish Protocol of Deeds," he had made a will in 1813, but I have not been able to locate it. Even though I have come across a record of his death in the archives of the Cathedral of the Immaculate Conception (stating that his widow was Reine Martineau, a native of Roussillac), I have not found his grave

Bridgens' illustration of the Gru Cru Palm, which appears to be growing in an area that may be south Trinidad. It shows an estate house, outhouses and factory. In the foreground is a planter on horseback in conversation with presumably one of the slaves. Because Bridgens may have spent some time sketching flora and fauna in the deep South, he might just have caught François or François fils one morning on his sketch pad! (Richard Bridgens, circa 1820, Trinidad, courtesy Adrian Camps-Campins)

in the public cemetery in Port-of-Spain. This has led me to believe that he may have been buried on one of his plantations in the South of the island.

What follows is an account of the fortunes of his children and their descendants. His eldest son, François *fils* who had been in control of running the estates, bringing in the crop, exporting the produce, handling the accounts, registering the slaves, and paying the taxes, would soon face serious challenges, not the least of which was his failing health. Other problems loomed with the Slave Amelioration Regulations published in 1823 to be operative from 1824. This would mean that property values would fall, credit would dry up, and mortgages could be foreclosed.

In 1824, the family was affected when Bellevue estate, 353 acres, was sold at the doors of the Tribunal for debt and was bought by one of François' creditors for a sum below its true worth. Fr. Anthony de Verteuil in his book, *The Black Earth of South Naparima*, records a notice that appeared in the *Port-of-Spain Gazette* of 19th April 1826 (pp. 147–149):

> "Obliged to quit the colony for reasons of health, François Besson requests all persons having claims against himself individually or against the Estates of La Romaine or La Grenade to present them within one month."

Fr. de Verteuil notes:

> "In fact from the 13th April François Besson had been legally discharged from the administration of his late father's property. He had apparently been a kind master towards the slaves as far as we can judge and was regarded with favour by at least some of them. The records of the estates on which no punishments were given for the quarter of the year ending 29th September 1824 include La Romaine Estate of which he was proprietor and manager and we presume that his kindness also extended to the slaves on La Fortunée.

> "Whatever the case, when the slaves on the Besson estates realised that they would soon have a new master of unknown quality they were very disturbed. At least three of them from the Besson estates (out of 40 for the whole of Trinidad) availed of the Compulsory Manumission clause in the new legislation of 1824. This allowed a slave who applied for manumission through the Protector of Slaves to be appraised by an official appointed and on payment of that sum to the recognised owner, to be given freedom."

On the 17th April 1826, Reine and Poly, two female slaves of La Fortunée plantation, applied for freedom; also on the 17th, Renette Marie, of Bellevue plantation; on September 19th Victoire Young of La Fortunée plantation. The *Port-of-Spain Gazette* for the above dates records:

> "The slaves hereunder named having with the assistance of the Protector and the Guardian of Slaves applied to His Honour the Chief Judge for the purchase of their freedom: Notice is hereby given to all

persons, having or pretending to have, any Right, Title or Interest in and to the said slaves . . . to attend before His Honour the said Judge by themselves or their agents on the 21st day of September, then and there to prefer such claims as they shall or may have in or to the said slaves. Victoire Young, Plantation registered as the property of the heirs of François Besson Snr. deceased, and belonging to the Plantation, La Fortunée, situated in the Quarter of South Naparima. (*Port-of-Spain Gazette* on indicated dates) Are we to conclude that François' leniency to his slaves led to the insolvency of the estates?"

The health of François *fils* may have taken a turn for the worse The *Port-of-Spain Gazette* of 17th May 1826 carried the following notice:

"Mr. François Besson having been definitely discharged from the administration of the property of his father since 13th April last, the undersigned heirs hereby give notice that the property which they hold in common, has since the 14th April been administered by Messrs Itier and Roux, merchants of Port-of-Spain, in whom all persons still having claims against the said Succession are requested to present themselves. Reine Martineau, widow Besson, for herself and her two minor children. François Guira, for his son, Simon Antonmattei, for his son, Joseph Roux, for his wife, François Besson, Jean Besson, Vincent Besson, Elizabeth Besson, Pierre Besson."

It would appear that François and his third wife Reine had two more children after the births of Frederick and Vincent: I have not found a registration, birth or baptismal certificate for these children. With regard to François Guira, who claims for his son, we see that Angelo Guira married Jeanne Besson in the presence of Louis Cortes and Louis Latour in 1840. It is not clear whose daughter she might have been. I have also noted the marriage of Louis Cortes and Andrienette Besson in 1839, in the presence of François Besson (=*fils*). I have not been able to ascertain the relationship of Joseph Roux or his wife or Simon Antonmattei to the family.

Being mindful of the changing times, and with François *fils* perhaps gravely ill, the family would now attempt to salvage what it could from the ailing plantations, while making an attempt to start a business in Port-of-Spain. On the 18th May 1826, the following notice appeared in the

Gazette: "The subscribers have entered into partnership under the firm of François and Pierre Besson from the 18th April last. François Besson Pierre Jean Besson." [92]

During that period, François *fils* travelled to France, perhaps for his health, perhaps to avoid his creditors, or perhaps even to avoid the dissatisfaction of his family for his handling of the administration of the estates. He died about five years later in 1831. The place of his burial is not known. It was around that time that François, the third by that name (I will refer to him in future as François III), the grandson of François Besson de Beaumanoir, took Benoît Olivier, perhaps an in-law into partnership as co-proprietor of La Romaine estate. In the South Naparimas, there were two plantations; in Guapo four, and in Moruga one, that was either owned or controlled by the extended family. Their eventual closure or loss through bankruptcy would be a disaster. The investment of almost 50 years in Trinidad, made after closing down the Grenada establishment, from 1788 to 1838, would prove to be a substantial loss of capital and one wonders if the family's interest would have been better served had they remained in Grenada.

In his *The Corsicans in Trinidad*, Fr. Anthony de Verteuil records (p. 21):

> "... in the district of La Brea-Guapo, adjacent to Oropuche, there were eighteen estates, all under the management of their resident proprietors. This was part of the money-making frenzy which gripped Trinidad for the first 20 years of the nineteenth century. There was a positive desperation to make quick money from sugar cultivation. Slaves were pushed to exhortation and death, and inefficient estates failed and were sold before the doors of the Court, only to be bought up by other speculators, often on borrowed money. By 1823, the crop for the fairly recently opened-up La Brea-Guapo area was, 1,613,946 pounds of sugar.

92   There is no record of the partnership registered by François and Pierre Jean Besson in the Colonial Bank's records.

Within a few years, though, the poor soils were exhausted and the Slave Amelioration Order of 1824 signaled the changes that were to come. These changes saw numerous mortgages foreclosed, and the disappearance of credit. The *coup de grâce* came with the emancipation of the slaves (1838) and the area then returned to the wilderness. The abandoned sugar mills and their boilers remained to rust and be engulfed in the jungle, until these long forgotten relics were rediscovered and brought to light again when the oil industry moved in after 1910."

In 1838 the British government paid to plantation owners sums of money that were meant to compensate them for the emancipated slaves. The Besson extended family received a temporary financial shelter by these payments; this would have gone a long way in dealing with debts already incurred and would have helped the members of the family to set themselves up in the growing town of Port-of-Spain. It did not compensate for losses made on the purchase of land, live stock, plant and machinery, as well as other expenses incurred.

Listed below is an account of payments received from the British government.

Recipient	No. of Slaves	£ - s - d
La Fortunée estate	71	3,444 - 9 - 3
For François Besson, Pierre Besson, Vincent Besson, Marguerite Besson, (?) Roux, Dominique Antoinnattai, Jean Besson, Pierre Jean Besson, Charles Besson, François Guira, Bellevue estate	31	1, 633 -17 - 3
For the heirs as listed above. La Romaine estate	37	1, 850 - 0 - 11
For Francis Besson and Benoît Olivier, Jean Besson, S. Naparima	2	118 - 2 - 9
Pierre Besson, S. Naparima	1	54 -2 - 8
Jean Besson, S. Naparima	1	74 -2 - 6
Jean Besson, Port-of-Spain	1	44 -4 - 7
François Besson, Guapo	1	51 -2 - 8
Pierre Jean Besson, Guapo	1	51 -2 - 8
François Besson as attorney, South Naparima	10	588 - 19 - 2

The ex-slaves, with emancipation, left the estates to experience freedom. It must be remembered that no form of compensation was paid to
them and for a great many, the old, the sick, the disabled, and the many
who would go in search of employment, confused by their new status,
life would be hard. Without support, they would know poverty, and
be homeless.

Fr. Anthony de Verteuil, in his *The Black Earth of South Naparima* writes
(pp. 147–149):

> "The Bessons continued to soldier on in South Naparima, for they may
> have salvaged some money from the sale of Bellevue Estate. As late as
> April 1846, Vincent Besson applied for 25 East Indian Immigrants for
> his estate in South Naparima, financed, presumably from his share in
> La Romaine. It has not been possible to establish a firm date as to when
> the Besson family had all ties of ownership of estates in South Napa-
> rima completely severed."

The abolition of the slave trade in the British Empire, when followed
twenty six years later by emancipation,[93] marked the beginning of the closing of an epoch in the history of the world. This epoch had been fueled

---

93 On 28 August 1833, the Slavery Abolition Act was given Royal Assent. This paved
the way for the abolition of slavery within the British Empire and its colonies. On 1
August 1834, all slaves in the British Empire were emancipated, but they were to be
indentured to their former owners in an apprenticeship system which meant to be
abolished in two stages; the first set of apprenticeships was to an end on 1 August
1838, while the final apprenticeships was to end two years later on 1 August 1840.
On 1 August 1834, "an assemblage of old black men, women and children . . ." who
were addressed by the Governor at Government House in Port of Spain, Trinidad,
about the new laws, began chanting: *"Pas de six ans. Point de six ans, Pas de six ans, nous
ne voulons pas de six ans, nous sommes libres, le Roi nous a donné la liberté.* These words
were spoken by a young spokesman represented in good French, and with eloquent
and respectful tone." Eventually taken up by the crowd and drowning out the words
of the Governor. Peaceful protests continued until a resolution to abolish apprenticeship was passed and de facto freedom was achieved. Full emancipation for all was
legally granted ahead of schedule on 1 August 1838, making Trinidad the first British
colony with slaves to completely abolish slavery. *"Pas de Six Ans!"* In: *Seven Slaves &
Slavery: Trinidad 1777 - 1838,* by Anthony de Verteuil, Port of Spain, p. 371-379.

by what was probably an unprecedented greed for wealth and a lust for power; resulting in a frightening degree of inhumanity.

However, towards the end of the 18th century, the idea was conceived in Europe that it was the natural condition of humankind to be in possession of unassailable rights, and that these human rights originated in nature. Thus, human rights cannot be granted via political charter, which would imply that they are legally revocable and hence merely privileges.

This period, the 1800s, was characterised by the awakening of a sense of understanding of a common humanity shared by all mankind. These times bore witness to the hope that reason would triumph over bigotry and superstition; it did see the beginning of the end of feudalism and the irrelevance of dogma and autocracy. These years are significant because they mark a point in time when ideas that sought to enlighten humanity to have confidence in a shared condition, in which reason was advocated as the primary source and legitimacy for authority, took root. These years also saw the birth of egalitarianism, a political doctrine that holds that all people should be treated as equals and have the same political, economic, social and civil rights, understanding that all mankind is possessed of ideals held in common that may be positioned as loftily as its imagination could aspire.

In the Besson family, these sentiments would have touched the generation of François' grandchildren, perhaps sending Jean and Pierre Jean Besson to the Wars of Liberation in South America and prompting several members of the family to join a Freemason's Lodge.

The abolition of the slave trade in 1807, notwithstanding the reasons that would be later given for it, undoubtedly indicated a shift in moral values in England, if not the Western world, and will be taken as the starting point of the British colonial narrative that would obtain for some one hundred and fifty years. This period was "a specific historical conjuncture."

The ideals of the Enlightenment would over time take root in the hearts and minds of those who would then live in these islands under British crown colony rule, and would eventually find expression several generations later in their quest for political maturity.

This form was common to all the British colonies and used for the compensation of slave owners at the time of the abolition of slavery.

...pbell of the Parish of St Andrews...

Six years and upwards to whose services   *she   is*   entitled.

PREDIAL UNATTACHED.	NON PREDIAL.	REMARKS.
predial Attach		
— Do — 1		
— Do — 1		
— Do — 1		
— Do — 1		
	non predial	
Feild do 1		
Do — 1		
Do — 1		
Do — 1		
" —	*non predial*	
" —		1
— " —	*non predial*	
9	5	Lu
	Margarate X Campbell	
	mark	

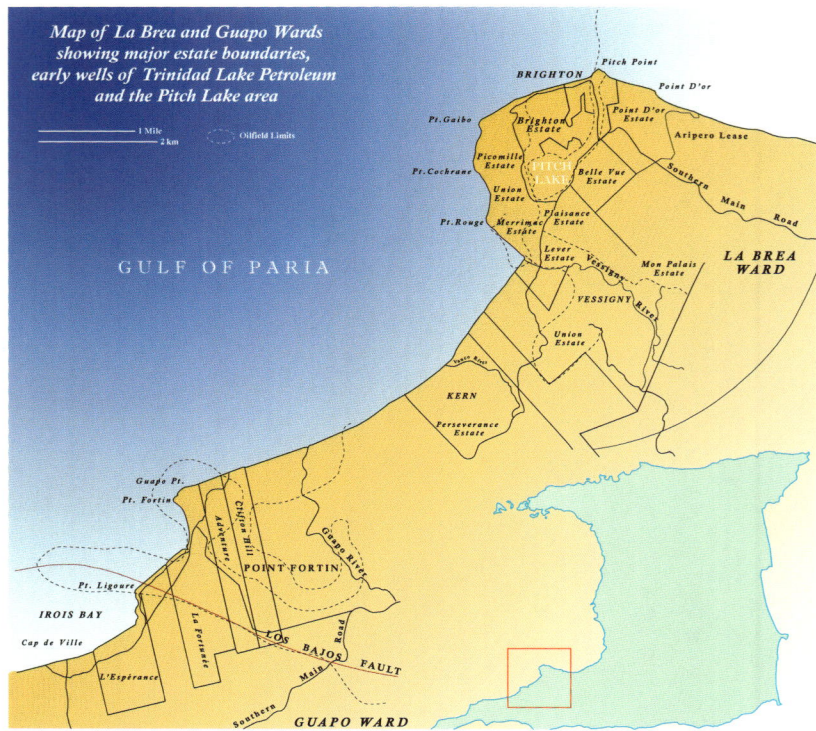

A detail of a map of the South Western peninsula of Trinidad that shows some of the plantations that would have been owned by François and by his descendants over a period of some fifty seven years (1788-1845). (After Higgins, p. 93)
Bellevue estate, from its somewhat slightly elevated position, overlooks the Pitch Lake, with which it shares a common border. It enjoys a charming view of the surrounding countryside as well as the spectacular prospect of the Gulf of Paria, where in the distance the Venezuelan mainland, Trinidad's North Western peninsula and the islands in the Dragon's Mouth may be seen. The Gulf of Paria appears as a vast lake surrounded by mountains and could have been reminiscent of Lake Geneva or the lochs of Scotland to the early Europeans who settled in the South of the island.
La Fortunée estate, also owned by the Besson family in a manner similar to Bellevue, also occupied a parcel of land that rose above the surrounding countryside, offering views of thick forest and a vast expanse of sea. These estates as well as La Romaine and others in the Guapo Ward and in the South Naparimas, that were owned or controlled by the family, lay on lands that would become world famous before the turn of the 20th century for the rich oil deposits that lay beneath their surfaces. The lands in South Naparima and in Guapo were sold for less than their real value. The irony is that on those same acres, within 70 years, oil was found in commercial quantities. Wells were brought in at Bellevue and La Fortunée and other sites that would have been Besson estates in Guapo in the 1800s. Because these lands had been granted either as Spanish crown grants or at a time when Spanish law was in force, the family would have possessed the subterranean rights to all minerals found.
Opposite: A map of Port-of-Spain of 1845 by Assistant Commissioner of Population, Manuel Sorzano. This map shows the locations of the various institutions that would have served the growing town. It also indicates the area of the reclamation of the foreshore project commenced some years before. The Besson family, in the period after the loss of their plantations, settled in Port-of-Spain. Because the house numbers in the streets running East to West start on the Eastern end of the town, it may be possible to get an idea of where they may have lived in the period of their settling there.

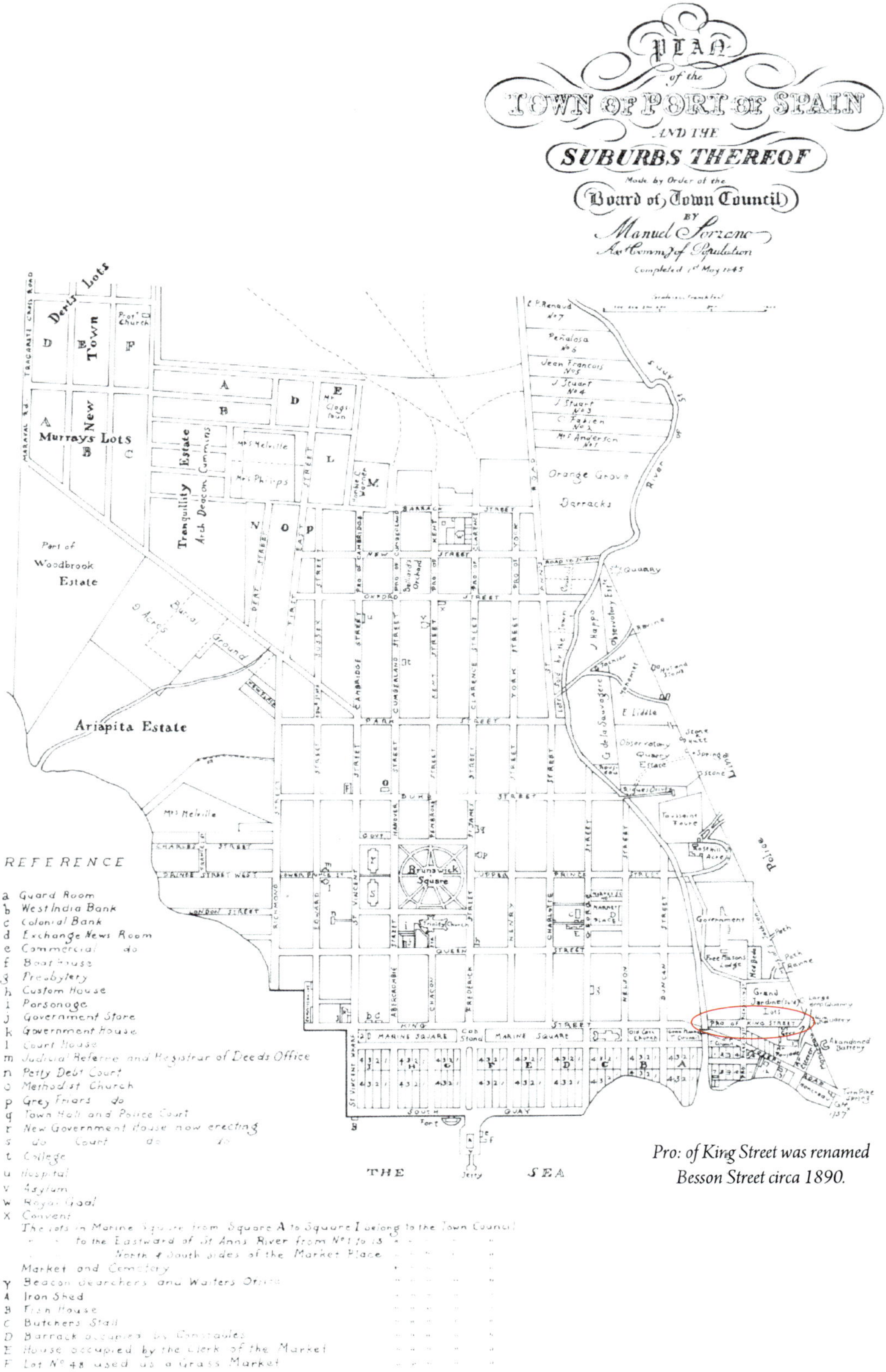

Pro: of King Street was renamed Besson Street circa 1890.

THE 19TH CENTURY
DESCENDANTS OF FRANÇOIS
6

The end of the slave trade, followed by emancipation over time, brought to a close the family's interest in the South of the island: in all, some seven plantations at one time or another had been either owned or controlled by François and his son, grandsons, and their relatives. [94]

The loss of the plantations in the decades after 1838 was fraught with difficulties for the pioneer families. Brereton tells us in her *History of Modern Trinidad* (pp. 82–83):

> "But the real crisis came in 1846. In that year the Sugar Duties Act was passed by the British Parliament, providing for the gradual equalisation of duties on foreign and British sugar. This meant that the British West Indian producers had lost their preferential position on the British colonial sugar market, and that they now had to compete on equal terms with cheaper producers. The Act caused a drastic fall in sugar prices, and a loss of confidence on the part of British merchant firms and mortgage holders in West Indian sugar estates. This situation was compounded by a disastrous financial crisis in Britain in 1847-48, which led to the failure of a number of firms that were heavily involved in the West Indian trade. In 1847 the failure of the West Indian Bank brought commercial transactions of every kind to a halt.

> "The Colonial Bank in Trinidad had to suspend payments temporarily and only just survived without total collapse. Trinidad was hard-hit by this double-edged crisis, and it was in these years that the sugar industry faced its severest difficulties. Thirteen estates were abandoned in 1838-48, [among them may have been La Romaine and La Fortunée owned by the descendants of François] which compared well with other colonies in the period. But Governor Lord Harris reported in 1848 that during the first decade of freedom, 159 estates (the great majority) had been operating at a loss: after running expenses had been met, insuf-

---

94   Trinidad slave registers, index to claims [T 71/939]

The house at right in the photograph is the Besson property and residence in Port-of-Spain at Numbers 3 & 4 Marine Square, later 1 Besson Street, where members of the family lived from the 1800s to the 1920s; the street on the left is Besson Street. François may have bought this property and a part of the neighbouring one from Marcilna Robles in 1806. (The Index to the Spanish Protocol of Deeds) Theresa Adèle Besson, daughter of François fils, married Pierre Alphonse Ganteaume from this house (1840.) Her sister Victorine, also married from the house, British officer William Bishop by special license. Scipio Besson lived there to the age of 101.His relationship to the family is unclear, he may have been a slave. Other members of the family, including Frederick Besson and his son, Charles Frederick Besson, son and grandson of François Besson and his wife Reine, also lived there. It belonged to Noel Bowen, a grandson of Jeanne Alciña Carige, née Besson, when it was demolished in the 1970s to build Riverside Plaza. (de Verteuil)

ficient money was left to cover the cost of property maintenance. The resulting deterioration in the condition of the estates caused a decline in the market value of Trinidad plantations.

"Writing in 1848, the Attorney-General noted 64 petitions of insolvency have been filed: estate after estate thrown upon the market with no purchasers found. . . 'Many estates have been abandoned from the inability to raise money on the faith of the coming crop.' He instanced the Jordan Hill estate [an estate that had been run by François *fils* as attorney for its owner] in South Naparima, making an average annual profit of £3,000 in the 1830s, which had just been sold for a mere £4,000: also, he said, 'men here wonder not at the sacrifice of the vendors, as much as at the rashness of the purchasers.'"

Twenty years after emancipation there would be an attempt to start a business by the family, led by Charles François Besson. But this too was to

François' Third Marriage to Reine Martineau

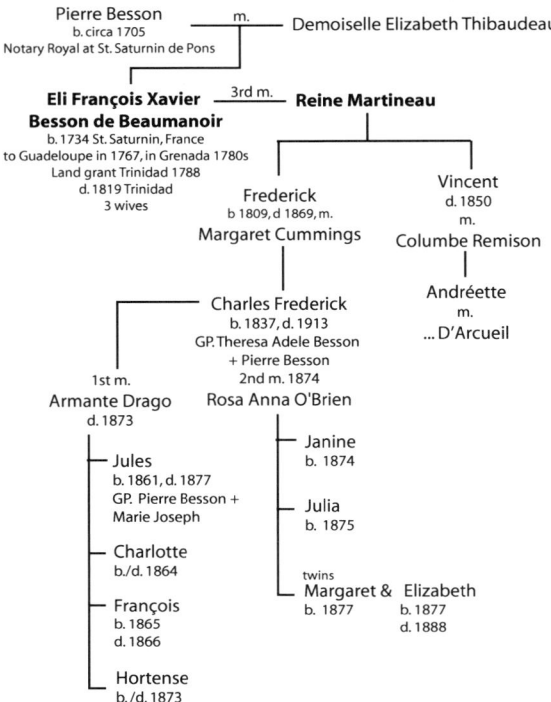

come to an end with the early deaths of so many young men, who may have worked for the family business, particularly its founder Charles François Besson and his son Charles Joseph, both of whom died almost simultaneously in 1872. The family never recovered financially.

The Besson family, mired in poverty, and seemingly unable to produce other ambitious or purposeful personalities, unfortunately would live in East Port-of-Spain, no longer possessing country estates; would suffer through the yellow fever and cholera epidemics in the following 30 years, losing many, young and old, boys and girls, during this terrible period.

As mentioned, François Besson de Beaumanoir, died in 1819; he was 85 years old. After the death of his wife Elizabeth, he had had two sons with Reine Martineau, his third wife. One was Frederick, born 1809, who married Margaret Cummings and who died in 1869 at age 60. They lived at 3 and 4 Marine Square, later Besson Street. Frederick's son, Charles Frederick Besson was born there in 1837 and died there in 1913. He married first Amante Drago, they had four children, all of whom died in infancy. Upon the death of Amante, he married Rosa Anna O'Brien. They had four children, the last two being twins. François' and Reine's other son was Vincent, whose date of birth I do not know. He married Columbe Rennison and died in 1850. Vincent had owned 14A Henry Street in

A view of Port-of-Spain from la Ventille, by M.J. Cazabon circa 1855. The figures in the foreground
seem to match the subject of the story in the text above. Frederick Besson, 1809–1869, son of François
and his third wife Reine, lived at 1 Besson Street. He may have had a "Freed African" indentured to him,
who took the name, Frederick Besson. The group of houses and the street just behind the figures appear
to be Besson Street or the start of Old St. Joseph Rd. or both. See photograph on p. 101.
(Courtesy Belmont Harris Trust and Geoffrey MacLean)

1838. He sold it in 18? (date unclear) to M. Besson. Neither of these two sons of François' last marriage would have male descendants and as such their line came to an end.

I discovered the will of a Frederick Besson, dated 1870, that begins "I Frederick Besson, a native of Africa, now residing in the district of Mayaro..." This is of interest because he may have been one of the "Freed Africans" brought to Trinidad in the mid-19th century, and probably indentured to Frederick Besson. He may have consequently taken the name. The watercolour, by Cazabon, above, may be of the two Fredericks looking out on the family's property on Besson Street. The family of Frederick Besson, "native of Africa" lived on Old St. Joseph Road and later at Irvin Lane and St Paul Street, and in other parts of East Port-of-Spain. Some members of this family still reside in Laventille. Frederick also owned lands at Mayaro. His children were Joseph, Felicianne and Marie Marguerite Besson. They are connected to the Nicholson, Mills and Grimes families. The Besson family of Toco may be the descendants of Joseph, son of Frederick, native of Africa, this is unclear because of the condition of the records. What is clear is that Antoine Besson, son of Joseph Besson had cocoa lands at Toco in the 1910s–30s known as Humbug estate and The Boundary estate. These lands passed to his wife Francis. Upon her death in 1931, Fanny Marie Borde, her sister, became sole executrix.

François *fils*, son of François Besson de Beaumanoir, who had been born in Grenada in 1766 and had married Marie Ruim or Roume, died in 1831 at age 65. Their eldest son, also called François III (born in Grenada in 1796 had married the daughter of an old colleague of François' from his Grenada period, Marie France Olivière) died in 1866, aged 70 in Trinidad. He had bought a property at 1A Henry Street in Port-of-Spain in September 1848. Their surviving children were Charles François born 1816, who married Rose Cephaline Darmanie, and then Rose Latour; Victorine born 1820, married a British army officer, Willam Bishop; Theresa Adèle born 1821, married Pierre Alphonse Ganteaume de Montou, a French Royalist planter of Mayaro; and Jeanne born 1822, who married Louis Latour of Perseverance estate, Moka.

Jean [95] (born 1797) brother of François III, was born in Grenada died in 1840 in Trinidad aged 43. He had married his cousin Elizabeth La Prade. They had one child, a son, Jules, born 1839, who died with no descendants in 1877. Jean had bought a property at 65 Duke Street in June 1839.

Pierre Jean, youngest brother of François III and Jean, was born in 1805, also in Grenada. He married twice, first Henriette Faut-Huerne of the United States, and then Rose Laurencine Darmanie, a sister of his cousin Charles' wife. He passed away in 1852. He had purchased a property at 4 Henry Street from Vincent Besson, [96] François' son by his third marriage to Reine Martineau, in March 1839.

---

95   Jean Besson, Pierre Jean Besson, Charles François Besson, Charles Frederick Besson were members of Lodge United Brothers 251 S.C. Lodge records.

96   In the will of Vincent Besson, died 1867, leaves all his worldly goods for his daughter Andriette Darcueil. We also found Trooper Vincent Besson, of the Port-of-Spain 1st Troop, who under the command of Major A.P. Lange formed part of a contingent that represented local forces at the coronation of His Majesty King Edward VII in 1901.

Charles François Besson (b.1816) son of Marie France Olivière and François III would buy this property from Pierre Jean in February 1843. Pierre Jean Besson, like his brother Jean, according to information sent to me by Frederico Ganteaume Pantin, Venezuelan historian, was also involved in the Wars of Liberation on the South American continent.

There are documents, no longer in my possession, authorising him to be paid for the shipments of "ball shot and powder" made to Angostura on the Orinoco River in 1823, signed by Simón Bolívar. Both he and his brother Jean were members of the Masonic Lodge, Lodge United Brothers 251 S.C. and were given Masonic diplomas, sometimes referred to as "passports", that would have served as introductions to Masonic circles in Venezuela during this period. [97] Masonic records show that Jean left for Angostura to join the South American Wars of Liberation in 1823.

The Colonial Bank records [98] show that Charles François Besson, the son of François III, was in correspondence with the London principals of the Colonial Bank in 1844. Charles François Besson & Company's correspondence with the Bank really begins in 1858 and continues on through to 1873. He owned a property at 18 Charlotte Street in 1864. He also bought 3 Hanover Street in 1865.

Charles François Besson's first wife, Rose Cephaline Darmanie died in 1841. He had a son with Rose Honoré, a woman of colour, out of wedlock, whom he acknowledged on the baptismal record as his child, who was born in the year of his wife's death. His name on that record is Thomas Alexander Joseph Besson. About a year following the birth of Thomas Alexander, Charles François married Rose Latour, with whom he had two girls and a boy, Charles Joseph, who was born in 1847 and died in 1872 at the age of 25 with no issue. Charles François also died in 1872.

The business was wound up. With the deaths of both father and son in 1872, this branch of the family came to an end. Charles François Besson's eldest daughter of his first marriage, Rose Louisa, born 1836, married

---

97   Records of Lodge United Brothers 251 S.C.
98   Rouse-Jones, M. *The Colonial Bank Correspondence 1837-1885* pp. 47 & 22.

Valentine Ganteaume de Monteau, daughter of Marie Joséphine Besson and Henri Peter Ganteaume senior. (Bedford)

Alex Ganteaume de Monteau, daughter of Pierre Alphonse Ganteaume and his first wife, Elisa Monier de la Quarrée. (Bedford)

This picture shows: Leonine Ganteaume, third lady from left, back row; the fifth, Elisa O'Connor née Ganteaume; the sixth, Isale O'Connor née Ganteaume, married to Henri de la Bastide; the seventh Henri Peter Ganteaume. In the middle row left, Henri de la Bastide, and the third lady on the left is Mathilde O'Connor née Ganteaume. The two older ladies sitting on the right may be Amélie de la Bastide, née Besson, and her cousin Adèle Ganteaume, née Besson.
(Photo source and information: Terry Bedford née Ganteaume).

The Descendants of Paul Darmanie

François' First Marriage to Marianne Esnard

François' Second Marriage to Marie La Prade

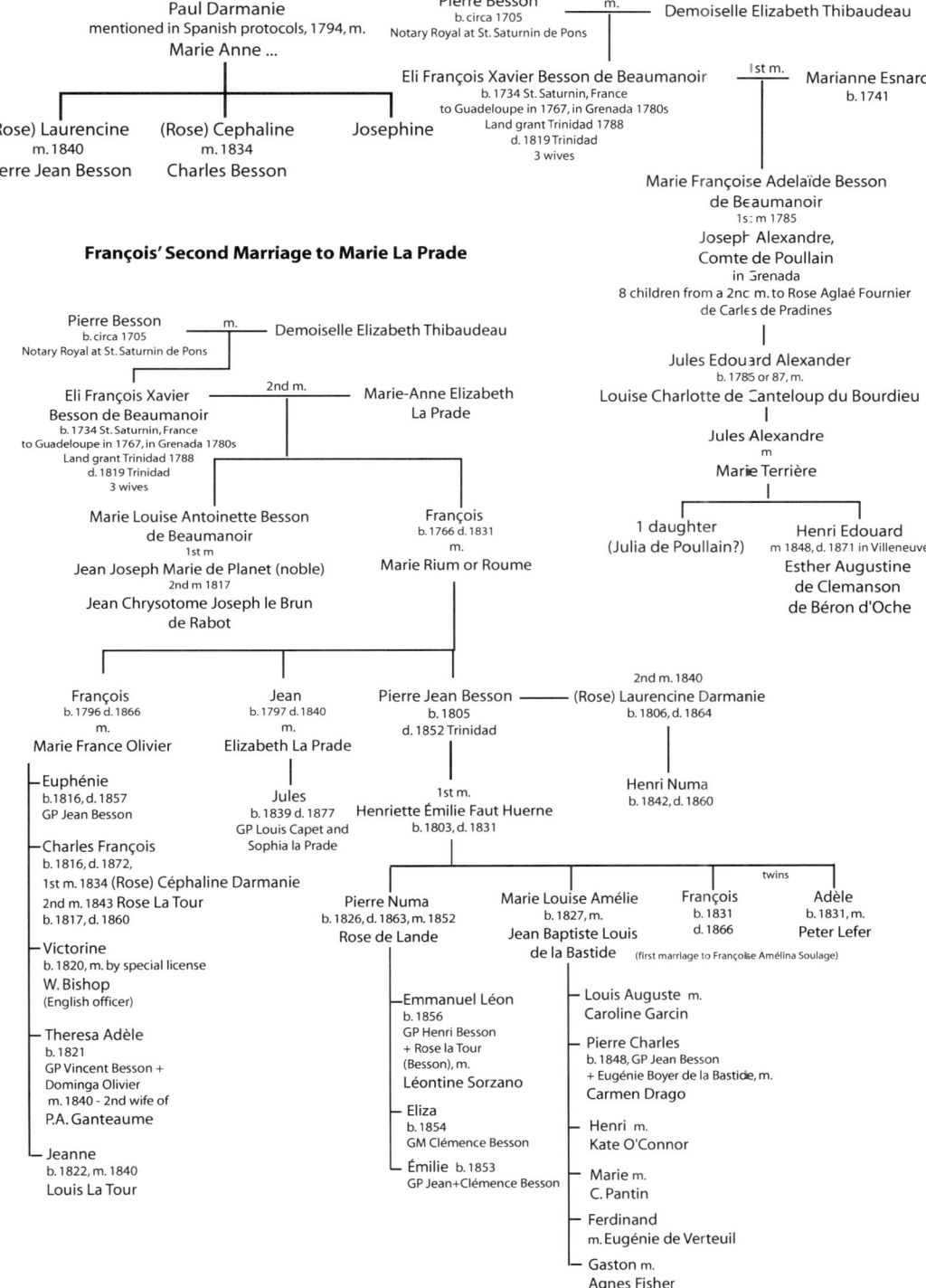

James Lynch O'Connor Marriage to Sophie Lefer

James Lynch O'Connor — m. — Sophie Lefer

Daniel Louis
b. 1823
Merchant
m. E. Bernard
no issue

Philip Charles
b. 1825
Merchant
m. Mathilde Ganteaume

Eneas Felix
b. 1828
unmarried

- Sylvester
- Daniel Louis
- James Lynch

James Lynch
b. 1829
Magistrate
m. J. Devenish

- Charles
- 2 daughters

Léon Dennis
b. 1831
Crown Solicitor
m. Egle Lefer

- Sophie
  m. R. Kernahan
  Surveyor General
  7 children
- Arthur
  Crown Solicitor
  m. M. Sellier
  4 children
- Charles
  Surveyor
  m. J. Sellier
  8 children
- Edward
  Jesuit Priest
  Stoneyhurst College
  England

Arthur
b. 1833
unmarried

Josephine
b. 1839
unmarried

James Lynch
b. 1861
Planter
m. H. Zepero
7 children

Kate
m. H. de la Bastide
Merchant
his mother was
Amélie Besson
13 children

Mathilde
m. V.H. Wehekind
Solicitor
4 children

Daniel
died in infancy

Denis
d. 1884, aged 17

Phillip Taaffe
b. 1870
Planter
m. M. de Gannes
8 children
one of these was
Emmett "PET"
m. Thora Brand

Eliza Marie
m. Henri Peter Ganteaume jr.
Barrister
7 children
his mother was
Marie Besson
his grandmother was
Adèle Besson

Philip Charles O'Connor, son of James Lynch O,Connor married Mathilde Ganteaume. She was the daughter of P.A.M.A. Ganteaume and his first wife, Eliza Monier de la Quarrée. (DeLa Bastide)

Louis Lefer, son of Jean Baptiste and Aurélie Sophie Asseline Lefer. The Lefer family came to Trinidad before 1822. They were Louis Christophe, Auguste François, Amable Felix, and Sophie Eleonora Euphrosin, who married Dr. James Lynch O'Connor. Their descendants are numerous through marriages with the O'Connor, Bernard, Ganteaume, Devenish, de la Bastide, Wehekind, de Gannes, Kernahan, Sellier, Besson and de Boissière families. (After an oil painting by M.J. Cazabon. Pocock)

Below: The six O'Connor brothers and their sister Josephine. The only one that could be identified is Philip Charles, seated, at left. They were the children of Dr. James Lynch O'Connor and his wife Sophie Lefer. (O'Connor)

François Alphonse Ganteaume, son of Pierre Antoine Marie Alphonse Ganteaume and his first wife Eliza Monier de la Quarrée, (seated right) with his second wife Lucie Vessigny (behind him with hand on his shoulder; his first wife was Eugénie Lefer). The girl at the right side of the photo is their daughter Marie, who married Louis de Meillac. The young man on the left is their son Henri Dieudonne Alphonse, and the girl standing in the middle is his daughter Simone who married Jean Quesnel. The other old lady standing is probably François Alphonses' sister Mathilde, who married Philip Charles O'Connor, and the girl sitting is Eliza Marie, their daughter who married Henri Peter Ganteaume jr. (Navarro)

François Besson & Marie France Oliviere

Pierre Besson
b. circa 1705
Notary Royal at St. Saturnin de Pons
— m. — Demoiselle Elizabeth Thibaudeau

Eli François Xavier
Besson de Beaumanoir
b. 1734 St. Saturnin, France
to Guadeloupe in 1767, in Grenada 1780s
Landgrant Trinidad 1788
d. 1819 Trinidad
3 wives
— 2nd m. — Marie-Anne Elizabeth
la Prade

François
b. 1766 d. 1831
m.
Marie Rium or Roume

François
b. 1796 d. 1866
m.
Marie France Olivière

Charles François
b. 1816, d. 1872,
1st m. 1834 (Rose) Céphaline Darmanie
2nd m. 1843 Rose la Tour
b. 1817, d. 1860

Theresa Adèle
b. 1821
m. 1840 - 2nd wife of
P.A. Ganteaume

Marie
Armantine
Joséphine
b. 1845,
m. 1834 Henri
Peter Ganteaume sr.

Eliza O'Connor and her husband Henri Peter Ganteaume jr. with three of their 9 children: Odette (baby), Hélène (in front) and Gèneviève (on chair).
Henri Peter's mother was Marie Besson; she was the daughter of Charles François Besson and his second wife Rose Latour. His grandmother was Theresa Adèle Besson. She was the daughter of François Besson III and his wife Marie France Olivière. They were the parents of Charles François Besson. Eliza O'Connor's parents were Philip Charles O'Connor and Mathilde Ganteaume. (Bedford)

Ganteaume Marriages to de la Quarrée & Besson

Eliza Monier
de la Quarrée
— 1st m. — Pierre Antoine Marie Alphonse
Ganteaume de Montou
b. 1802, d. 1860
— 2nd m. — Adèle Besson

François Alphonse
b. 1826
1st m. Eugénie Lefer
2nd m. Lucie Vessigny

Eliza
m. Alexis de Verteuil

Clémence
m. Henri J. Pantin

Alix
m. John Agostini

Henriette
m. George Pantin

Corinne
m. Charles Pantin
Their son, Frederick married Mercedes de Tovar

Mathilde
m. Philip Charles O'Connnor

Eugénie
m. Léon Guiseppi

Henri
Dieudonne
Alphonse
m. Milliy Hancock

Marie
m. Louis de Meillac

Simone
m. Jean Quesnel

Alphonse
André
Sophie
m. Maurice Rostant
Clémence
Holy Orders
Lenore
m. L. Rostant
Mathilde
m. John Taylor
Eliza
m. Frederick Scott
Louise
m. Robert Reid
Eugène

2 sons, 3 daughters
youngest daughter
Eliza Marie
m. Henri Peter Ganteaume jr.
Barrister
his mother was
Marie Besson
his grandmother was
Adèle Besson
7 Children

sisters

Henri Peter sr.
m. Marie Armantine
Joséphine Besson

Marie
m. Adolf Wuppermann

Albert
m. Andriette Fanovitch

Léon
m. Tucker

George
m. Leonie de Bot

Harris

Anthony

Felix
m. Léonie de Bot

Edgar
m. Maria Luisa de Tovar

Lucie
m. Emmanuel Cipriani

Victorine
m. Ehlers

Paul

Charles

Ferdinand
m. Ethel Rooks
Léonie
d. 1958
Eugène
Henri Peter jr.
m. Eliza Marie O'Connor
Patrick
m. Elizabeth Robinson
Hector
May
Valentine
Adolph
d. 1915
Arthur
d. 1912

Odette Valentine
m. Sydney Hargrave
Gèneviève
m. Otto Scott
Hélène
m. William Beavan
Marcelle
m. Victor Quesnel
Louis Edmond
m. Lilia Elena Rother
Marie Élise
c. 1930
Andrée Christine
Spinster
Thérèse Amélie
Principal informant
for this family tree
m. Victor Bedford
Marguerite
m. Esme de Verteuil

It is thought that this may be Jean Louis Baptiste de Jacques de la Bastide, écuyer, who married in 1841, Marie Louise Amélie Besson, daughter of Pierre Jean Besson and his wife Henriette Emilie Faut-Huerne.

Henri de Jacques de la Bastide, the son of Marie Louise Amélie de la Bastide, née Besson and her husband Jean Louis Baptiste de Jacques de la Bastide. He married Kate O'Connor.

Lucy de la Bastide, the grand-daughter of Marie Louise Amélie de la Bastide, née Besson. She married Victor Louis de Gannes, he was the son of Joseph Gaston de Gannes and Sophie Cipriani.

Henri de la Bastide sitting in rocker with daughter Lucie (hat) and Louis "Philippe" de la Bastide next to her. The others in the picture I believe are Wehekinds. Philippe's wife Marie Leonie "Audrey" Wehekind is to the far right. Sitting on Henri's knee may be Claire de la Bastide, Marcelle "Bibi" de la Bastide or France de la Bastide. (Photos: Paul de Jacques de la Bastide)

A group of de la Bastide brothers and cousins, circa 1880.

Marie Louise Amélie Besson was born in 1827. She was the daughter of Pierre Jean Besson and Henriette Emilie Faut-Huerne. She married Jean Baptiste Louis de Jacques de la Bastide. Their eldest son, Louis Auguste, married Caroline Garcin. Their second son, Pierre Charles, who was born in 1848, married Carmen Drago (front row right). Their other son, Henri, married Kate O'Connor, daughter of Dr. James O'Connor and Sophie Lefer; their daughter, Marie, married Charles Pantin, grandson of P.A. Ganteaume and his first wife. Ferdinand, their last child, married Eugénie de Verteuil, the daughter of Alexis de Verteuil and Eliza, daughter of P.A. Ganteaume and his first wife. The Dragos were Italian from Genoa.

Left to right standing: Joseph Paul 'Raymond' de la Bastide, Marie Amélie Cécile Joséphine 'Finotte' de la Bastide, Anna Alix Marie Carmelite 'Netta' de la Bastide, Marcelle 'Bibi' de la Bastide, Roderick O'Connor, Charlotte Martine de la Bastide, Margaret 'Peggy' O'Connor, Edmond Marie Gérard 'Chouquine' de la Bastide, Brian O'Connor, Marie Ange Marthe 'Martza' de la Bastide.

Standing in front of 'Bibi' is Marie George Daniel 'Dandy' de la Bastide (father of Paul de la Bastide and Danny Gianetti). Sitting to his left in the middle is Mathilde Louise O'Connor (née Ganteaume), wife of Phillip Charles Auguste O'Connor.

Sitting far right is Carmen Delores de la Bastide (née Drago), wife of Pierre Charles de Jacques de la Bastide. Charles Frederick Besson, a grandson of François' third marriage, married Amante Drago in 1860. They had four children, all of whom died in childhood.

Finotte, Netta, Martza and Charlotte are all sisters of Joseph Paul Raymond, were the children of Pierre Charles de la Bastide and Carmen Dolores. None of these children ever married.

'Bibi', elder sister of 'Dandy', also died a spinster. 'Chouquine' is 'Dandy's' elder brother.

Peggy, Roderick and Brian O'Connor are issue of James Lynch and Honora 'Nora' Lynch (née Zepero). James Lynch O'Connor is son of Phillip Charles and Mathilde Louise. (de la Bastide)

Pierre Jean Besson's Descendants

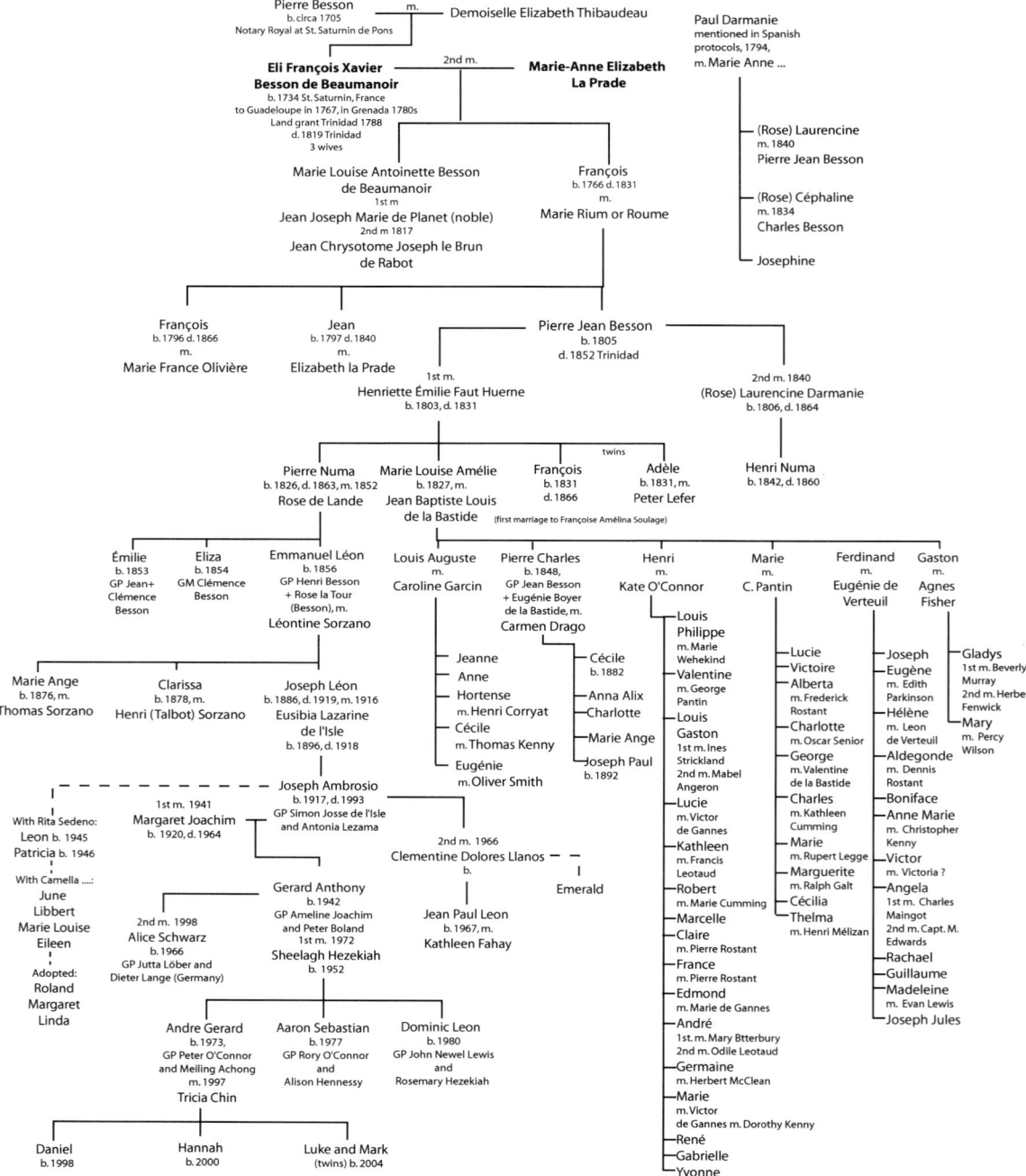

in1856, Jules de la Bastide. Another daughter, Marie Camille Josephine, born 1841, married Louis Fifi, and his third daughter, Cephaline, born 1838, never married. Charles François with his second wife, Rose Latour had three children, Johanna Marie, born 1844 who never married; Marie Armantine Josephine, born 1845 who married Henri Peter Ganteaume, the son of her aunt, Theresa Adèle, Charles François' sister, who had married Pierre Alphonse Ganteaume; and Charles Joseph, born 1847.

The legitimate male line of the Bessons would continue with Pierre Jean Besson, uncle of Charles François, who was born in 1805 in Grenada. As mentioned above, Pierre Jean had married first Henriette Faut-Huerne, and they had two boys and two girls: Pierre Numa, born1826, Marie Louise Amélie, born 1827, François, born 1831, and Adèle, born 1832. Of these, François died in 1866, childless. Marie Louise Amélie married Jean Baptiste Louis de Jacques de la Bastide. Adèle married Peter Lefer. [99] Upon Pierre Jean's wife's death in 1832, possibly in childbirth, he married his cousin, Charles François' wife's sister, Rose Laurencine Darmanie, she died in 1843. They had one child, a son, Henri Numa Besson, born 1842, who died at age 18, in 1860 with no issue.

The Colonial Bank's records at the University of the West Indies contain the correspondence of P. Besson, presumably Pierre Numa, son of Pierre Jean and Henriette Faut-Huerne. In 1865 he lived at Queen Street. His business exported agricultural produce and imported dry goods, and also N. Besson & Co., which would have done the same, and may have been a company started by Pierre Numa Besson, son of Pierre Jean Besson.

Pierre Numa married Rose de Lande d'Aussac, who may have come from the United States as she was his mother's second cousin. They had one son, Emmanuel Léon and two daughters, Marie Emilie, born 1853, and Eliza, born 1854. I have found in the Catholic Cathedral's records that in 1874, Eliza Besson married Jules Ernest Attale, son of Henry Attale. In 1880, Marie Emilie Besson married Augustine Savary. Pierre Numa died at age 37, in 1863. [100]

---

99   Cathedral of the Immaculate Conception records of baptisms, marriages and deaths, as well as the Registrar General's Office in Port-of-Spain.

100   Pierre Numa Besson was made a Mason at Lodge Eastern Star 368 S.C. in 1856. This Lodge had as its first Worshipful Master Paulin Josse de L'Isle in 1854 (*Lodge records*). The name Numa appears as a middle name for several Trinidadian men from the

Perseverance estate house at Moka in Maraval, was the home of Jeanne Besson, born 1822, and her hus-
band Louis Latour. Jeanne was the daughter of François Besson III and Marie France Olivière. She took
into her home the children of her husband, Louis Latour, and Léonide (Lorraine) Besson, as teenagers,
upon the death of their mother who may have been a person of colour. It is likely that Louis Latour and
Léonide, also called Lorraine Besson may have had a plaçage relationship over several years. The chil-
dren's names were Frederick Louis Latour and Louise Ultima Latour. I have not been able to discover
the parentage of their mother. In her will she leaves them, as teenagers, in the care of their father, Louis
Latour. Louise Ultima Latour married Jules Cipriani, also known as Cipriani de Rose or Jules De Rose
Cipriani, reputed son of Léon Cipriani and a woman of colour by the name of Rosalie Labastide, (she
may have been a relative of the Bessons and de la Bastides). One of their children was Michael, "Mikey"
Cipriani, sportsman and pioneer aviator. Jules de Rose Ciprianis' sister, Marie Alix, married Charles
James Milne.This house and its extensive grounds, gardens and cocoa fields was eventually bought by
Albert Henry Cipriani (Baba), son of Albert Henry Cipriani, brother of Emmanuel Cipriani, who had
married Lucy Ganteaume, whose mother was Theresa Adèle Besson, the second wife of Pierre Alphonse
Ganteaume.Albert Henry's (Baba) brother was Captain Arthur Andrew Cipriani, several times Mayor
of Port-of-Spain. He was a labour leader, and champion of the poor. Perseverance estate passed into
the hands of the Battoo family and was used as a music hall for several years, until it was eventually
abandoned, and destroyed by fire in the 1980s. (Photo: Paria / Carr Collection)

Louis Latour and his wife Jeanne, née Besson, had two sons, Paul and
Alexander. It would appear that Alexander never married. Paul did marry and had one son, Dr. George Louis Latour, who married an English
person. Their son, Frank Louis Latour married Kathleen Bishop and had
Marion, Pamela, Marcel, and Charmaine Latour.

Above: Michael Cipriani prior to his leaving for Europe in 1914. Seated, perhaps one of his sisters, possibly with members of the Latour family. (Photo: Paria, St. Mary's College, Duruty)
Below: Michael Cipriani and his aeroplane (Photo: Garth Lyder)

Cumberland House on Abercromby Street was built for Louisa Ultima Léonisa Latour by her husband Jules Cipriani. She was reputed to have been the most beautiful woman of her generation. They were both coloured people, products of the 19th century plaçage and were the parents of the famous aviation pioneer Mikey Cipriani. Jules did quite well in business and built this house. (Paria)

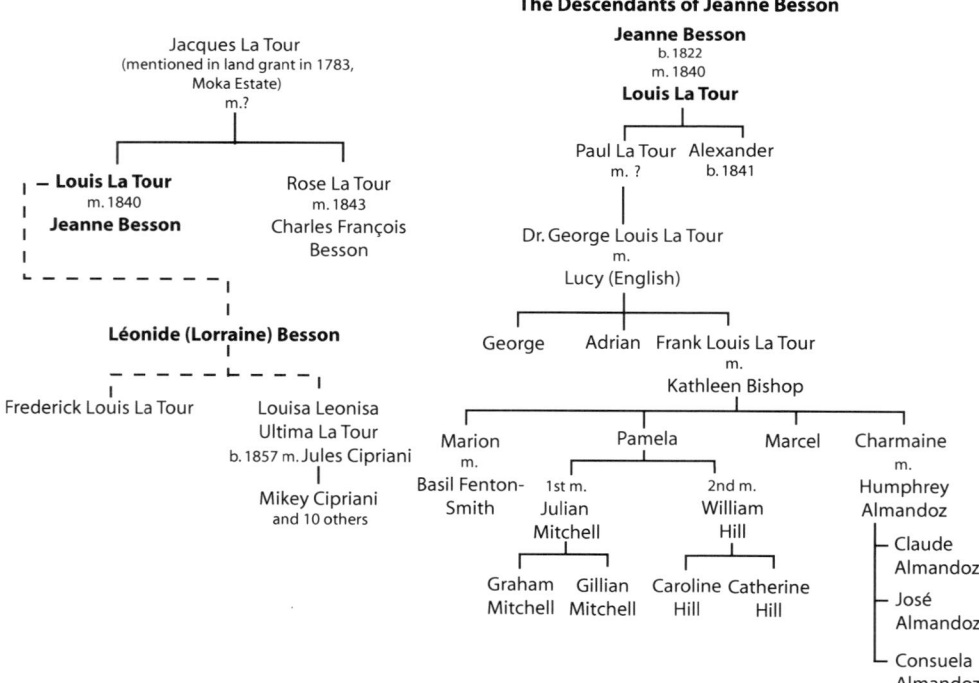

With this rate of deaths among the males in the family, and the unmarried state of so many of them, it would be only Emmanuel Léon Besson, son of Pierre Numa Besson and Rose de Lande (born 1856, died 1928) who lived at Arima, who would now continue the legitimate male descent of the Besson name in Trinidad. The early deaths of so many of Emmanuel's male relatives of the previous generation, his father's early death, at 37, and the loss of their business interest, meant that he may not have been possessed of any sort of fortune and possibly had not received much education. The family did not have an opportunity to become wealthy and to join in with the other French Creole cocoa planter families who were to create fresh fortunes in the cocoa economy from the 1870s to 1930s.

The only will I was able to find of a woman of colour with the Besson name turned out to be a person who had a *plaçage* relationship with a man who was married to a white Besson woman (see Appendix III)

Louise Ultima Latour was the daughter of Louis Latour and Leonide Besson, who was a woman of colour. Leonide left her children, a son and a daughter in the care of their father, Louis Latour, who brought them up in his household together with his own children. He had married Jeanne Besson, the daughter of Marie France Olivière and François III, the youngest sister of Charles François and no doubt a relative of Leonide Besson, the mother of his reputed children.

Louise Ultima Latour married Jules Cipriani, reputed son of Leon Cipriani and the woman of colour, Roseilie Labastide, who may have been related to the Besson and the de la Bastide families. Jules became a successful merchant of Port-of-Spain. He built a mansion on Abercromby Street, called Cumberland House. The union of Jules and Louisa Ultima produced ten children, amongst these were a few professional men. The most outstanding of them was Michael (Mikey) Cipriani. Some of their children married persons of European descent. The present Jobity and Walker families are amongst their descendants.

---

mid 19th-century to the 1900s, George Numa Dessources, Ferdinand Numa Rat, Pierre Numa Besson, Henri Numa Besson, Joseph Numa Boissière and perhaps one or two others that I can't bring to mind. Numa, a 4th or 3rd century B.C. Etruscan king, is said to have founded Guilds or Colleges of builders and artificers in Rome. (*The Scottish Workings of Craft Masonry, Complete and Accurate.*)

This house, above, on the corner of Oxford and St. Vincent Streets, still in existence at the time of writing, was where Marie Camille Josephine Besson, born 1841, daughter of Charles François Besson and Rose Latour, came to live upon marrying Louis Fifi. It had been bought by him from the Blache-Fraser family and has been lived in by her descendants for some four generations.
Below, the front entrance.
(Photos: Alice Besson)

THE CHILDREN OF
CHARLES FRANÇOIS BESSON
& ROSE HONORÉ
7

As previously related, Thomas Alexander Joseph Besson, illegitimate son of Charles François Besson and Rose Honoré, was born in 1842, shortly after the death of his first wife Cephaline Darmanie (who may have died in child birth in 1841). He may have been supported in his youth and was given a start in life, as he appears as a landowner in Arouca in the 1870s. He married a woman of colour, they were to have several children, amongst these was a daughter, Angelina. She married a widower from Canton, China by the name of Chan. Some time after their marriage Chan changed his name to Alexander Besson. He opened a shop on the corner of the Eastern Main Road and Lopinot Road and apparently prospered. In his will he left several properties as well as cash for his wife and children.

Amongst their several descendants were two island scholarship winners who attended Queen's Royal College. [101] One of them was George E. Besson, who won the island Scholarship in 1909, and Dr. William Willesbert Besson, who was born in 1901 and won the island Scholarship in 1920. Their brothers were John Besson, Charles Alexander Besson, a druggist, and Henry Alexander Besson who lived at Arima. Henry's son was Herman Alexander Besson. Herman became Crown Attorney of Montserrat, Solicitor General, and a High Court judge of Trinidad and Tobago in the 1970s. Herman's sister, Elsie, never married. Herman married Gweneth Gumbs of Tortola; their children were Herman, Noel and Sandra Bes-

---

101 Information on Dr. William Besson and his family is taken from the following sources: a letter written by Elma Reyes to Alison Hennessy in March 2000; the will of Alexander Besson, formerly Chan of Canton, China; correspondence to me from Daniel Hinton of New York, who is George Besson's descendant; and *The Life and Times of a Trinidad Scholar (1901 - 1989)* by Dr. William W. Besson, edited by Jean Besson.

son. William and Henry's sister, Edna, married a British aristocrat by the name of Milne-Home, a relative of the first Governor General of the Federated West Indies, Lord Hailes. They lived at Golden Grove in 1970. Their son, William (Bill) Milne-Home, lives in Australia. Dr. John Besson, Dolly Joseph, née Besson, Gordon Besson formally of Belle-Smythe Street, Woodbrook and Ann Besson of Edinburgh, Scotland, Daphne Besson, London, England, Chris Besson-Knorich of Germany, as well as Gregory Anthony Besson, son of Ursula Besson, are also a part of this extended family.

The widower, Chan, however, had a daughter, who had come from China with him she was called Ellen, or sometimes Ah Chee, "Elder sister." She married James Qui You of China, their daughter Ayin married (?) Hezekiah. Their son Oliver, would marry Theresa Watkins and have four daughters Judy, Alison, Rosemary and Sheelagh. Sheelagh married me, Gerard Besson.

Another son of Rose Honoré and Charles François Besson was Leonardo Charles Besson, he was also acknowledged by his father on his baptismal record. He was born in 1843. Amongst his several descendants were Cleton Besson and his sister Abdonies Besson. They were both cocoa estate owners of Cantaro, Santa Cruz. Cleton Besson, who married Matilde Lezama, was the ancestor of several lines of Besson descendants. Amongst them was Bernard Charles Besson, of 23 and 25 Mount Moria Road, San Fernando, Postmaster, in 1916. He was one of the first students of St. Mary's College in 1863 and died in 1919 (Source: Fr. Anthony de Verteuil). His son Charles Besson had children; Frank, Hamel, and Julia Besson. Frank's children were: Rachael, Cheryl, Patricia, Brian, Ian, Janice, and Jacqueline. Hamel's were: Hamilton and Alvin. Julia had no children.

THE BESSONS
IN FREEMASONRY
8

Before we continue the story of François' descendants in Trinidad, it may be of interest to give an account of the family's association with the order of Freemasonry, and also of their involvement with people and events in Venezuela. Because Freemasonry and the role it played in the thinking of men in the late 18th century will form part of an important argument in part 2 of this book, I will now give a brief account of it and tell something of its activities in Trinidad during François' time and later in the lives of his grandsons.

There were several Bessons who were Freemasons in Trinidad over a period of 180 years. There is no indication that François or his son François *fils* were members of a Masonic Lodge. As mentioned earlier, Julien Besson had joined a party of insurgents in 1813; they had gone to Venezuela under the Command of Santiago Mariño to join Simón Bolívar's Wars of Liberation, and were to be remembered as "The Immortal 45." Interestingly, although Julien Besson was not a Freemason, many of the "Immortals," including Mariño, were. [102] Julien's relationship to François, as discussed previously, is unclear; he may have been the son of Stanislas Besson of Grenada and a godson of the Grenadian revolutionary, Julien Fédon.

The question that is often asked is: Why did so many Catholic men, despite the order having been banned by the Church, become members?

The origins of the order and of its rituals are ingeniously hidden in an obscure mythology, mostly for the benefit of persons who would wish to speculate on them. Insisting on a universal brotherhood, which transcends race, class, and national boundaries, Freemasonry with its underlying philosophy of "Equality" was to influence several of the great reform-

---

102 Santiago Mariño de Acuna visited *Les Frères Unis*, later Lodge United Brothers in 1809 (Seemungal, Paper 74). It is not clear where he was made a Mason. or if he was a member of this Lodge.

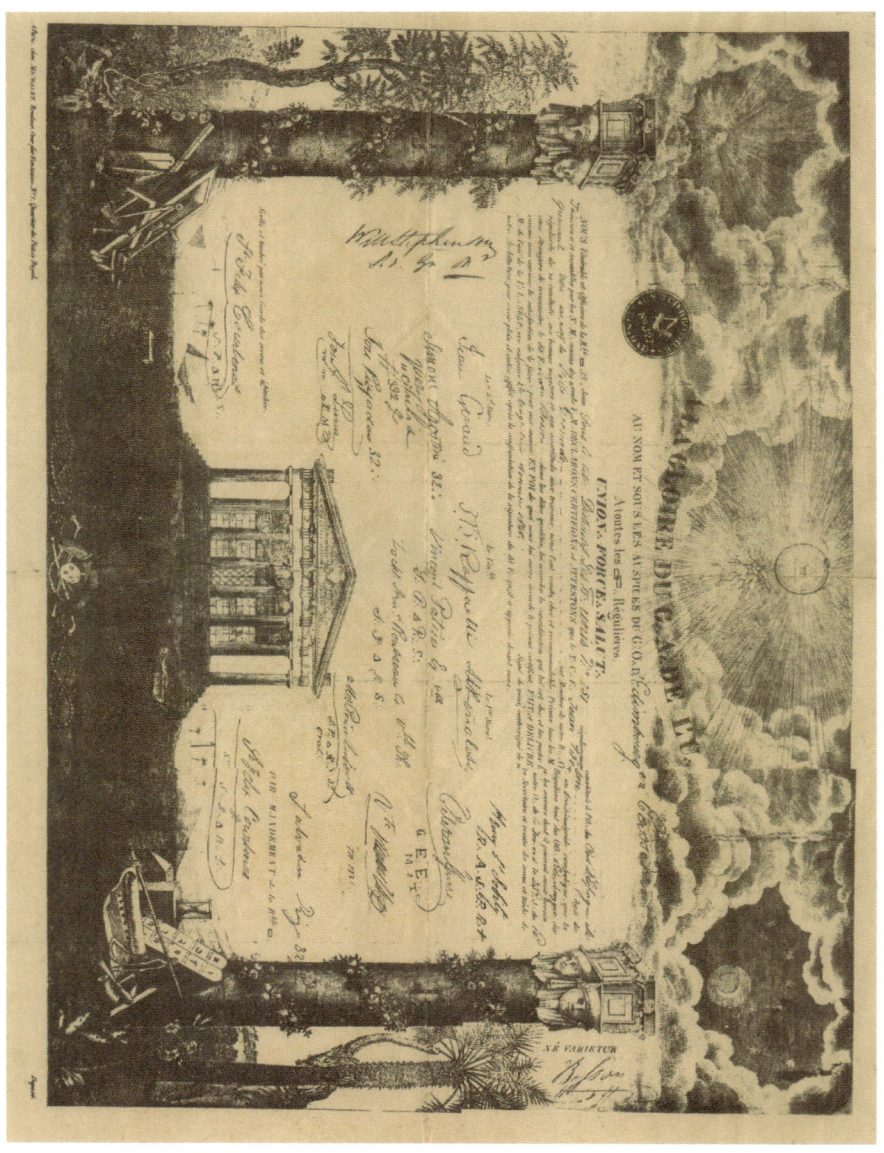

Masonic Diploma that was given to Jean Besson. It bears the signatures of Vincent Patrice, Simon Ago-stini, Vincent Julia, José Pujadas, Zacharie Rousseau, Michael Lubault, St. Felix Courbenas, Salvador Rizo. All signed S.P.R.S. or 32°. Also, Henry Joberty R.A., Peletan Guise G.E.E. This Diploma is dated 23rd December 1840. Jean Besson's signature is directly above this caption. (Seemungal)

ers of the 18th century (David Hume, Voltaire, Diderot, Montesquieu, Rousseau and others) with its teachings and by its example. Over time, it would come to influence the shift in moral values that characterised the age of Enlightenment. The system of plantation slavery, for example, aroused little protest until the 18th century, when rationalist thinkers of the Enlightenment criticized it for violating the rights of man, and Quaker and other evangelical religious groups condemned it as un-Christian.

The founders of the order were in accord with the ideas expressed by rationalists such as Thomas Paine, in writings such as *The Rights of Man,* a guide to Enlightenment ideas, and *The Age of Reason*, in its promoting of reason and freethinking, and its arguments against institutionalised religion and dogma. Because of its egalitarianism it was attractive, particularly to the growing British and European middle class in the 18th century.

Attracting men of different rank and calling, it was probably the only institution, apart from the Church, in which both nobles and commoners met as equals and where their roles in society could be reversed. Under the aegis of the order the class system in England and on the continent became less rigid, and more flexible.

In the highly structured society of the time, this in itself was revolutionary. By its central dictum that all men are created equal and that to become a member of the order, a man had only to be free and believe in a Supreme Being, it attracted the progressive-minded men of the period. As a secret society, or, as it is sometimes portrayed, "a society with secrets," a cabal, it conveyed the notion that it was able to control events from behind the scenes. That too was attractive, for at times this is true. It bound its membership through the shared experience of its rituals within a supportive network, as expressed by its motto, "Brotherly Love, Relief and Truth." [103]

It would be true to say that many Freemasons were revolutionaries (equally true is the opposite) and created or influenced revolutions in the Americas (North and South) and also in France. [104] It should also be borne in mind that a great many members of the order were sent to the

---

103 In 1855 Joseph Numa Boissière, the son of a slave, born in slavery, was admitted to the Craft at Lodge United Brothers, 251, S.C.

104 George Washington, Simón Bolívar and Francisco Miranda were Masons.

guillotine in France and in the Caribbean for being Royalists, condemned by men who were themselves Freemasons. And Freemasons were on both sides, the British and the American, during the War of Independence.

Quite apart from all the above, it was very fashionable, *avant garde*, to be a Freemason; it set one apart, in one's own eyes, and, one hoped, in the eyes of others.

Pierre Jean Besson and his brother Jean, grandsons of François, were both members of Lodge United Brothers, *Les Frères Unis,* as it was originally. So too were Jean Besson, [105] son of Pierre Louis and nephew of François; as well as Charles François Besson and Charles Frederick Besson. Pierre Numa Besson was a member of Lodge Eastern Star 368 S.C. and visited Lodge United Brothers frequently. [106] The period, the 1820s, is of interest to us, as it was in those years that several families came to Trinidad from North America. Some were American of British origin, and others were of French; some came from Pennsylvania. Several of the men of those families were Freemasons. [107] It was from one of those families that Pierre Jean Besson was to find a bride. Her name was Henriette Émilie Faut-Huerne; her brother, Pierre, was also member of Lodge United Brothers. They may have been the grandchildren of the French General, Pierre Huerne who had written to Benjamin Franklin on the 20th June 1778 desiring to go to America under Franklin's patronage [108] to support the revolutionaries fighting against British rule.

From information gathered by Lionel Seemungal, District Grand Librarian, Jean Besson, grandson of François, appears to have left for "An-

---

105 Jean Besson, son of Pierre Louis Besson and a woman of colour, nephew of François, died in the Royal Gaol in December 1840. He had been imprisoned for debt, became ill and died there. He had been made a Mason at L.U.B. in 1823. He resigned his position in the Lodge before going to prison. He was one of several coloured men to become Freemasons; another was Philip Langton, initiated May 1789. (Lodge records)

106 Minute books of Lodge United Brothers 1856-1859.

107 The de Lande D'Aussac family, into which Pierre Numa Besson married, may also have come to Trinidad via the United States.. Records of Lodge United Brothers.

108 Benjamin Franklin Papers, University of Pennsylvania 1705-1788, B F 85, 1778 A L S 2 p. From P. Huerne.

gostura, on the Orinoco River in some haste" [109] in 1823. He had left "forthwith," taking with him a Masonic Diploma signed by the leading Masons of Trinidad. Masonic Diplomas were sometimes seen as "passports" or "travelling documents," and would have been used as letters of introduction to Masonic circles in Venezuela.

Simón Bolívar, as well as other South American revolutionaries, was a Freemason. Pierre Jean Besson also received a Masonic Diploma and was also involved in the wars on the South American continent. As previously mentioned, I had in my possession a document authorising him to be paid for shipments of arms to Venezuela, which was signed by Bolivar. This had been sent to me from Venezuela by Frederico Ganteaume Pantin.

Francisco Nicolas, Count de Tovar, along with many other notables, was a supporter of Simón Bolívar and the Wars of Liberation. He was philanthropic and a liberal in inclination. Alexander von Humboldt wrote on his efforts as, "Nobly occupied with the necessary measures for the gradual abolition of Negro slavery in these regions . . ." [110] Two of the Count de Tovar's granddaughters would marry a grandson and a son of Pierre Alphonse Ganteaume. Mercedes de Tovar y Zeresa would marry Frederick Pantin de La Guerre, the son of Charles Pantin and Corinne Ganteaume. Corinne was Pierre Alphonse Ganteaume's daughter with his first wife, Eliza Monier de la Quarrée. Mercedes' sister, Maria, married Edgar Ganteaume; he was the son of Pierre Alphonse Ganteaume and his second wife, Adèle Besson. Both these marriages may have taken place in the 1840s in Venezuela. It is of interest that the children and grandchildren of these two marriages were to marry each other in much the same manner as their cousins were doing in Trinidad. It is a family tradition that these two young men, Frederick Pantin and Edgar Ganteaume, went out to Venezuela to help in the establishment of that country's Rail and Postal services. [111] The well-known portrait of Santiago Mariño was painted by a de Tovar.

---

109 From a letter written to the author by Seemungal in 1983.
110 von Humboldt, Viaje. . ., iii, p. 94 in Mijares, Augusto, *The Liberator*, p. 62
111 Bedford, Theresa, oral traditions of the Besson and Ganteaume families.

In a flotilla of small craft, the "Immortal 45" set out to conquer South America. Led by Santiago Mariño, Julien Besson took his chances in the squalls of the Boca Grande, off Chacachacare. (M.J. Cazabon, courtesy Geoffrey MacLean. Inset: Detail of portait of Mariño, de Tovar.)

The island of Chacachacare, off the coast of Trinidad and of Venezuela, had been presented to Gerald Fitzgerald Carige of Coolmine (Ireland), by the Spanish Crown upon his marriage to Maria Rosa de Ortega. [112] Their daughter, Maria Atanacia married Santiago Mariño de Acuna in 1787. Maria Atanacia's nephew, Pierre Carige, son of her brother William, married Jeanne Alciña Besson. Jeanne Alciña is of interest in that her father, Jean Besson, was the son of Pierre Louis Besson, nephew of François, and Marie Nerge, a woman of colour. Jeanne Alciña's mother, Eliza, was the daughter of Jean La Prade (who would have been a relative of François' second wife Elizabeth La Prade) and Sophia Laborde, also a woman of colour. According to the wills of both her parents, Jeanne Alciña, who had married Pierre Carige in 1838, was left properties in Port-of-Spain. She was a product of the *plaçage,* and a beneficiary of the "cult of the will" (as may have been her parents) and as a result, so would be their descendants.

---

112 Geraldine Carige was a grandson of the Earl of Meath and of the Earl of Desmond. Maria Rosa de Ortega was the daughter of the Marquise de Ortega. *Our Ancestors.* An unpublished manuscript by Olga Mavrogordato 1966, (Rowena Scott.)

Her husband Pierre Carige, who was of European descent, also inherited several town properties from his father and had retained a sizeable portion of land on the island of Chacachacare (see Appendix IV).

Their children, in turn, married Europeans, whose children became members of the professions. Their descendants today are to be found in the Bowen family. Dr. Edward Bowen and his brother Noel Bowen are both remembered as respected members of the medical and the legal professions. Dr. Edward Bowen's children are Valerie, Marjorie, Diane, Andrew, Edward and Noel Bowen. These examples are not unique as there are several other families, products of the 18th and 19th century colonial experience who were to benefit from the recognition of their European fathers, gain the respect of their peers and live successful and productive lives in the colonial society of the day and to the present.

The membership of Lodge United Brothers 251 S.C. during the first decades of the 19th century was made up of several Corsicans, as well as many men who had been friends and colleagues of François in Grenada, and others who would be relatives and in-laws, present and future, of his sons, grandsons and granddaughters. To name a few: Charles de la Barquerie de la Barrère, Cipriano Cipriani, Cousteau de l'Isle, Pierre Huerne, Jean, Joseph Etienne and Charles Maingot, J.B. and Paul Leotaud, Henri Lequin, Pierre Lange, A. Guiria, Thomas Mathurin de Gannes de la Chancellerie, Henri & Antoine de Jacques de la Bastide, Louis A. A. de Verteuil, Louis Maury de La Payrouse, Manuel Sorzano de Tejada, Pierre de Bot, Jean Garcin, Louis Marie Soulage, Auguste Lefer, Augustin de Lande d'Aussac, Jean de Boissiére, Jean Louis Jobity, André and St. Rose Espinet[113] and others. Several of them were to marry women whose fathers or brothers were themselves members of the order.

The Roman Catholic Church in Trinidad, during the colonial period, was regarded by the British colonial authorities as a powerful influence. In

---

113 Agostini, Cappedella, Caracciolo, Cipriani, Franceschi, Giuseppi, Piché, Pictri, Raffaelli, Vessiny, Vanneschi, Antonmattei, as some of the earlier members (1790s-1820s).Seemungal, Lionel, *Notes on Members of Les Frères Unis (from 1813 Lodge United Brothers 251 S.C.) from its transfer to Trinidad in 1794.* Paper 74.

fact, politics in the Crown colony, if one could describe them as that, were arranged along the lines of Catholic influences and interest, and Protestant influences and interest. Although Crown colony rule as expressed by the governor of the day was absolute, these influences and interests were at times played out in the colony's Legislative Council, and tended to influence the colonial government's policy, with regard to education for example.

The Church in Trinidad was guided by the Vatican's policy, which was framed by encyclicals, Papal Bulls. After the capitulation to the British in 1797, the Church in Trinidad, although treated with fairness by the authorities, and despite being the largest religious community, did not yet have the episcopal strength to challenge the French planters and adventurers, who formed the membership of Lodge United Brothers. Neither did the Church want to be seen as questioning an Act of the British Parliament that had recognised Freemasonry. What altered the status quo in Trinidad was the Papal Bull QUARTI CURA of 1864, issued by Pius IX. This encyclical was effectively brought to bear as a moral force.

The Catholic Church, never accepting that freedom of conscience might be considered a natural right, positioned as a grave mortal sin, membership in a secret society. This meant excommunication, which meant that the sacraments were not available to a Catholic Freemason: he could not enter a Catholic church, assist at Mass, marry, baptise his children, bury his dead, confess his sins, and receive the last rites. The stigma attached to his family could prove unbearable to them, and to him. He, and his family, could be shunned in certain social circles. One must bear in mind the pervasive (in all aspects of life) influence of religion during this time.

Another factor which was to alter the Catholic presence in Lodges in Trinidad was the episcopal succession of strong bishops, which began with Vincent Spaccapietra, second Archbishop of Port-of-Spain, whose term ended in 1859. The episcopal succession continued in Trinidad under effective administrators and archbishops who promulgated the encyclical of 1884 HUMANUM GENUS, by Leo XIII.

LODGE UNITED BROTHERS NO. 251 S.C.
BY MICHEL JEAN CAZABON

In this watercolour of Lodge United Brothers by Cazabon, the old Queen Street footbridge may bee seen. The building was built in 1803-1804, and is today, apart from the gaol on Frederick Street, the oldest purpose-built building that has been in continuous use in Port-of-Spain. (LUB)

This policy may have dissuaded many new members and caused resignations from the Lodges. [114] This may have been reinforced by the work of the clergy in the parishes. Guilt, social pressure, the enduring presence of superstition and the domestic pressure of fearful wives and daughters, would have served to tip the balance.

This saw a radical change in the membership of Lodge United Brothers. The deathbed recantations of members, who were beseeched by their families to leave the order, became news to be reported with relish and to be remembered in history. [115] In the diaries of Abbé Armand Massé,

114 Henry Kirkham Collens wrote in his annotations to J.M. Bodu's *Trinidadiana*: "Independent order of Good Templars. This order did not last many years - all Catholic members were forced to renounce membership by the Church authorities as it was a secret order. This order was founded by C.F. Stollmeyer and Dr. Robert Knaggs, whose brother Samuel Knaggs was Colonial Secretary, and Col. J.H. Collens, Inspector of Schools, all very powerful in colonial Trinidad in the 1870s."

115 Bodu's *Trinidadiana* reports the deathbed "reconciliation" of Paulin Josse de l'Isle, first Worshipful Master of Lodge Eastern Star. Henry Kirkham Collens wrote in his an-

The Wilderness on Pembroke Street may have been the home of Jeanne Alciña Besson, born 1840 in her later life. She was the daughter of Jean Besson and Eliza La Prade. Jean Besson's father was Louis Pierre Besson, possibly the nephew of Eli François Besson, and a coloured woman, Marie Nerge. Eliza La Prade's father was Jean La Prade, and her mother was Sophie Laborde, also a coloured woman. Louis Pierre Besson and Jean La Prade were related through marriage, in that Eli François' second wife was Elizabeth La Prade. They were the products of the 19th century custom of plaçage and both inherited town properties. Jeanne Alciña married Pierre Carige, born 1825. He was the grandson of Géraldine Carige of Inchquin. Their daughter, Marie Alciña, married a Welshman by the name of Edward Bowen.

The house figures in Trinidad's history in that Pierre Carige's aunt Maria was the wife of General Santiago Mariño, one of the leaders of the wars of liberation of South America. Their descendents, the Bowens lived there for several generations. The Wilderness was later turned into a primary school, St. Monica's, and was demolished in the year 2004.

(Photos: Alice Besson)

1878-1883, Vol. IV, for example, one finds: "There was joy lately in the Freemasons Lodge of Trinidad: the Governor [116] took his place among them. Today their sorrow is great because the head of the Lodge, a Catholic, has renounced Freemasonry and has been genuinely converted. 20th April 1882."

Of the 27 names of new members admitted to Lodge United Brothers in 1822, only two were British—one assumes Protestant—and the others, French and Spanish names, were Catholics. Of the 56 names of new members admitted between 1855 and 1860, almost all had either British or German names, with the exception of four, and one was Charles François Besson with Pierre Numa Besson as a visitor from Lodge Eastern Star, a newly-formed Lodge consecrated in 1856. It had as its first Right Worshipful Master, Henri Paulin Josse de l'Isle, who would be the grandfather of Eusibia Lazarine de l'Isle, Joseph Léon Besson's wife (Joseph Léon was Emmanuel Besson's son). By the 1860s, Lodge United Brothers no longer worked in French. [117] There were also few members with French names. Charles Frederick Besson, grandson of François Besson de Beaumanoir, died in 1913, and was buried with Masonic honours. He had lived at 1 Besson Street, Port-of-Spain.

---

notations to Bodu: "Funeral of Paulin de l'Isle - 'Reconciled' to the church, that is he renounced Freemasonry and died 'fortified with her sacraments'; this does not reconcile with the funeral of Maxwell Phillip with 'Masonic honours'. Bodu was pro Catholic, so in his report on the death of Maxwell Phillip P.M. Royal Prince of Wales Lodge, he does not say, with Masonic honours. Another well-known Freemason, Daniel Hart, who died in 1869, received Masonic honours at his burial. This was also not mentioned by Bodu."

116 Sir Sanford Freeling K.C.M.G. Governor of Trinidad in 1880, was a member of Royal Prince of Wales Lodge in 1881, as was Sir Clement Courtenay Knollys K.C.M.G., who was Colonial Secretary and acted as Governor of Trinidad and Tobago on occasion. *Royal Prince of Wales Lodge records.*

117 Notwithstanding the apparent flight of the French Creole Masons from Lodge United Brothers, the Black and coloured membership continued through the 19th century into the 20th. To name a few of the more well-known men of colour: J. Boissière, F.O. Webb, A.E. Grell. A.P. Mathison, A. Richards, A.C. Blondel, W. Aleong, E. Lazare, M. Phillips, (from 1850-1900). *Lodge records.*

A view of Mount Tamana from Arima. In the middle distance, left, the spire of the Mission church of Santa Rosa de Lima at Arima, with the roofs of the town just visible above the trees. The Besson family would make their home there from the last decade of the 19th century to the present, a very long way, and some two hundred and fifty years from the little village of Tanzac in western France. (M.J. Cazabon, courtesy Belmont Harris Trust and Geoffrey MacLean)

THE BESSON FAMILY TO THE PRESENT DAY
9

To bring the story of the descendants of François forward to the present day, let us continue with Emmanuel Léon Besson, son of Pierre Numa, grandson of Pierre Jean, great-grandson of François *fils*, and great-great-grandson of Eli François Besson de Beaumanoir. There is no evidence to show that Emmanuel received or inherited any property. He was only 17 when his father, Pierre Numa died. The Registry Department in Port-of-Spain possesses no wills of Bessons related to this line of descent; the substantial town properties owned by the family may have been passed on to others or sold off to provide cash to maintain the many girls born in this period. Emmanuel's sisters, as we have noted, were Eliza Besson who married Jules Ernest Attale, and Marie Emilie Besson who married Augustine Savary. It would appear from the Arima records, [118] that Emmanuel went to live there with his mother's family (the de Landes, who had received a Spanish grant in Arouca in 1784) and was brought up on a cocoa estate in the heights of Guanapo in the mountainous valleys north of Arima. This isolation would have served to break the links with some of his other relations and also to place him in a situation where his very limited prospects did not hold out a particularly bright future.

It could also have been the point in time when memories of the family's origins and recent history were lost: François' position in the French government in Grenada; his wealth and prominence; the situation of his sons and grandsons; their entry into the plantation economy in Trinidad; their success at sugar cultivation and their ultimate failure when the plantation economy changed. In Emmanuel's time, there were very few family members left who could perpetuate the family's stories as living memory, as oral history told around dining room tables and front galleries on windy afternoons for the benefit of the young people. Connections to the family in France would perhaps have been lost and forgotten in this period.

As a young man, Emmanuel must have experienced a great sense of loss. The loss of his father at a young age was bad, and with hardly any close male relatives, no land to make a living from—his life looked bleak. Good fortune brought him into contact with a lovely young woman, to whom he proposed marriage, by the name of Marie Léontine Sorzano. She was the great-granddaughter of Don Manuel Tomás Sorzano y Tejada, [119] who had arrived in Trinidad in 1780 and had been a high-ranking civil servant for the Spanish crown during the administration of the last Spanish Governor, Don José Chacón. The Sorzanos were wealthy and land-owning, and came from a distinguished Spanish *Grandee* family.

---

118 The Arima Catholic Church, Santa Rosa, records, as well as the Arima Town Hall records.

119 Manuel Sorzano was made a Mason in 1789 and joined Lodge United Brothers in Sept. 1795. It is of interest that apart from being a Catholic he was also a Spanish government official.

They lived at Sorzano Street in Arima. This marriage and its connections, the family's landholdings and prestige, would have served to offer opportunities for Emmanuel to restart the family's fortunes, but it does not appear that he took advantage of this. He simply became a cocoa planter and worked for his father-in-law. He appears to have lived a very quiet life at Arima in the bosom of the Sorzano family at Mausica and Trianon estates, during what was known as the cocoa boom. The cocoa estates of Trinidad did very well. Those French Creoles who had land made a fortune during the last thirty years of the 19th century. [120]

Emmanuel and Léontine had two daughters, Marie Ange, born in 1875, who married her cousin Thomas Sorzano [121] and Clarissa, born in 1878. In 1886 Emmanuel and Léontine had a son who was christened Joseph Léon Besson. Joseph Léon might have been born at a house in Green Street in Arima. He may have had a simple education at the Arima Boys' R.C. School, although this is perhaps unlikely, because few boys, coming from a European, landed, French/Spanish family in colonial Trinidad would have done so. However, the St. Mary's College records do not go back further than 1916, so we have no idea of the sort of education that Joseph Léon or his father Emmanuel might have had. By the time Joseph Léon was 16 or 17, he most certainly would have gone to work on one of his mother's, the Sorzano's, cocoa estates.

No family photos have survived; in fact, the only mementoes we possess of the Besson family of those days are three silver table spoons engraved "E.B." which were given to me upon my marriage to Sheelagh Hezekiah by my cousin Pauline Gellizeau (the daughter of Marie Ange, sister of Joseph Léon Besson, who had married her cousin Thomas Sorzano). There is also the Besson family grave at Lapeyrouse cemetery in Port-of-Spain, where two imposing gravestones mark the graves of the wives of Pierre

---

120 Franklin, C.B. *Yearbook of 1916* shows over 1,000 cocoa estates; of these, persons with French names owned 126 of perhaps some of the larger ones.

121 The children of Marie Ange and Thomas Sorzano were: Louis Ambrose, who married Edith Williams, a person of colour, Mark married a Venezuelan, Barbara married Andre Devenish, Marie Pauline (Polly) married Hector de Gannes-Gellizeau, Val married Robert Cipriani, and Lena married Guy Maingot.

Joseph Ambrosio Besson
1917–1993

Jean Besson: Henriette Faut-Huerne, who died in 1831 and Rose Laurencine Darmanie who died in 1864.

At the age of 30, Joseph Léon married Eusibia Lazarine de I'Isle, also of Arima. She was the daughter of Henri Josse de l'Isle and Isabella Luces. The de l'Isle family, like the Bessons, de Landes, de la Bastides, and other French families, had arrived in Trinidad in the 1780s. They too had received a Spanish land grant. They were well-off property owners in and around Arima, and also cocoa planters. Their son and only child, Joseph Ambrosio Besson, my father, was born 22nd March 1917 at the home of Eusibia's parents in Arima at a house also in Green Street.

By the following year, 11th April 1918, Eusibia was dead, age 23, of enteric fever. In her will, she left to her husband Joseph Léon Besson, in trust, the estate that she had inherited from her late father. She further states that the proceeds from the cultivation of the estate should go to the education and maintenance of her infant son, Joseph Ambrosio Besson. By the following year, 3rd September 1919, Joseph Léon, her husband, died, aged 33, also of enteric fever, leaving Joseph Ambrosio Besson an orphan of two years old.

At this point, the history of the Besson family in Trinidad hits a new low. The boy was brought up by his mother's brother, Simon Josse de l'Isle, and his family in Arima in unfortunate circumstances. He was, from all accounts, treated as a charity case, and not brought into the closeness of the family. The proceeds from his mother's estate were reabsorbed by the family and for reasons unknown, his education was perhaps even more rudimentary than his father's. He did not attend St. Mary's College in Port-of-Spain. He did not inherit anything from his mother's estate. He was a victim of the "cult of the will." There was no particular care given to him as a boy, and he grew up, it has been suggested, as a stable hand on the de l'Isle cocoa estate in Sangre Grande. That he was ill-treated by his uncle, Simon, was remembered by Josephine Lezama, a granddaughter of Simon de l'Isle, who related that he wore the clothes of his older cousins. She said that he wore small boy's clothes, even as a teenager, and that he acquired few social graces, and was placed at an early age outside the perimeter of polite society. His various relatives, members of his extended family all knew him, some pitied him, others avoided his company. This was related to me by Maurice and Basil de Gannes, and Emanuel (Noche) Lange, all of whom knew my father, Joseph Ambrosio Besson, and have generally corroborated this account of his upbringing.

Joe Besson, also known as "Boysie", was left to fend for himself and to make his way in the world, which he did with considerable charm. He married, in 1941 Margaret Joachim, my mother; she was the daughter of André Joachim [122] and Ella Boissière, both coloured people, and products

---

122 André Joachim, my maternal grandfather, was the grandson of Orevatté, a slave on the estate of Joachim Frontin, who may have been his grandfather, a French manwho had received a Spanish land grant in Mayaro in 1782. Andre Joachim's wife, Ella Lousia Boissière, my maternal grandmother, was the great-granddaughter of Zuzule, a slave belonging to Jean Valleton de Boissière of Champs Elysées, Maraval, recorded in Trinidad in 1792. The children of these pre-emancipation unions received legacies, land, household objects, perhaps cash, from their European forebears. In the case of André Joachim, he carried his father's first name as a surname. He inherited land in Mayaro from his mother Améline Joachim. My grandmother's family had carried the name of Boissière for two generations by the time of her birth, also inherited property in Port-of-Spain left to them by Jean Valleton de Boissière. They were both beneficiaries of the "cult of the will". *Registrar General's office records and family tradition.*

of the 19th century custom of *plaçage*, descendants of African women born in slavery who had had relationships with French colonial pioneers who had come to seek their fortunes in the New World in the closing decades of the 18th century.

He knew very little about his family, except that the first Besson to come to Trinidad was called François, and that he had been a *"Chevalier"* from France. He also said that he was related to "everyone", meaning the descendants of the French planter families who had come to Trinidad in the 1780s, attracted by the terms of the Cedula of Population. He had a gold ring, very worn, with some obscure markings on it, and this he left for me.

End of Part One.

Part Two.

INTRODUCTION
TO THE SECOND PART

In a real sense all historians are revisionists, as all try to make some new contribution that would serve to alter our understanding of the past. In this book, I am attempting to alter the criteria of identity formation of Caribbean people along the lines of what I call the "cult of the will." This cult or obsession, and the politics it has produced, apportions a false sense of inherited victimhood and entitlement to some, and to others inherited guilt and social embarrassment. It locks us in a perpetual state of irresponsibility and powerlessness, and makes us prisoners of the past.

As such, in the first part of this book, I set out to challenge one aspect of the "cult of the will": a tendency in post-colonial Caribbean historiography and historicity that seeks to stereotype people of the past as members of socioeconomic groups or classes and to diminish the role of the individual. This tendency seems to facilitate the stigmatisation of Caribbean people of European descent, or those who appear so, through the projection of negative concepts of "slave master" and "colonial master" to modern-day individuals for political and ideological purposes. As such, an ethnic minority in our midst is stigmatised— this is one of the more unfortunate legacies of the 20th century and one that in my view has no place in modern society, academia and politics.

As an example, in the first part of this study, I touch upon the circumstances that established a French colonial family in the Caribbean in the mid-18th century, and give some instances of the racial and political conflicts of those times that were brought about by the excesses of colonisation and plantation slavery. I endeavour to arrange these against the backdrop of the swiftly changing world events that characterised this period.

I also discuss the relationships between European men, enslaved women and women of colour, both free and enslaved. These relationships were sometimes called *plaçage* (concubinage), and I look at the lives of some of the children born of these unions, and at the beneficial or, at times, deadly consequences that the products of those relationships may have experienced or even occasioned.

In the second part of this study I am striving to change the reader's mind in a fundamental way about a specific criterion of the "cult of the will": the creation of narratives as tools for identity-formation. In understanding how, why, and for what purpose a new narrative, a new interpretation of history, was introduced at the time of Independence in 1962 by Dr. Eric Williams (1911-1981), and the consequences of his revision of history were, I invite the reader to alter his or her understanding of the past, and leave the "cult of the will" behind—because its essential premise is the fallacious concept that "history is destiny".

For the purpose of understanding the term "narratives" in this study, I would like to quote Professor Brereton, who in her paper *Contesting the Past: Narratives of Trinidad and Tobago History,* observes:

> "Historians and social scientists agree that nationalisms and national identities, ethnicity and ethnic identities, are all constructed or invented at specific historical conjunctures, and that the creation of narratives about the past is always an important aspect of this process."

In this second part of the study, I explore what this definition means with respect to Dr. Williams' deconstruction of British imperial history with Independence in 1962 for the purpose of creating a new historical narrative concerning events in our past. This new narrative I shall call the "Eric Williams narrative".

I suggest that the political personality of Dr. Eric Williams was shaped by the 18th century Afro-French Creole plantation experience, and the manner in which this was lived and expressed in the 19th by the coloured middle class, of which he and his extended family were a part.

I argue that painful events in his family's past, the powerful political influences at play in the late 1930s, and his immersion in Caribbean history, made Williams a prisoner of the past.

I suggest that his 'wounded personality' was incapable of accepting that notwithstanding whatever the reasons given for the abolition of the slave trade in 1807, it was, when enacted and enforced, a major step taken by Great Britain in the advancement of Western civilisation.

I suggest that Dr. Williams may have been influenced, perhaps even manipulated, by C.L.R. James and other ideologues, who may have had knowledge of his personal circumstances and psychological weaknesses.

I argue that Williams' clever use of black nationalism was a method to gain power so as to alleviate his anger and disappointment, to assuage a raging "Inward Hunger" and will attempt an explanation as to why he expressed strong racial antipathy towards Indians and French Creoles.

Also cited in Professor Brereton's paper is American psychologist Barry Schwartz, who wrote:

> "Recalling the past is an active constructive process, not a simple matter of retrieving information. To remember is to place a part of the past in the service of conceptions and needs of the present."

This observation will be applied to this study, so as to discover the roots of the racial prejudices that dog us to this day, in the hope that it may shed some light on Trinidad and Tobago's current problematic sociopolitical condition.

Professor Brereton continues in her paper:

> "All postcolonial states, in particular, have undergone a process of national self-creation, a process of identity formation involving 'a recasting of history to produce a usable past' as Howard Johnson has said of Jamaica."

Against these observations, I pose these questions: did Dr. Williams' new narrative and the political culture it engendered provide a useful process for identity formation and give us a usable past, one that could be placed at the service of the present? If not, shouldn't we now revisit our recent past, the Independence period of the 1960s, with a view to refashion a more usable future — especially against the societal and political challenges that were created by the Williams narrative, that now appear to be undermining the institutions of the state and contribute to eroding the moral fibre of the society?

Should we not now review that point in time, Independence, when we experienced a shift in moral values that caused this collapse of moral and civic responsibility, which is precipitated by an entrenched sense of victimhood combined with unearned and often undeserved entitlement?

I pose these questions in this second part fairly certain that at the time of writing, a crisis of credibility faces the political culture created by Dr. Williams, possibly signalling the end of this incarnation of the more than fifty year-old regime.

I suggest, finally, in this second part of *The Cult of the Will,* that a new, New World narrative, a different view of the past, may be upon us, one endowed with empowerment and responsibility, and one that, in the words of Professor Ramesh Deosaran, " … holds a better promise for spiritual growth, and the shaping of a common humanity."

The Queen's Royal College, successor to the Queen's Collegiate School, was the alma mater of a significant number of men, including the Hon. Dr. Eric Williams, who would help to shape the future of Trinidad and Tobago. The building was opened on the 25 March, 1904. (Paria)

THE INTELLECTUAL ROOTS OF THE ERIC WILLIAMS NARRATIVE
1

In this chapter, I will explore some of the intellectual influences that may have conditioned the young Eric Williams during his time spent in England at Oxford University, which led him to challenge the British colonial narrative, its interpretation of history, with a different reading of the events that resulted in the abolition of the slave trade.

In my opinion, his encounter with his former teacher C.L.R. James and his circle in the London of the late 1930s and their Marxist/Trotskyite world-view, may have helped to shape the thinking of the young, impressionable Williams. James had become a scholar-activist and sociopolitical theorist. He was addressing an audience of anti-colonialists in Africa, the Caribbean and radicals worldwide. Acclaimed as "the black Plato of our time," James can be viewed as both product and pioneer of Caribbean modernism.

James' political practice was two-fold in that he moved in Trotskyite circles while collaborating with Trinidadian intellectual and revolutionary George Padmore; Jomo Kenyatta from Kenya; Jamaican activist writer, Amy Ashwood-Garvey; Trinidad-born communist and feminist, Claudia Jones and other pioneers of Pan-Africanism, Pan-Caribbeanism and anti-colonialism. Their work influenced nationalist activists like Williams, Norman Manley of Jamaica and Kwame Nkrumah of the Gold Coast, later Ghana.

This milieu of Pan-Caribbeanism, Pan-Africanism and international socialism may have resulted in Williams internalising the inherent moral relativism [123] of those ideologies, stimulating him to apply it to a recasting of history: a counter discourse to the dominant narrative of the Western world.

Dr. Eric Williams' recasting of history contested one of the basic moral positions that had underpinned the British colonial narrative: the conviction that the slaves in the British Empire had been freed as a result of the late 18th century English sense of injustice and moral outrage at the mistreatment of African slaves in the British colonies.

His doctoral thesis: *The Economic Aspects of the Abolition of the Slave Trade and West Indian Slavery,* which according to him, the authorities at Oxford had threatened to fail because they did not like his views, [124] was seminal in recasting history for the creation of a different understanding of the past. It became the first step in formulating a new historiography for his homeland, and the Anglophone Caribbean.

---

123 In philosophy moral relativism is the position that moral or ethical propositions do not reflect objective and/or universal moral truths, but instead make claims relative to social, cultural, historical or personal circumstances. Moral relativists hold that no universal standard exists by which to assess an ethical proposition's truth. Relativistic positions often see moral values as applicable only within certain cultural boundaries (cultural relativism) or in the context of individual preferences (individualist ethical subjectivism). An extreme relativist position might suggest that judging the moral or ethical judgments or acts of another person or group has no meaning, though most relativists propound a more limited version of the theory. In moral relativism there are no absolute, concrete rights and wrongs. Rather, intrinsic ethical judgements exist as abstract, differing for each perception of an ethical outlook. (Wikipedia)

124 Deosaran 1981, 22

In his thesis, Williams dismissed the reason given by British historians for the abolition of the slave trade, arguing that abolition was largely an act of British foreign policy. According to him, both abolition and emancipation were political and economic expedients, and the humanitarian campaign was merely a ploy to distract from Britain's true intentions.

Williams successfully repositioned Caribbean history in his book *Capitalism and Slavery,* an adaptation of his doctoral thesis. In it, Williams sought to diminish the claim of moral or religious motives, as expressed by the British philanthropists and Evangelicals such as William Wilberforce, Thomas Buxton, Thomas Clarkson and many others, including Chief Justice L.C.J. Mansfield, who in 1772 handed down the following judgement in England: "The state of slavery is so odious that nothing can be suffered to support it but positive law. Whatever inconveniences, therefore, may follow from the decision, I cannot say this case is allowed or approved by the law of England. Therefore let the black go free." [125]

Williams condemned the abolitionists as "hypocrites" for describing slavery as a crime against humanity. He compared slavery to conditions in Europe. He wrote, "The age which had seen the mortality among indentured servants saw no reason for squeamishness about the mortality among slaves, nor did the exploitation of the slaves on the plantations differ fundamentally from the exploitation of the feudal peasant or the treatment of the poor in European cities." [126]

It is not without significance that Williams' view did not take into account that the abolition of the slave trade and the emancipation of the slaves, for whatever the reasons given or the causes explained, whether as an expeditious economic necessity, a political trick to achieve a moral position, or an act that was based on a sense of 'justice and humanity,' when passed into law by the government of the United Kingdom in 1807 and in 1836, were in fact significant moral achievements, and that these laws, when enacted, demonstrated a major advancement of Western civilisation.

---

125 Wooding 1968, 146. Wooding comments that this judgement "established for all time the tradition of personal freedom which the common law upholds."

126 Williams,1964, 34f

The view that the slave trade was abolished for economic reasons and political expediency rather than for humanitarian inclinations, which he supported by rigorous research, may have appealed to Williams' state of mind, as someone, as we shall see, who was inclined to believe in conspiracies. Later this position would serve a political purpose, in that it would make sense to many who were prepared to accept the idea that the British had not spoken the truth in their rendering of history, and that people had been made victims of a conspiracy that with held the truth about the abolition of the slave trade, as well as be made to suffer from colonial injustice and racial prejudice.

Williams drew on many sources for his doctoral thesis. Perhaps the most evocative for him may have been C.L.R. James' history of the Haitian Revolution, *The Black Jacobins*, which as Simon Lee suggests was a deconstruction of the hegemonic Western fantasy of history:

> "James likewise deconstructs the flawed moral philosophy of both the Enlightenment's and the French Revolution's pursuit of freedom, sustained by totalising yet blind Hegelian discourses, as logically how can freedom be built on slavery? In presenting the Caribbean version of the Haitian Revolution, James initiates profound Creole discourses, some of which have gone unappreciated to this day. By demonstrating that the revolutionary impulses of the French Revolution were far more radically manifested in the Caribbean, he places the region emphatically in the realm of global modernity.
>
> James writes in *The Black Jacobins*, 'The blacks were taking their part in the destruction of European feudalism begun by the French Revolution, and liberty and equality, the slogans of the revolution meant far more to them than to any freeman'" (*The Black Jacobins.*) [127]

James encouraged Williams to embark on a revolutionary, yet altogether scholarly approach to rewriting history in his doctoral thesis, which sought to expose, from their point of view, the lies and hypocrisy of the British colonial establishment, both in its interpretation of history and in the governance of their island home.

---

127 Lee, Simon: Literary Foundations: "CLR James's contribution to initiating Creole discourses and defining Creole Space," typescript, emailed to the author.

James published *The Black Jacobins* in 1938; Williams defended his thesis at Oxford in 1939. James claims to have influenced Williams' choice of topic, as Boodhoo relates: [128]

"Williams: I am to do a doctorate, what shall I write on?

James: I know exactly what you should write on. I have done the economic basis of slavery emancipation as it was in France. [129] But that has never been done in Great Britain, and Britain is wide open for it. A lot of people think the British showed goodwill. There were lots of people who had goodwill, but it was the basis, the economic basis, that allowed the goodwill to function." James continues "I sat down and wrote what the thesis should be with my own hand, and I gave it to him.... I saw the manuscript quite often, I read it three or four times."

In *The Black Jacobins*, Williams claims to have found the important insights with which to challenge his entire colonial conditioning. For example, James writes "The revolution had awakened them, had given them the possibility of achievement, confidence and pride. That psychological weakness, that feeling of inferiority with which the imperialists poison colonial peoples everywhere, these had gone." (p. 197)

It could be argued that with *The Black Jacobins,* James "effectively founded modern Creole discourses of history, historiography and historicity."[130] C.L.R. James' account of the slave uprising of Saint Domingue at the turn of the 18th century, in which he explores anticolonialist and Marxist paradigms, is replete with descriptions of the struggle between the races, or as he puts it, the classes: the African slave, the Creole slave, the mulatto, free, not free; the whites, the bourgeoisie, small and otherwise. "I was a highly trained Marxist and that was the person who wrote *The Black Jacobins*," recalls James in an interview with the BBC. As a radical Marxist historian, James' imagination may have been stirred by Trotsky's history of the Russian Revolution and perhaps by Oswald Spengler's, *The Decline*

---

128 James in interview with KAS-KAS, p. 36, from Boodhoo, Ken *The Elusive Eric Williams p.159*

129 In fact this is a very minor aspect of *The Black Jacobins.*

130 Lee, Simon, op. cit.

of the West. The epic scale of these histories is echoed in his account of the Haitian Revolution. Williams writes in the bibliography to *Capitalism and Slavery*:

> "Special mention must be made of two studies which present in a general way the relationship between capitalism and slavery. The first was a Master's thesis by W. E. Williams: *Africa and the Rise of Capitalism.* [131]

> The second and more important was C.L.R. James, *The Black Jacobins, Toussaint L'Ouverture and the San Domingo Revolution* (London, 1938.) On pages 38-41,[132] the thesis advanced in this book (*The Black Jacobins*) is stated clearly and concisely and, as far as I know, for the first time in English."

The three pages that so moved Williams contain James' attack, on what appears to him, as the conspiracy by "a venal race of scholars, [i.e. historians,] profiteering panders to national vanity, (who) have conspired to obscure the truth about abolition." [133] This conspiracy, according to James, was meant to trick the European powers and eventually, the former slaves and their descendants in the colonies into believing that humanitarian motives were behind these moves, a conspiracy to obscure the truth about the abolition of the slave trade and in so doing allow the English to gain a popular moral position.

This period in history, between the two World Wars, was formative for the future of Europe, and for the world at large in the long term, it witnessed the passing away of an epoch, the end of the European empires, and has been described as the end of legitimacy and of the age of difference. James, as a Marxist and Trotskyite, was involved in a world wide endeavour to create a new narrative, a new worldview. He must have understood plainly that to change the politics of people, one needs first to alter their understanding of the past. Therefore James' approach to history was to rewrite it.

---

131 Published by the Division of Social Sciences of Howard University in 1934

132 Pages 38-41 refer to the first, 1938 edition of *The Black Jacobins.* In the Vintage Books edition of 1989, pages 51-54 are the relevant text.

133 James may have been referring to Sir Reginald Coupland, a scholar of Imperial History at Oxford, attacked by Williams, and used by James.

To achieve this change, James needed to discover the inner, concealed intentions of the British 18th century parliamentarians and then expose their supposed collusion with as much empirical evidence as possible, and in so doing, bring to light the secret machinations of 'the powers that be' so as to demonstrate how the British government had sought to conspire to delude the gullible, the morally motivated, the do good-ers, the slaves, causing them to accept as truth what was perceived by them on the surface of things.

James' depiction of the events in Haiti and the life of Toussaint L'Ouverture contains a description of what he perceives as a conspiracy between Prime Minister Pitt and the abolitionist Wilberforce. This exposé of a conspiracy, to which we will return in some detail, may have been one of several elements contained in James' work that served to shape the thinking and fire the imagination of the young and impressionable Eric Williams. Another may have been on a more subtle level, and could reveal how their relationship and their mutual endeavour may have been formed by their empirical research. This concerns Vincent Ogé, who was a young mulatto man from Saint Domingue, living in Paris in the 1790s, whose circumstances were strangely reminiscent of their own relationship.

Ogé fell under the influence of Maximilien Robespierre, the revolutionary who dominated the Committee of Public Safety in that period of the French Revolution commonly known as the Reign of Terror. Robespierre and other revolutionaries controlled a radical organisation called *Société des Amis des Noirs*, which was an anti-slavery society that had been founded in 1788 in Paris by Jacques Pierre Brissot.

During the late1930s, in writing *The Black Jacobins.* James was absorbed (and probably Williams as well for his own doctoral work) in the machinations of the French revolutionaries. The British 18th century historian Bryan Edwards in *The History Civil and Commercial of the British Colonies In the West Indies* (1807, 43) comments on the *Société des Amis des Noirs*:

> "Ogé had been introduced to the meetings of the *Amis des Noirs,* Friends of the Blacks, under the patronage of Gregoire, Brissot, La Fayette, and Robespierre, the leading members of that society; [in a manner not dissimilar to Williams', admission into James' circle of Pan Caribbean,

Pan African ideologues, communists and would be revolutionaries]
and was by them initiated into the popular doctrine of *Equality,* and *the
Rights of Man."*

[…] "Here it was that he [Ogé] first learnt of the miseries of his condition; the cruel wrongs and contumelies to which he and all his mulatto
brethren were exposed in the West Indies, and the monstrous injustice
and absurdity of that prejudice, 'which (said Gregoire) estimating a
man's merit by the colour of his skin, has placed at an immense distance
from each other the children of the same parent; a prejudice which sti-
fles the voice of nature, and brakes the bands of fraternity asunder … *it
is not surprising that the efforts of this society should have operated powerfully
on the minds of those who were taught to consider their personal wrongs as
the cause of the Nation, and driven some of them into the wildest excesses of
fanaticism and fury."* (Emphasis mine)

Williams would later identify his own deprivations and suffering with
his audiences', and carry forward this identification in his development of
nationalistic politics in Trinidad and Tobago in the 1950s, and in so doing
implement the Williams narrative.

James writes of Ogé in *The Black Jacobins:* "Such were his talents that it
was said of him that there was no position to which he could not aspire"
— a sentiment that he often expressed of his "star pupil and devoted ad-
mirer", Eric Williams. (p. 68)

Some years later, Williams, in discussing the Haitian revolution in his
book *From Columbus to Castro* (p. 247) writes of Ogé, his memories and
feelings for those times evidently still vibrant,

"The young spokesman for the mulattos, breathed fire and brimstone:
'We will not remain much longer in degradation […] We can raise as
good soldiers as those of France. Our own arms will render us respectable and independent. Once we are reduced to desperate measures,
thousands of men will cross the Atlantic in vain to reduce us to our
former condition' "

[…] "The prophecy was correct except in one important particular:
Ogé was not speaking for the slaves […] Advised by a friend to launch
an immediate uprising of the slaves, Ogé rejected the plan as too radi-

cal; property before race. With a handful of followers, he was soon rounded up, tried, and broken on the wheel […] The mulattos in their turn, having learned the lesson of Ogé, decided to call out the slaves."

Interestingly, four years later in 1795 in Grenada, another mulatto Republican revolutionary, Julien Fédon, did call out the slaves.

There is a sense of *déjà vu* in all of this: Vincent Ogé had been guided by the French revolutionary leader in Paris, Maximilien Robespierre, to start the mulatto uprising in Saint Domingue in 1790, an uprising that failed, but one that served as a trigger for the start of the real event a short time later.

This is remarkable similar to the manner in which another revolutionary ideologue in London in the 1930s, C.L.R. James, while reading and researching the 1790 material for the purpose of writing *The Black Jacobins*, published in 1938 was able to influence the thinking of Eric Williams, who defended a thesis in 1939, later published as *Capitalism and Slavery*, which served the purpose of Pan Caribbean, Pan African anti-colonial resistance, and ultimately caused the deconstruction of an aspect of the British colonial interpretation of history.

Robespierre and Ogé — James and Williams: this coincidence of master and pupil, some one hundred and forty years apart, allows one to perceive perhaps the template in which Williams was handled by James and helps to position Williams' thinking more with those of the 18th century revolutionaries, than with those of the 20th.

Both Williams (born in 1911) and James (born 1901), would have had family members who were not so far removed from "slavery days." Williams could draw from his experiences as a mixed-race product of the historic process that had taken place in these islands and empathise with *The Black Jacobins*. In a real way Williams' doctoral thesis could be seen as an extension of the discourse initiated in *The Black Jacobins*. Both these works recast history along the lines of moral relativism.

Williams could empathise with that half-world shown by James in the second chapter of *The Black Jacobins*, "*The Owners*," which describes the alleged collusion between the British Prime Minister Pitt and the social reformer, Wilberforce. As a pragmatist, Williams could relate to the economics of the situation, and as a student of history, based on his research into primary sources, he could appreciate the changes that had been made in terms of the geopolitics of the day. As a person with a somewhat cynical turn of mind, he would make his own choices based on his interpretation of the information.

"The Owners" also explores the pathetic conditions of the coloured people of Saint Domingue. It describes the humiliating grades of colour that ultimately took one to the inevitable glass ceiling that divided "whiteness" from the rest of the world.

Williams may have been able to name and count the gradations of shade and colour in himself. He was born at a time when people knew of such things. He would have been able to identify these variations in his mother, father and grandparents. His father's father was a *zambo*, half Carib, half black. Ernest Laborde, [134] the Williams' family historian, described Williams' father's mother as having the appearance of a white woman, a European, in skin colour, features and hair texture. Perhaps she may have been seen as a *marabou,* in the proportion of 88 to 40 parts European and African or a *sacatra,* in proportion of 72 to 56 respectively. Williams wrote that one of his father's problems that had prevented his advancement had been his colour: his father thought that he was too dark-skinned.

All these issues were the inevitable consequences of the slave trade, its liaisons, its sensuality, its secrets, and the products of its unions and their social challenges. How was the product of miscegenation to attain respectability? How was he/she to enter that parallel society, which the historian Pierre Gustave Louis Borde assures us existed; one that possessed a limited but coveted access to the European, aristocratic, well-connected, extended family; to which one was actually related?

This dilemma may have been of particular significance to Dr. Williams, whose antecedents in the Afro-French Creole, patois-speaking Catholic

---

134 Ernest Laborde of St. Vincent gave his research material to Flora Gittens, Eric Williams' sister, who gave it to me. I did a number of interviews with Flora in the 1980s for a history of the de Boissière family, which was published in 1993 by the author Michael Pocock, *Out of the Shadows of the Past.*

society of Trinidad with its highly developed sense of social status, had found themselves victims of broken promises, collusion and conspiracies that had deprived them of their legacies. Williams could therefore relate to the duplicity and hypocrisy of the colonial administration that was implicit in James' chapter.

Pages 38 to 41 in the 1938 edition of *The Black Jacobins* are well worth examining at length as they illuminate the formation of an important aspect of Eric Williams' political personality: his predilection for conspiracy theories; his suspicious nature and later a distrust of even his closest advisors.

James writes: "A venal race of scholars, profiteering panders to national vanity, have conspired to obscure the truth about abolition. Up to 1783 the British bourgeoisie had taken the slave trade for granted."

From this beginning, James goes on to recount the Jamaican Assembly's fears of insurrection. He next discusses the loss of America, which changed the Atlantic trade situation, pointing out that England had benefited from these changes, although the West Indies had not. He goes on to describe the benefits of growing sugar cane in India as opposed to the West Indies, and quotes Randle Jackson who in 1793 said to his company's shareholders, "it seemed as if Providence, when it took from us America, would not leave its favourite people without an ample substitute; or who should say that Providence had not taken from us one member, more seriously to impress us with the value of another." To which James remarked:

> "It might not be good theology, but it was very good economics. Pitt and Dundas saw a chance of capturing the continental market from France by East Indian Sugar. There was cotton and indigo. The production of cotton in India doubled in a few years. Indian free labour cost a penny a day. (...) But the West Indian vested interests were strong, statesmen do not act merely on speculation, and these possibilities by themselves would not have accounted for any sudden change in British policy, it was the miraculous growth of San Domingo that was decisive. Pitt found that some 50 per cent of the slaves imported into the British islands were sold to the French colonies. It was the British slave-trade, therefore, which was increasing French colonial

C.LR. James "I denounce the schol-
arship of European colonialism, but
I respect the learning and profound
discoveries of Western civilisation."

produce and putting the European market into French hands. Britain was cutting its own throat".

James' argument is scholarship with a purpose. According to him, Pitt was concerned solely with the economics and geopolitics of the day:

"And even the profits from this export were not likely to last. Already a few years before the slave merchants had failed for £700,000 in a year. The French, seeking to provide their own slaves, were encroaching in Africa and increasing their share of the trade every year. Why should they continue to buy from Britain? Holland and Spain were doing the same. (...) Pitt was in a hurry; it was important to bring the trade to a complete stop quickly and suddenly. The French had neither the capital nor the organisation to make good the deficiency at once and he would ruin San Domingo at a stroke."

James' interpretation of history is generally silent on the increasingly vocal movement against the slave trade that was gaining prominence in England at the time. James does not give much credence to the abolitionists' claims that the true British national interest rested in ending the slave trade.

Additionally, James attributes Pitt's choice of parliamentarian and social reformer William Wilberforce to spearhead the pro-abolition movement to cunning political strategy:

"By 1786, Pitt, a disciple of Adam Smith, [135] had seen the light clearly. He asked Wilberforce to undertake the campaign. Wilberforce ... had

135 Adam Smith, 1723-1790, was a Scottish moral philosopher and a pioneer of political economy. He was the author of *The Wealth of Nations*, published in 1776, the first modern work on economics which expounds the free market. Smith believed that while human motives were often driven by self interest, the competition in the free market would tend to benefit society as a whole by keeping prices low, while still building an incentive for a wide variety of good and services. (Wikipedia)

Thomas Henry Williams and his son, Eric Williams. (Patricia Gittens)

a great reputation, all the humanity, justice, stain on national character, etc., etc., would sound well coming from him … In 1787 [Pitt] warned Wilberforce that if he did not bring the motion in, somebody else would, and in 1788 he informed the Cabinet that he would not stay in it with those who opposed. Pitt was fairly certain of success in England. With truly British nerve he tried to persuade the European Governments to abolish the trade on the score of inhumanity."

James uses this information to support his claim that Pitt's urgency to have the trade abolished was economically and politically driven. According to James, the French traders were reaping significant profits from the colony of Saint Domingue, a colony whose economy was based chiefly on sugar produced by slaves. Importantly, the British slave trade had played an integral role in many of these slaves being taken to Saint Domingue. Abolishing the slave trade would therefore weaken, if not destroy, France's economic position.

However, the fact that there were many powerful individuals with significant vested interest in the West Indies in sugar and the slave trade proved a formidable challenge. Assuming a moral high ground, arguing that the slave trade was "a stain on the national character" would be the quickest, most expedient means of effecting abolition.

It did not suit James' purpose in *The Black Jacobins* to bring the attention of the reader to the phenomenal rise in the annual number of petitions to parliament for abolition, nor to the diversity of interest that this opposition took. This opposition, which included denominational pressure groups, such as Swedenborgians, Quakers, Baptists and Methodists, canvassed actively for the abolition of the slave trade. Some of these denominational pressure groups may have included Freemasons and could have been influenced, to some extent, by the order's philosophy, 'That all Men are Created Equal," [136] and perhaps because of its potential for networking.

---

136 One Mason in particular, William Hutchinson of Bernard Castle, was instrumental in the dissemination of a small colophon circular woodcut executed by the engraver Thomas Bewick. It showed a chained Negro slave kneeling in supplication. Originally commissioned by the Committees for the Abolition of Slavery, the image has an apt superscription "Am I not a Man and a Brother?" , a translation of the Greek

The order had gained in influence in the United Kingdom, particularly in the 'City of London,' amongst the bankers and investors, and also in the Colonial Service in the various far flung imperial enterprises of the time.

James' discovery of the inner workings of a hidden conspiracy on the part of the British government, is remembered by Williams in his *British Historians and the West Indies,* where he credits James as mounting "one of the first challenges to the British interpretation of the abolition of the slave system." (1964, 163–164). The exciting memory of those times, when the great colonial conspiracy was unmasked by himself and James in the London of the late 1930s, was to remain with Williams and be expressed in his election campaigns some twenty years later. Vidia Naipaul in his *A Way in the World* (1994, 38) describes going to Woodford Square in the mid1950s and listening as "the speakers on the Victorian bandstand had talked of history and suffering and the great conspiracy of the rulers, and had suggested that redemption had come at last." Naipaul also comments that the politicians "… on the band stand spoke of old suffering and current local politics. They spoke like people uncovering a conspiracy. " (1994, 31)

James had demonstrated to Williams how colonial politics worked: the truth is hidden, then history is written "by people constantly seeking for triumphs of humanitarianism." The alleged complicity between Pitt and Wilberforce to hide the true intentions of the British government resulted, according to James, in the politicising of a gross lie: that the abolition of the slave trade, followed by emancipation, was due to a sense of moral responsibility, justice and humanity, which in turn had lent credibility to the British government's right to govern its colonies. Williams would echo, in fact amplify this view, making it an important argument in his doctoral thesis and later politicising it in the book *Capitalism and Slavery,* for the purpose of destroying British credibility. (Williams 1964, 45)

---

epigram of Aratus of Soli. The woodcut later became a famous Wedgwood porcelain plate design. Stewart, in: *Franc-maçonnerie et politique au siècle des Lumières: Europe-Amériques,* p.148

Eric Williams, then, also rewrote history for a purpose. In *Capitalism and Slavery,* a work that absolutely challenges the national image and tradition of England's historical interpretation, Williams accepts the part played by the abolitionists but trivialises Coupland's argument that behind Mansfield's legal judgement lay the moral judgement established in precedent, and that this marked the beginning of the end of slavery throughout the British Empire. He comments on Coupland: "This is merely poetic sentimentality transliterated into modern history," echoing James' observation about history being written "by people constantly seeking for triumphs of humanitarianism." Yet William Hutchinson's expression of the principles of justice and humanity, sincerely felt and increasingly popular, and increasingly held by a wide cross section of the British public, as well as very influential persons in the 1800s, may lead one to dispute James' and Williams' claims. Stewart writes: [137]

> "They [abolitionists, Quakers, Freemasons, Methodists and other persons who subscribed to the anti-slavery sentiment at the time[asserted that all men, irrespective of their colour or race, possessed divinely bestowed natural rights. Their ideas of natural justice were based mainly on Christianity because they argued that the slave trade abrogated God's good order in society through the imposition by slave traders and slave owners of a harsh human power between God and some of his creatures [the slaves]. Indeed, the continuance of the slave trade prevented the operation of Christian benevolence, which they said arose from men's innate ability to distinguish good from evil; a concept that was crucial in English Enlightenment sensibility. Cruelty against fellow creatures with God-given souls [the slaves] was an unjust and even blasphemous misuse of power."

Williams is able to identify the point at which the slave trade abolition bill came before the House of Lords (Hansard, VIII, 679-683. Feb. 6, 1807). He points out that this was when a discussion might have arisen with regard to whether economic and political expediency or humanitarian impulses had been the motivating factors in ratifying the legislation.

---

137 Stewart, Trevor in Révauger 2006, 144

He writes:

> "When the slave trade was abolished in 1807, the bill included a phrase
> to the effect that the trade was 'contrary to the principles of justice,
> humanity and sound policy.' Lord Hawkesbury objected; in his opin-
> ion the words 'justice and humanity' reflected on the slave traders. He
> therefore moved an amendment excluding those words. In so do-
> ing, he confined the necessity for abolition solely to expediency. The
> Lord Chancellor protested. The amendment would take away the only
> ground on which the other [European] powers could be asked to co-
> operate in abolition. The Earl of Lauderdale [138] declared that the words
> omitted [justice and humanity] were the most essential in the bill. The
> omission would lend colour to the suspicion in France that British abo-
> lition was dictated by the selfish motive that her colonies were already
> well stocked with Negroes. 'How, in thus being supposed to make no
> sacrifice ourselves, could we call with any effect upon foreign powers to
> cooperate in the abolition?'" (1964, 178)

Ultimately the Lords voted for the original version, inclusive of the
words "the principles of justice, humanity and sound policy."[139]

---

138 James Maitland, 8th Earl of Lauderdale, (1759-1839). He was in 1780 a member
of the faculty of advocates, a member of parliament, 1780-84. From 1789 a member of the House of Lords. He was an opponent of Prime Minister Pitt on various
issues with regard to France, and was thought to be a sympathiser of the French
Revolution.

139 British parliamentarian James Fox's last great achievement as secretary for foreign
affairs (Pitt had resigned in 1801) would be the abolition of the slave trade in 1807.
Though Fox would die before abolition was formalised, he oversaw a Foreign Slave
Trade Bill in spring 1806, which prohibited British subjects from contributing to
the trading of slaves with the colonies of Britain's wartime enemies, thus eliminating
two-thirds of the slave trade passing through British ports.
On 10 June 1806, Fox offered a resolution for total abolition to Parliament: "this
House, conceiving the African slave trade to be contrary to the principles of justice,
humanity, and sound policy, will, with all practicable expedition, proceed to take ef-
fectual measures for abolishing the said trade …" The House of Commons voted
114 to 15 in favour and the Lords approved the motion on 25 June. Fox said:
"So fully am I impressed with the vast importance and necessity of attaining what
will be the object of my motion this night, that if, during the almost forty years that I
have had the honour of a seat in parliament, I had been so fortunate as to accomplish

Eric Williams and C.L.R. James undoubtedly challenged the orthodoxy of the times, attempting to rewrite history together, fortified by moral relativism. They may have sought to peer through the empirically-perceived veneer of things to the hidden truth beneath, convinced perhaps by the words of Karl Marx: "The final pattern of economic relationships as seen on the surface . . . is very different from, and indeed quite the reverse of, their inner but concealed essential pattern." [140] This would have been a very inspiring notion for conspiracy theorists.

Several arguments have been advanced for the cause of the decision taken by the British parliament for the abolition of the slave trade, among these is the view that such a law as the abolition of the Slave Trade Act was almost certain to be passed; the growing power of the abolitionist movement was one aspect of the debate. Another was one of timing and may have been connected with the Napoleonic Wars (1803-1815) of the time. For it was during these years that Napoleon took the retrograde decision to revive slavery, which had been abolished during the French Revolution, and to send his troops to re-enslave the people of Haiti and the other French Caribbean possessions. The British prohibition of the slave trade gave the British Empire the high moral ground upon which they were able to build the narrative of "Justice and Humanity."

On the diplomatic level, the British government secured at the Congress of Vienna in 1815 a general statement from the European powers condemning the slave trade, and was able to arrange an agreement with Spain to limit the slave trade to south of the equator in exchange for British waivers on loans as well as a payment in cash of £300,000. Spain signed a further agreement in 1817, which provided for the abolition of slave trading even south of the equator, in return for a further cash payment of £400,000. [141]

---

that, and that only, I should think I had done enough, and could retire from public life with comfort, and the conscious satisfaction, that I had done my duty." Mitchell. (2007). Charles James Fox. *The Oxford Dictionary of National Biography* (internet)

140 Marx, Karl, *A Contribution to the Critique of Political Economy,* 1859 (internet)
141 Johnson, Paul. *The Birth of the Modern,* p. 328.

The Act's intention was to entirely outlaw the slave trade, not only within the British Empire. But the trade continued and captains in danger of being caught by the Royal Navy would often throw slaves into the sea to reduce the fine. In 1827, Britain declared that participation in the slave trade was piracy and punishable by death. Between 1808 and 1860, the Royal Navy's West Africa Squadron seized approximately 1,600 slave ships and freed 150,000 Africans.[142] In the decades that followed the abolition of the slave trade, the Royal Navy did become "the policeman of the world."

Action was also taken against African leaders who refused to agree to British treaties to outlaw the trade, for example against "the usurping King of Lagos," who was deposed in 1851. Anti-slavery treaties were signed with over 50 African rulers.[143] This, however, did not prevent other African kings from selling slaves to Europeans. Despite treaties signed between Britain and the United States, Britain and Portugal, and Britain and Brazil, the Atlantic slave trade continued for several decades, causing the Royal Navy to run a blockade in the mid Atlantic, where slave ships were boarded, their cargoes taken off, and in some instances brought to Trinidad and to Tobago, where as 'Freed Africans' they made their lives.

Dr. Williams would carry his economic/expediency conspiracy theory for the abolition of the slave trade forward into his political life He would develop a political programme that would exploit these ideas. His revisionism narrative pilloried the European population in Trinidad and Tobago as not only descended from slave-owners, but also of inheriting their guilt, while ignoring the complicity of the Africans who had sold their fellow Africans in exchange for trade goods.

This would be enhanced by his shrewd use of black nationalism. These ideas, expressed by him in a professorial style with strong racial overtones were at times rendered with humour, or anger, while making use of the vernacular, in a calypso or Midnight Robber-talk delivery, that educated, enthralled and entertained. These ideas were to be as readily embraced as they were easily politicised.

---

142 Loney, William. R.N. *The West African Squadron* (internet)
143 Loosemore, Jo. *Sailing Against Slavery* (internet)

At the time, and to the present, a great many people, including his political opponents and detractors, would share in his cynical outlook. In so
doing, they would reject the existence of any truth in the moral impulse
of late 18th century English people, as expressed in ideas such as "justice
and humanity." They would understand little of the significance of the political leverage of those in England who were profoundly offended by and
against the slave trade on sincerely felt moral principles.

It would be difficult, if not impossible for them to appreciate and accept as truth the sincerity of the religious conviction held by a vast quantity of people at the turn of the 19th century, expressed in the idea that
"… Cruelty against fellow creatures with God-given souls [the slaves] was
an unjust and even blasphemous misuse of power." [144] And further, that
the abolition of the slave trade was in truth, and in fact a significant moral
achievement, and that these laws (the abolition of the slave trade and
emancipation), when enacted and successfully enforced, demonstrated a
major shift in moral values in the Western world.

It would appear that by the 1950s and 60s, there had been a shift in
moral values per se, and people in general could feel that 'in this day and
age' they could accept Williams' cynical reasons for the abolition of the
slave trade—even without agreeing with his brand of politics, or without
reading *Capitalism and Slavery*, or without getting other views on the subject. Or, even understanding that they were themselves experiencing 'in
this day and age' a shift in moral values—that it was, in some way, 'modern' to hold a cynical world view with regard to notions such as "justice
and humanity." To many, Williams epitomised this modernity.

Dr. Williams and his challenge to the orthodoxy of his time has left a
lasting impression on the politics of the Caribbean as well as on the historiography of the region. It has proven to be of lasting significance. As
Solow Engerman remarked, Williams "defined the study of Caribbean
history, and its writing affected the course of Caribbean history… Scholars may disagree on his ideas, but they remain the starting point of discussion. … Any conference on British capitalism and Caribbean slavery is a
conference on Eric Williams." [145]

---

144 Stewart, in Révauger 2005,148
145 Engerman, Stanley and Solow, Barbara: *British Capitalism and Caribbean Slavery: The*

A view of the waterfront at Port-of-Spain in the 1850s. The building in the foreground stands in the Spanish Fort San Andrés, this was where slaves when disembarked from the slave ships anchored in the stream were sold. (M.J. Cazabon, courtesy Belmont Harris Trust and Geoffrey MacLean)

THE SOCIAL STRATUM OF THE WILLIAMS FAMILY
2

Because being either *victim* or *victor* of the colonial experience is central to this discussion, in this chapter, I will outline the makeup of the colony's society and the development of its Afro-French Creole, generally mixed-race, "coloured" middle class, of which Williams was a part. I will also discuss the entry of the Indian indentured workers and give some idea of how they were received and perceived by the society on the whole. The population of the colony, based on the census taken in 1946, numbered 557,970. Some 46% or 261,485 were of African descent; 195,747 (35%) were East Indians; 14% (78,775) mixed or coloured; 15,283 (2.7%) Europeans (British officials, businessmen and professionals, locally-born European, English and French Creoles); 5,641 Chinese (1%); and 887 (0.2%) people from the Middle East.

Legacy of Eric Williams, compilation of essays based on a commemorative symposium held in Italy in 1984, p. ix (internet)

Trinidad's indigenous black and coloured population descends, in the
first instance, from the approximately 20,656 apprentices (former slaves)
who had been emancipated in 1834, and from the Free Blacks and People
of Colour who had benefited from the terms of the Cedula of Population of 1783 and who numbered about 12,000 persons in a population of
some 35,000 at emancipation 50 years later.

Trinidad' indigenous white population descends from the some 2,500
Europeans, mostly French, at the time of emancipation. These French
colonists, invited by the island's Spanish Government, had established a
plantation economy worked by slave labour over a period of about fifty
years, between 1783 and 1834. They were responsible for a great many,
but certainly not all of the 20,000 emancipated slaves. [146]

Because the majority of these people, African, European and mixed, had
originally come from the former French colonies, they were Catholic, and
French and Creole (patois) speaking. They tended to share a common syncretic culture, developing the nuances that would over time define them as a
group. Some were related to each other, and most, if not all, were connected
as a result of the shared experiences of the plantation economy.

For all of the 19th and well into the 20th century Trinidad, on the surface of things, gave the impression, certainly to visitors, of being a French
territory. Charles Léotaud in his memoirs [147] notes that in the census of
1891 there were some "200,000 inhabitants, representing every people in
the world, including 60,000 coolies imported from East India. Two thirds
of the population speak French, or at least French patois." Newspapers,
in the first decades of the 19th century, were published in the French
language. Calypsos were sung in French patois up to the 1930s, and the
carnival, with a great many of its characters, the folklore and the folk traditions, including children's games, music and cuisine, were all expressed
with a distinct French flavour. *Picon,* a type of rough humour, expressed in

---

146 An American planter, William Burnley, was reputed to have been Trinidad's first mil-
     lionaire and the island's largest slave owner.
147 Léotaud, Charles. *Memoirs of an Honourable Gentleman.* Edited by Dillon and Clau-
     dette Léotaud, p. 23.

patois, like calypso, could contain subtle disparaging attacks on the British colonial establishment. Carnival was itself confrontational; the *cannes broulées* riots of the 1880s were seen as a threat to the authority of Crown colony rule. The island's law courts employed French/English interpreters. Women, black, coloured, and some French-descended, dressed in the colourful costume of the French islands. The architecture of the town, particularly east of Frederick Street, displayed a French character similar to that of Fort de France in Martinique. It was considered useful, indeed important, that new arrivals to the island learn to speak and understand French patois, as it was considered the *lingua franca* (a language that is adopted as a common language between speakers whose native languages are different) of the colony. For over a century and a half, the European and African-descended people in Trinidad produced a discernible subculture that may be described as Afro-French Creole. It was in a sense, a *subversive* subculture to the British colonial system, developed by people who felt that their land was occupied by a foreign power.

Some of the French patois-speaking Free Blacks and People of Colour had been wealthy land and slave-owners. By the early 19th century, Trinidad's Afro-French/English Creole society had produced a small black and coloured educated middle class, which boasted a few university-trained professionals. Compared to other black and mixed people in the neighbouring islands, they had already gained a head start. Among these were the well-known Philippe, Romain, Beaubrun, Saturnin, Cadet, Boissière, Regis, Bicais, Rambert and Langton families, who, as historian P.G.L. Borde noted, *"formaient une seconde société parallèle à la première, et non moins distinguée qu'elle."* [148]

During the mid-19th century, approximately 6,580 freed Africans augmented the population. Rescued from Portuguese slave ships in the mid-Atlantic by the Royal Navy, they had never known slavery, and were to retain their religious beliefs and their cultural, tribal and personal identi-

148 Borde, 1982

ties. Among their descendants are the Antoine, Besson, Ducurew, Robertson, Carter, MacShine, and Carr families. These, despite their retention of African religious and cultural forms, adopted the Afro-French cultural practices and style, including French patois and Catholicism.[149]

An ever increasing number of the "fortunate few" after emancipation benefited from the system of public education or rose by their own endeavour and joined the ranks of those coming from other islands, who were leaving behind them lives of indigence and ignorance. Among these were families from Barbados who, like the Woodings, would rise quickly in the professions. After the 1860s we find individuals like Charles Preudhomme David K.C., the first man of African descent to sit on the colony's Legislative Council; John Jacob Thomas, educator; C.H. Phillips, barrister; James Hobson, magistrate; Samuel Carter and Joseph Lewis who owned a newspaper; A.E. Hendrickson, K.C.; E.E.S. Pollard, K.C.; L.A. Wharton, K.C.; Hon. Vincent Brown, K.C.; M.M. Philip, Solicitor General; and E.A. Robinson, K.C., to name a few of the more prominent in a generation where there were at least a dozen or more of that ilk in public life and hundreds more in less prominent positions. Although subject to the racial prejudice and limited opportunities of Crown Colony life, they made the most of what was offered in terms of the benefits of a structured civil society: opportunities for education and a stable family life in which self respect was inculcated, and where the pursuit of respectability and the benefits of religion played important roles.

The black and mixed-race population, in 1946, was a combination of extended families, some established for several generations in this island, and of a great many immigrants from other West Indian islands. West Indian immigration to Trinidad had commenced from the mid-19th century. Between 1871 and 1911, 65,000 people had come from other islands. In the 1920s and 30s, just before the Second World War, more than 80,000 people came from the other islands to share in Trinidad's prosperity. Many of these were poor, rural and basically primary school-educated, if at all. They came mostly from the Lesser Antilles, some, those from Grenada, St. Lucia, and Dominica were Catholic and spoke French

149 Henry, Frances. *He Had the Power, Pa Neeza, The Orisha King of Trinidad.* p. 23.

patois. They came from islands where there were a few European planter and merchant families; a handful of British officials; some black and coloured middle class families and a large African-descended population. Importantly, many of the immigrants had little experience of the racial diversity or cosmopolitanism that distinguishes Trinidad from all the other Caribbean islands.

In all Caribbean islands, African New World slavery had a longer history than Trinidad, in some instances dating back to the early 17th century. In these islands, merchant/planter oppression, the culture of servitude and the lifestyle on the whole, had not much changed since emancipation. These immigrants would have brought the memory of those experiences with them to Trinidad. West Indian immigrants would join the urban poor in the overcrowded, squalid and unsanitary conditions of East Port-of-Spain and in other areas of the island, especially in the South, where labour was needed to clear the forest and build the infrastructure for the growing oil industry. The thousands of small islanders experienced great poverty, especially during the world-wide depression of the 1920s and 30s with all its attendant problems, expressed with ill health, poor physical and psychological conditions, malnutrition, domestic violence and alcohol abuse. The Eric Williams narrative, when eventually presented to the population of Trinidad and Tobago in 1956 and in the 1961 election campaign, would be heard by all these different people in different ways, depending on their circumstances.

By the beginning of the 20th century these black, mixed immigrant families, would have been caught in a cycle of poverty. For a few, there may have been a view of themselves as survivors, or perhaps even as victors, with a sense of pride and achievement.

All were, in the main, loyal to the British Empire. Their understanding of moral and civic responsibility united them. This understanding was created to a considerable extent by religion and by the cult of Empire worship, and the institutionalisation of a devotion to social deference and to authority, which was invested principally in the white race. Justice was available, but racial prejudice was supported and at times enforced with the full implementation of the law.

People understood that one earned one's limited place in colonial life and generally did not entertain a feeling of entitlement. There was, at all times, during the 19th century and into the 20th, a collective memory of slavery; some may still have borne the physical marks of slavery at the end of the 19th century. This was characterised by the debates as to whether emancipation should be marked as a day of remembrance. They would have had a quarrel with history, quite naturally, and some would have understood that history was not destiny.

A valid narrative about the past, and the understanding of their present circumstances, was in formation. This was expressed in civil society with a growing political consciousness with pressure groups such as the Reformist movements at the turn of the 19th century and later with forms of black pride expressed in organisations like those inspired by Marcus Garvey, and various spiritual and religious forms. These were always repressed by the colonial administration.

Let us now look at the Indian segment. East Indian indentured workers were introduced from1845 to 1917; in all a total of 143,939 arrived in Trinidad. After serving five years of indentureship those who opted to stay on in the colony generally continued an agricultural lifestyle and were encouraged to remain rural, where their conditions both on the sugar estates and in the communities that developed on the periphery of the estates have been described as "degrading and coercive." [150]

The Indians had entered a hostile environment on the estates and in urban life. The long-established population took some time to realise that as a group the Indians had come to stay. There was generally an unsympathetic attitude towards them, which was shared by the European-descended, the colonial administrators, the urban middle class and the black people, both poor and otherwise. In the urban areas, the Indians held the mostly low status jobs and were perceived as miserable and suffering. Indian men, women and children appeared as street dwellers. In the context of their culture, some became mendicants; this was misunderstood by non-Indians.

---

150 Brereton 1981, 110.

Often malnourished and ill with hookworm infestation, malaria and leprosy, they were seen as abhorrent. Institutions such as the Leper Asylum, the hospitals and the House of Refuge appeared to be at times disproportionately populated by Indians creating an impression that Indians as a whole, in the judgment of society, could be perceived as inferior beings. [151]

In 1917, 70% of the Indians were agricultural workers, maintaining religious forms, cultural practices, retaining their names, and forming strong family ties, village and community interest. A handful of East Indian families would eventually make their way into the colonial establishment. [152] The social development of the Indian segment of the population tended to be quite separate from the Creole life. "This is strikingly illustrated by the reluctance of Indian men to cohabit with Creole women, despite the shortage of Indian women. As late as 1871, the Protector of Immigrants believed that no single case of cohabitation of male or female with Creoles existed and up to 1917 such cases were very rare." [153] This may have been perceived as very strange by the Creole population, where miscegenation had been the common practice for centuries. The shortage of Indian women at times caused crimes of passion, and this, compounded by the retained memory of the Indian Mutiny of some fifty years before, resulted in a type of characterisation that associated Indians with a potential for mass violence.

Over a short time, Trinidadians from various walks of life evolved a variety of stereotyped perceptions about Indians and generally distrusted them. For example, "Indians were regarded as deceitful and prone to litigation; there was no understanding that the Indian might not understand

---

151 The nature of a basically racist colonial society as existed in Trinidad and Tobago could easily arrive at views such as this, or for example that the Portuguese and later the Syrians, were not regarded as socially white, and black people, because of the pseudo scientific notions of race at the time, were seen as a sub species of the human race.

152 "In 1921 only 187 Indians were classified as 'officials and professionals.'" Brereton 1981, 110 ff

153 ibid.

the moral force of an oath in a Western court, or that he was often forced into litigation — for instance, to inherit his father's property if he died without a will, since the vast majority of Indians in the period were illegitimate in the eyes of the law." [154] British law that is, which at the time did not recognise Hindu and Muslim marriage.

The Indians became caught, through no fault of their own, in the politics of the day, which was being enacted in the island's Legislature, between the planter and merchant interests, which promoted the idea of cheap labour, and other interests that had formed around individuals who represented local concerns, meaning those who wanted reform of the island's colonial status. Indian indentureship was perceived, especially by the black and coloured middle class professionals, as symbolic of the power and the privilege of the British colonial establishment.

There was hostility directed to the idea of imported Indian labour, because it affected black Trinidadian workers in the context of competition for wages in the labour market. Indians were at times vilified and stereotyped as willing to work for starvation wages; their frugal lifestyle appeared as ludicrous. It was felt that Indian immigration drove down wages and was the cause of unemployment and hardship among the black workers. Strong arguments were made that Indian immigration "had become by then merely a weapon to allow planters to control the labour market by depressing wages to starvation levels."[155] These ideas were popularised by newspapers such as the *New Era* and the *San Fernando Gazette*, which represented the view of the coloured and black middle class. This group consistently opposed Indian immigration publicly and at times bitterly, by enunciating the more offensive forms of stereotyping.

The notion of perceiving the Indian population as not really belonging to the island's overall population, when coupled with other negative stereotyping, produced in the minds of the generation of Afro-French/English Creole people, born in the opening decades of the 20th century, as well as in the West Indian immigrants, a deep prejudice against

---

154 ibid.
155 ibid.

a large and differentiating group of the population, in such a derogatory manner that when it was politicised in the 1950s and 60s, it would have lasting consequences. Interestingly V.S. Naipaul describes in his *Way in the Word,* page 35, he, being in Woodford Square in 1961 or 62, and listening to the speakers on the Victorian bandstand and feeling, as, he supposed some whites who were also there did, excluded, and having the sense of "the ground move below him"! He writes: "Much of the hostile feeling released by the sacrament of the square would have focussed on the Indians, who made up the other half of the population"

Some of the black, brown and to a lesser degree, Indian, ordinary people of Trinidad and Tobago benefited from a more or less steady economy, bolstered from the 1870s by the demand for the island's cocoa, which was highly regarded. Increasingly, some became owners of cocoa lands, so much so that by 1916 only 126 out of more than 1,000 cocoa estates were owned by persons with obvious white French Creole names. The remainder, with the exception of those cocoa holdings owned by the large British concerns Gordon Grant & Co. and Cadbury, belonged to Trinidadians of every condition. These estates, some large, over 200 acres, some small holdings, provided the colony with a trickle-down economy that a wide cross section of the society profited from.

The cocoa boom generated employment both in an expanding civil service, in which the French Creoles and black and coloured worked, but were kept well below the inevitable glass ceiling, and also in the several private firms (some owned by coloured people) that exported the island's produce and imported goods. The expanding cocoa economy provided them with upward mobility, education opportunities, an improved standard of living and the possibility of owning their own home.

The expansion of the railway also created opportunities as new towns and villages came into existence and old towns were revitalised, providing opportunity for respectable employment as tradesmen, teachers, post masters/mistresses, midwives etc. In this period of economic and infrastructural development, a few coloured families owned businesses: some large like that of George and Louis Alston, brothers, whose firm, over time, would become an important conglomerate; A.P.T. Ambard, owner of the

Port-of-Spain Gazette newspaper and a founder member of the Trinidad Turf Club; the Maillards, whose *El Popular* general goods store stood on the corner of Frederick Street and Marine Square; Grell's Bakery on Frederick Street; the Mathieu family's *Red Store* on Henry Street; Thomas and Son's *Mongoose Store* on Charlotte Street; *Eugene Boissière &Co.* on Marine Square and several others. In addition, the oilfields were being developed by the 1920s and 30s, and in the South of the island major retail, hardware and oilfield supply stores were established by coloured Trinidadians like the Montano, Dieffenthaller and Henkel families. The first generation of Indian entrepreneurs would appear in the 1940s with S.M. Jaleel's, aerated water factory, H.P. Singh, tailors and outfitters, and Battoo Brothers in transportation.

Notwithstanding the constraints of the times, the ambition, thrift and hard work of the black, coloured and Indian people during the colonial period served to produce a relatively high quality of life for many. Evidence of their achievement survives today in the gingerbread houses that were built by the middle class in the Port-of-Spain districts of Belmont, Newtown, Woodbrook; in parts of San Fernando around Rushworth Street; St. Joseph, Arima, Tunapuna and many other areas.

This is not to say that they were not affected by racism, unfair treatment, hypocrisy and often the sheer mendacity of the British officials and the local white establishment, which comprised French and English Creoles. The British Empire was built on a discriminating class system, which expressed itself as racist in the colonies and was maintained by the suppression of its subjects. Because of their success, the black and mixed-race middle classes felt this institutionalised oppression and racism keenly, resenting its continual obstruction of their aspirations. Often the press was their only recourse, as editor, Samuel Carter wrote: "A Crown Colony is a despotism tempered by the Press... In Trinidad, more than in any of the other Colonies, has the existence of the independent Press been an absolute necessity; in none has it done more good." [156]

Insults were endured, as for example when a coloured man from an old

---

156 San Fernando Gazette 14.4.1894, as quoted in: Brereton 1979, 96

established family was told to get up from a table by the manager of a San Fernando hotel, who felt that a person of partial African descent had no right to sit at the same table as a white man. He was reported to have commented that even during slavery, coloured men of a certain standing were freely admitted to all public places "within the scope of their social position." [157]

The cry for equality was heard, at times touchingly, as in the case of this wealthy, brown merchant's obituary:

> "Rich, educated, strictly moral, yet he felt he had no place in society, because of those social distinctions with which the country is cursed. And he was not without that manly pride which enabled him to be satisfied with a very small number of chosen companions rather than to court those whom he felt to be his inferiors morally and intellectually, and whose only claim to consideration consisted... in the purity of their Caucasian blood... He felt keenly the disabilities under which certain races, notably that to which he himself belonged, were subjected." [158]

There were also instances when the coloured middle class's sense of loyalty to the British Empire was affronted, as in the case of a public meeting that was organised to draw up an address of condolence to Queen Victoria on the death of a daughter, and the speakers were all European. A number of black and coloured people responded in the press voicing their objection:

> "Surely [the coloured people's] importance, advancement and loyalty are sufficiently conspicuous to entitle them to have their feelings expressed on the occasion by someone who is one of their unmistakable representatives." [159]

Professor Brereton writes:

> "In this period, it was the belief of the Colonial Office and of local officials that Creoles in general should not be appointed to certain strategic posts, and that coloured Creoles were especially objectionable as

---

157 New Era 10.6.1872, ibid. p. 97.
158 Obituary for Etienne Gouffe, Telegraph 22.5, 1872, ibid. pp. 97-98 .
159 Fair Play 23.1.1879, ibid. p. 98

candidates for these positions. Their appointment to judicial and mag-
isterial appointments was felt to be particularly unwise. For instance, a
Governor requested in 1871 that a British barrister be appointed Police Magistrate for Port-of-Spain: 'I hope to secure for the office both
the deference which would at once be paid to the judicial decisions
of an English barrister, and the entire freedom from all those habits of
thought, which, in opposite directions, control the minds of almost all
the natives of the West Indies, white, or coloured.'" (1979, 99f)

Notwithstanding the official position, the press, when owned by black
and coloured interests, spoke out advocating social justice for the 'natives'
(which did not necessarily imply the Indian community) of the colony.
This was the case when favouritism was shown time and time again to
white civil servants at the expense of their coloured counterparts, as this
letter illustrates:

> "One class is protected blindly, without regard even to decency and
> propriety; and other classes degraded with a similar disregard to
> prudence, common sense and even safety . . . The authorities show a
> lamentable want of discretion and judgement by irritating so often, so
> determinedly, and so unnecessarily, a sensitive race . . . The dominant
> race enjoys to the top of its bent everything it can desire, power, place,
> emoluments, social position. It lives, it luxuriates on the fat of the land.
> Why does it not enjoy itself quietly? and not every now and then insult
> the Children of the Sun by acts of gross injustice . . ." [160]

The black and coloured middle class were not exempt from criticism
from their own ranks, as Brereton observes. Speaking of J.J. Thomas, author of *The Theory and Practice of Creole Grammar*, she writes:

> "He was vividly aware that black and coloured West Indians were as
> guilty as whites of perpetuating colour and race prejudice. In a news-
> paper correspondence on the failure to celebrate Emancipation Day,
> Thomas wrote that they should stop harping on their grievances at the
> hands of the whites. For it was notorious, 'that the most fatal instances of
> skin prejudice have *not* their source among the whites.' Colour prejudice
> was rarely discussed honestly. It was normal to think of two classes: 'op-

---

160 Telegraph 19.5.1873, ibid. pp. 100 -101.

pressing and suffering being White and Ethiopic respectively.' This was hypocrisy, for in the West Indies, 'colour prejudice is a ladder with almost numberless rungs. It is a system of social aggression and retaliation.' West Indians of every shade were in some way, the ministers as well as the victims of this pernicious idolatry . . . For the sake of our cuticle we stand aloof, in mistrust or contempt, from our fellow-citizens . . . The earnest work of popular life remains undone, because we cannot, even for our common good, compromise the dignity of our epidermis.'" (1979, 105)

The tangled roots of racial prejudice run deep in our society, and continue to afflict us all in a variety of ways. Over time, a few of these middle class families became affluent, well-travelled professionals. From their number would come individuals who would help in the formation of institutions like the Reform Movement, the Workingmen's Association, the Cooperative Bank, the Building and Loan Association, and other organisations for the benefit of all. These decent folk were searching for the opportunity to take control of a destiny that would be uniquely their own.

The Williams family undoubtedly belonged to this group of Afro-French/English Creole middle class people with connections to families in the Lesser Antilles, who came in all shades, from darkest brown to apparently white, by right of history and descent. [161] In this relatively small society, they were almost all known to one another. A great many were related to one another in varying degrees and some also connected to the white English and French Creole families.

As the 20th century dawned, the black and coloured middle class could not help but feel a sense of pride in their racial heritage, and they challenged entrenched racism whenever they could. They possessed self esteem and had gained a place in the colonial sun through hard work, study, education and sacrifice. The ranks of the black and coloured middle class were increasingly swelled by families of Chinese, Portuguese, Syrian, Indian, and those of "other" descent, who produced university-educated individuals in various disciplines.

---

161 The Williams' were related to several distinguished brown, black and coloured families; i.e. Landeau, Bain, Hunt, Comissiong, Bailey, Redford, Boissière and Hamel-Smith.

By the 1950s, there were undoubtedly many *victors* of the colonial experi-ence distinguished by their sense of self-respect, unhindered by inhibitions and social insecurities. Unfortunately, thousands of them would eventually form the large waves of emigration from Trinidad and Tobago in the period of the 1950s and onwards, taking with them their collective memories, cul-ture, skills, socialisation and training for the benefit of others.

The 1940s was the start of the Cold War. Great Britain, having lost the will to govern an empire, was relinquishing its colonies. For the first time since the New World revolutions of the end of the 18th and of the begin-ning 19th centuries, dozens of new nations were being established at the same time. The baton of world leadership in the West was passed to the United States of America. With the Soviet Union as the main contender for the hearts and minds of the emerging countries, a socialist experiment for worldwide revolution was gaining popularity, and this form of poli-tics did not make these successful individuals, these *victors* of the colonial experience, seem desirable as future leaders to the ordinary person. They had neither the populist ideology nor the vernacular of contemporary black nationalists; they could not 'talk the talk,' the pseudo socialistic jar-gon; they could not get the support of "the masses, the workers, or the proletariat" and were collectively portrayed as "Uncle Toms", as apologists for the colonial powers, and as backing the wrong side.

ERIC'S NEUROSIS:
THE CULT OF THE WILL
3

The Williams', as a coloured family had suffered a serious setback in the context of Trinidad's colonial society in the closing years of the 19th century. As a result, Dr. Williams may have harboured a deeply felt sense of injustice and deprivation due to his family's unique circumstances, which I will relate in this chapter.

I will contend that his "wounded personality" or neurosis, which shaped his political personality, was partly the result of his family being victims of the "cult of the will."

To inherit, or not to inherit, money or property from one's European parent or mixed race relations was a crucial event that the coloured Creole child's future could hinge on. One could, as a result, become either a *victim* or a *victor* of the colonial experience.

In this chapter, I will outline how the Williams family was clearly a *victim* and how this experience affected Eric Williams' parents and later expressed itself in his political personality.

I am using the term neurotic in connection with Eric Williams because he often demonstrated obsessive behaviour and phobias, expressed with feelings of depression, fear of conspiracies, persecution, deprivation and victimhood. His sense that he and his family had been the victims of a conspiracy to deprive them both materially and socially was perhaps at times so strong that it may have become an obsession, perhaps a form of mental disorder, impairing contact to some degree with external reality, which is the definition of neurosis.

The sense of loss felt by Williams, his siblings and his parents, was all the more acute, in that on both his mother's side, the de Boissière family, and on his father's, the Williams/Hunt family, they were to lose out on the benefits of several (possibly three) opportunities to inherit money and property. As a result they had been deprived of the advantages of sharing in the wealth and prestige of their well-connected and respectable extend-

This watercolour by Michel Jean Cazabon may be of the great house and grounds at Rookery Nook in Maraval, which was owned by John Nicholas Boissière. He lived there with his wife Marie Aurélie née Soully and their numerous children. Also included in their family and living with them were Jules and Marie Eliza Boissière. They were the illegitimate children of John Nicholas. Dr. Eric Williams, a great-grandson of John Nicholas, would later work at the Caribbean Commission in Kent House, which was built on that site in the late 1940s. Williams would have been aware of this coincidence — his mother was not a stranger to the Rookery Nook household, where her father had been brought up. Did it contribute to his frustration? (National Museum)

ed white, pass-for-white (i.e. apparently European) and coloured family. [162] This prestige was highly regarded in 19th and early 20th century coloured Creole society, as it conferred acceptance and respectability, the chance of gaining an education and perhaps a profession, and owning property. These were key ingredients for upward mobility and served to alleviate some of the societal pressures and racist attitudes directed at black and mixed race people by the French and English Creoles, the British colonial

---

162 Flora Gittens recalled that as a girl she went to St. Rose's Girls' School and while in the company of other girls, watched a parade go by. Riding with the Governor was his A.D.C. Lieut. Jean de Boissière. "That's my cousin!" said Flora to her friend, who looked at her in disbelief and replied "Flora, you must be mad." Flora said that she understood then how absurd that must have sounded, and after the incident, she never again told anyone that she was related to the de Boissières.

Dr. Jean Valleton de Boissière, ecuyer, an ancestor of Dr. Eric Williams on his maternal side, may be described as a man of the Enlightenment. As a scientist and medical doctor, he was engaged in the scientific advancements of his time. He was known to have collaborated with Dr. Edward Jenner on a vaccine for smallpox. He conducted experiments, of a similar nature as those of Benjamin Franklin, with electricity and was associated with Franz Anton Mesmer in seeking medical cures through the use of magnetism and hypnosis.

He was a Huguenot and expressed Republican sentiments in his writings, this despite his being a nobleman. During the Revolution he served as a member of one of the revolutionary councils in Paris and in the Napoleonic era was a Mayor of the city of Bergerac. He never came to Trinidad. His son Jean de Boissière came to Trinidad towards the end of the 18th century. (Pocock)

establishment, and even the successful coloured elements of the society.

If the Williams' had enjoyed social acceptance, respectability, financial gain and their own home, they might have seen themselves as *victors* of the colonial experience and may, as a result, have had an entirely different outlook on life.

At the time of Eric's coming of age, in the 1930s and 40s, social respectability was "the be all and end all" of the black and coloured middle class. As Vidia Naipaul quipped, "they" could not be white, but they could be polite. The burden of the ignominy of slavery, [163] the disgrace of illegitimacy in one's past, compounded by racial prejudice, made this respectability a fragile affair, one that poverty or scandal could destroy, and which only education could validate and vindicate.

Eric Williams is sometimes portrayed as a black man with "some

163 Williams was born in 1911; his father in 1878, and his mother in 1888. Slavery had been abolished 40 years before his father's birth. The Fédon uprising in Grenada happened in 1795, 73 years before, and the Cedula of 1783, 94 years before his father's birth. There was no TV and people listened to the stories that the old told in the evenings. The oral tradition was strong. Flora Gittens knew her family's history and its anecdotes.

French Creole blood." [164] I do not see him that way. My own view of him, as a relative of my mother's family, the de Boissières, is somewhat different. He did not have "African hair," [165] but "good grass," as he was said to have remarked, and he and his family were known to be coloured people. Several members of his family were of a lighter complexion than himself. In the early years of the PNM, some thought that because of his hair texture, he should claim to be a dougla that is of both African and East Indian descent, which he refused to do.

Williams was a product of the 19th century Catholic, patois-speaking, inter-racial British colonial experience, who came from an old, [166] well-known coloured family, recognised as such, its antecedents drawn almost in their entirety from the Free People of Colour (a legal definition) of the period of the Cedula of Population, the end of the 18th century. This group, in the context of the society of that day, did not consider itself, nor was considered by others, as black. Because to be black in that context, would imply having African hair and perhaps even being a part of the labouring class, mostly African-descended. Later on in his life he presented himself as, and was indeed seen as a black man by many of his followers; over time, he has come to be characterised as black, particularly as this term became increasingly politicised.

The Williams/Hunt/Smith/Comissiong extended family was not typical. As we shall see, they were of a rather higher class as Free People of Colour were, and as such had higher expectations. Their ancestors (they were able to trace and identify six generations) and relations were property-owning, with townhouses in Port-of-Spain, St. George's, Grenada and

---

164 Brereton 2007, 5

165 Dr. Vincent Tothill, a Scottish doctor living in Trinidad in the 1930s, notes in his book Doctor's Office: "Among coloured people I have often heard it said that the social grades are very exacting, and are based on the amount of coloured blood in them. I do not think this is true, for I have met quite black people in the houses of the High Brown and High Browns in the houses of the Clear Skinned, and they obviously move in the same social circle. But I have noticed one very curious thing — it seems to be the hair, and not the colour, that is the real social bar." (p. 65)

166 Old in the sense of being in Trinidad "earlier than 1783", according to Ernest Laborde.

Kingstown, St. Vincent. They were better educated, [167] and certainly more respectable than many others, with three generations of marriage on Williams' father's side. His father's family retained an oral history that went back to "slavery days."

Dr. Williams' coloured ancestors were slave-owners in the early 19th century, as this account illustrates. [168] Phillippa Laborde of St. Vincent recalls that the Smiths were hot-tempered, and one of the brothers of Phillippa Susannah Smith, son of Sir Charles Smith [169] (see family tree) and Phillippa Comissiong, kicked a slave, who said that he would be the last man he would kick. According to Phillippa Laborde's account, on being kicked the slave told the master that he would place a curse on him and his descendants to the fifth generation and that during that time, Smith and his descendants would become poorer and poorer until they lost all they had. Soon after, the boy took to drink and as a result, much property was lost. The slave fell sick and, on his deathbed, sent to call Smith stating what he had done, indicating that he would like to undo the curse. But he was already too weak. [170] Eric Williams would have been in the fourth generation after Smith . . .

The Williams' family genealogy included such aristocratic British officers as Lt. Col. Sir Charles Felix Smith of West Herrington who commanded the local forces in Trinidad and acted as Governor of the colony in the 1820s, as well as Jean Baptiste Hunt, the coloured son of a Scots-

---

167 Eric Williams' great-uncle Louis Hunt attended St. Mary's College and his grand-mother, Onemia Hunt, had gone to St. Joseph's Convent. Thomas James Williams, Eric's grandfather, "had a good education for that time" (Laborde); he was born in 1855 Louis Hunt and his brothers were, according to Laborde, born in England and trained as book keepers "of the first class". They were Clairmonte, Alphonse, & Phillip, they were Anglicans and owned a business in San Fernando.

168 The Comissiongs, Eric Williams' father's grandparents, as Free Coloured People of means would have been slave-owning.

169 Phillippa Comissiong & Sir Charles Smith are reputed to have had several children out of wedlock, including Dr. Emil Smith. This became Hamil "to distinguish them from the illegitimate Smiths," said Laborde. His descendants became the Hamel-Smiths. The Hamel-Smiths have a different account. (Carmichael 1961, 153)

170 Laborde, Ernest, family notes, passed on to me by Flora Gittens.

Left, Thomas Henry Williams, Eric Williams' father, was a cousin of Alfred Comissiong of Grenada, right. They may have been both the great grandsons of Domingo Comissiong, a Genoan sail maker, and a woman of colour in Grenada, circa 1799. Domingo's daughter, Phillippa Susanna Comissiong (manumitted before her father's death) had a common-law relationship with Lt. Col. Sir Charles Smith, acting Governor of Trinidad, circa 1829. Their daughter, also called Phillippa Susanna, married Jean Baptiste Hunte, son of Col. G. R. le Hunte and a woman of colour, Sir G. R. le Hunte was Governor of Trinidad 1909-1916 and might have been a relative. The coloured mulatto upper class tended to have these sort of relationships, marrying within their set, as with the coloured Ciprianis and Bessons as seen in the previous paper. (Paria, Comissiong)

Some Members of the Comissiong Family, of Grenada: Sylvia, Leta Ruby, in the late 19th century, and Jenelle Comissiong when she won the Miss Universe title in 1977.

Eric Williams in the 1930s   *Terrance Comissiong in the 1900s*   *Eric Williams in the 1960s*

John Nicholas Boissière

Dr. Jean François, Count de Valleton de Boissière

Some Members of The Valleton de Boissière family in Trinidad

Left, John Nicholas Boissière, 1816-1886, Eric Williams' great-grandfather. Right, Eric's mother Eliza,1888-1969, the daughter of Jules Boissière, 1857-1930, who was the son of the man on the left. Below left, Jules' half brother Dr. Jean François, 1861-1942, son of Jean Nicholas. Jean François assumed the courtesy title of Count de Boissière in France in the 1900s. Right, Henri Armand de Boissière,1881-1937, father of the writer Ralph de Boissière,1907-2007, brother of Jean François and half brother of Jules. Henri Armand was a solicitor in Port-of-Spain and secretary of the St. Andrew's Golf Club. Eric's mother's father Jules and his sister Eliza were taken while young into the family of John Nicholas and his wife. They grew up with Henri Armand and Jean François as children together in the same house, Rookery Nook, in Maraval Trinidad. Williams would have an office there, at Kent House in Rookery Nook, when he worked at the Caribbean Commission in the early 1950s. Below right, Jean Gaetan de Boissière, 1901-1982, son of Jean François, who also used the title of Count in France, while in his 70s. At his left is Eric Williams in his late 60s, and in his 40s. Their resemblance is obvious; Jean Gaetan was Eric's third cousin. (Paria)

Eliza Williams née Boissière

Henri Armand de Boissière, father of the author Ralph de Boissière

Eric Williams

Eric Williams

Jean Gaëtan de Boissière

Saint Joseph Convent girls circa 1880. (Paria.)

man, Col. G. R. Le Hunte, [171] also a commander of British forces in the West Indies. Other ancestors were of the French nobility. Williams' grandfather's half-brother Dr. Jean François de Valleton de Boissière assumed the courtesy title of count while living in France in the 1920s; another half-brother, Armand, a solicitor, was secretary to the exclusive St. Andrew's Golf Club (they were both coloured men, Armand was the father of Ralph de Boissière, author). There were even Genoese sail makers. The founder of the Comissiongs of Grenada, Domingo Comissiong, was one such Genoese sail maker who had come to the West Indies in the 1780s. The descendants of his union with a woman of colour had achieved not only respectability but also considerable wealth as slave-owning estate proprietors, and later prominence. Terrence Bertrand Comissiong was Assistant Administrator of Grenada and the Grenadines in the 1940s. All this was extremely prestigious. [172] An item in Domingo Comissiong's will

---

171 Sir G. R. le Hunte G.C.M.G. was Governor of Trinidad and Tobago in 1909-1916 and may have been a relative of the above.

172 Joseph Thomas Comissiong, coloured man born in Grenada, who lived in Tobago and St. Lucia and was the son of Joseph Comissiong, a son of Domingo Comissiong, was Collector of Customs and Excise in Tobago in 1850. He cautiously stated his interest in being a member of the Anti-Slavery Society, despite the rules forbidding officials from opposing government policies. He was transferred to Sierra Leone to

is revealing of his character, it reads: "I will and desire that Nancy Comissiong mulatto woman belonging to the Honourable Thomas Bridgewater who I believe to be my daughter may be purchased if possible emancipated set free and released from all slavery and servitude whatsoever."

Phillippa Susannah Comissiong may have been a granddaughter of Domingo Comissiong (see Domingo Comissiong's will in Appendix 1). She is described as "wealthy" by Laborde, the family's historian. He wrote in the 1960s: "She is reported as having said that the buckles on her shoes contained diamonds." She and Sir Charles Smith lived in a *piaçage* relationship. Their daughter, Phillippa, married within her class the coloured son of Col. Le Hunte and a woman of colour, Jean Baptiste Hunt. The women of colour mentioned in the genealogical table were more than likely drawn from similar backgrounds, products of the *plaçage* of well-placed Europeans and coloured, light-complexioned women, who would in turn have been fathered by well-off Europeans.

Ernest Laborde, in his historical notes on the Williams family, states that Phillippa Smith may have died in 1871. "At her death her children had everything needed and funds sufficed." To this community, being remembered in the last wills and testaments of one's parent or parents was crucial. Apart from receiving money or property, it indicated a limited form of recognition by European relatives, at least in that generation. Importantly, it also meant acceptance by coloured peers who enjoyed a similar status; the coloured married within their group, at times to relatives and also to foreign born Europeans, so as to maintain or improve their complexions, hair texture and status and to retain or to expand landholding. Historian Pierre Gustave Louis Borde writes:

> "The Free blacks and People of Colour formed themselves into a second society on parallel lines [to the European aristocratic society in Trinidad [and not less distinguished than the whites. In the town, for the most part, they owned new buildings, and in the country they were gathered in the Naparima quarter where they set up sugar mills. Apart from the caste system which continued in Europe and in America in

hold the same position. (Craig-James 2008, 47)

spite of the French Revolution, these people enjoyed the same political
rights as the whites." (1982, Vol II, 308)

The inheritance of money and or property implied that in addition to
carrying the name of their European ancestor, they could also share in the
prestige of the well off European or coloured family. [173] This divided the
coloured community into those who might experience upward mobility,
education, social prominence, career opportunities, and perhaps some
wealth, and be free of most of the personal and social inhibitions and insecurities that afflicted black and coloured colonials, and those who would
not inherit anything.

Those who were not recognised as the offspring of their European fathers or well placed coloured relatives and therefore were not included in
their wills could eventually descend into poverty, eventually becoming
indistinguishable from the black working class; perhaps bitterly retaining
the memories of a previous generation. I call this phenomenon of the colonial era the "cult of the will."

Eric Williams' grandmother, his father's mother, Onemia Wilhelmina
Jane Hunt, was a "pass for white," a very light-complexioned person, perhaps "a marabou in the proportion of 88 to 40, or a quadroon of 96 parts
white and 32 black." (as C.L.R. James defines the proportions 1989, 38)
"Onemia looked like a European, but she said that she had Negro blood,"
according to Laborde. "She had long, straight, light-coloured hair and European features, spoke French and patois, and English with difficulty. She
died in St. Vincent on the 4th of September 1931." She was born in Port-
of-Spain on the 2nd April 1853. She was the daughter of Jean Baptiste and
Phillippa Hunt, née Smith. She was educated at St. Joseph's Convent.

---

173 In the will of Henri Boissière, he leaves his bedposts and all his clothes for his reputed
    son Louis, and his watch and chain for his other reputed son Alphonse, sons of Ro-
    salie Rose of Champs Elysées.
    The Philippe family of Grenada, who later settled in Trinidad, were also beneficia-
    ries of the will of their European ancestor. As such, they as Free Coloured People,
    were able in the 1820s to educate two of their sons in England, while maintaining a
    leasehold house in London at 33 Great Coram Street (McDaniel, Lorna, *Madame
    Philip-O*)

Onemia and her brother Louis Hunt (Eric Williams' great-uncle), inherited much property in Port-of-Spain from their parents. However, Onemia would soon lose her share of the inheritance. "He (Louis) was persuaded by the executor for the estate to join with him in defrauding the Trust. His sister, Onemia, was coerced into signing away her share," writes Laborde. [174] It would appear that some of the property was sold for non-payment of taxes as well. "Government intervened," and Louis left Trinidad to become a "globetrotter, said he reached Jerusalem." In effect, Louis Hunt conspired with the trustees of the estate to defraud Onemia of her share of the family's wealth; [175] this was to have unfortunate results a generation later. Laborde goes on to say that friends and relatives came to Onemia's rescue. Perhaps this was why she came to be influenced by one of the family's servants, a nanny who may have looked after her from birth, and who may have sought her best interest, considering her circumstances.

Onemia had come into contact with her husband James Thomas Williams, through her Negro nurse called in those days a 'Da'. In marrying James Williams born on Nevis in April 1855, [176] Onemia brought to a

174 Laborde family notes. Laborde writes that Louis Hunt would eventually live in Venezuela, "Said to be a member of the 'Cabinet' of the Venezuelan government, on the fall of that government, sought refuge in Montserrat, BWI. Married there Sarah Dyer of that island. Had four children: Charles, Clairmont, Reginald, Edmond." He returned to Venezuela, but later moved with his family to St. Vincent, where he was a merchant of the town of Barrovallie, children born there, Phillippa, Oliver, Ada. He returned to Trinidad in 1899, and then to Venezuela where he died in 1900. He was said to have left property there, which one of his sons, presumably Edmond went to Venezuela to try to and secure it. This is of interest as it may have been the third hope for an inheritance anticipated by the Williams family. Edmond settled there and died in Venezuela perhaps in the 1960s. Louis' son Charles married Victoria Hall of Montserrat. Their daughter Sarah Eugenia Hunt married Frederick Hubert Espinet, their son was Charles Sydney Espinet, the Editor of the *Trinidad Guardian.*

175 This family, according to Laborde, owned properties around the 'Convent corner' between Pembroke and Frederick Streets and by the Rosary Church, corner Park and Henry Street. Jean Baptiste Hunt died of cholera circa February 1853.Onemia claimed that the family "owned half of the properties in Frederick Street" (Laborde)

176 Laborde notes "The book 'A West Indian Fortune' speaks of a 'James Williams' and

close a steady evolution to whiteness or apparent whiteness in the Comis-siong-Smith-Hunt descent. Ernest Laborde, in his historical notes writes that James Williams was the "son of Sara Jane Williams née James, who was of Carib descent (long straight hair) and born in Nevis in 1830, and died in Trinidad in 1915. Sara Jane claims not to have been born a slave."

The Black Caribs had not been enslaved. Slavery had ended in 1838 in the British Empire. When the British took charge of St. Vincent after the Treaty of Paris in 1763, they were opposed by the original French set-tlers and their Carib allies. After a series of Carib Wars, and the death of the black Carib leader Satuye (Chatoyer), they surrendered to the British in 1796. The British considered the Black Caribs enemies and deported them to Roatán, an island off the coast of Honduras. In the process, the British separated the more African-looking Caribs from the more Amer-indian-looking ones. They decided that the former were enemies who had to be deported, while the latter were merely "misled" and were allowed to remain. Sara Jane born a mere 34 years after the deportation and was more than likely more Carib than black.

In "marrying" Mr. Williams, nicknamed "Old King", their son James Thomas Williams would have been considered a "Zambo," a mixture of Amerindian and African. [177] James Williams' father might have been of Af-rican descent, or perhaps of mixed Carib and African heritage. Known as "Old King" he was a "turnkey", a prison officer at the Royal Gaol in Nevis, as such he held a position of trust in the colonial service. Their son, James Williams was educated and was brought up a Methodist. He came to Trinidad before 1878 and operated a real estate agency in Port-of-Spain. He had come to Trinidad from St. Vincent in the company of another family, Mr. and Mrs. Israel Johnson. Mrs. Johnson's maiden name was Tet-ron, a French family resident in Trinidad from before the Cedula of 1783. They were the parents of Sir Edgar Gaston Johnson K.C., who became a mayor of Port-of-Spain in the 1920s. James and Onemia Williams, in hav-ing a family like the Johnsons as their patrons, would have been perceived

---

a 'Henry Williams' who lived in Nevis."
177 ibid.

by some other coloured families in Port-of-Spain as certainly poor but as "respectable." Onemia, according to Laborde, was shunned by some of her own relatives, but as a member of the Roman Catholic church in Trinidad, would have had friends and some family who would have helped and received her. [178]

James and Onemia had two children, Thomas Henry and Phillippa Williams. The birth of dark-complexioned children, like Thomas Williams, Eric's father, born in 1878, was not a social set-back, necessarily, as middle-class, respectable coloured people came in many shades. He had, though poor, a good education at Tranquillity Boys School, (Laborde) and possessed "the appropriate social qualifications," for his circle, contrary to what Professor Selwyn Ryan writes in his book *Eric Williams The Myth and the Man* (p. 13).

What Thomas Williams needed to do, and in fact did accomplish, was to marry a light-skinned person from a respectable, old coloured French Creole family; one as well recognised as his mother's, the Hunts, who were possessed of social prestige, and hopefully with some money and property. Thomas Williams did not have African hair, [179] and so, was able to marry "up" to a young woman, Eliza Boissière, who was of a fairer complexion than he, with "good hair" as well. She might have come into a little money or even inherited a house, but her family, too, as it would turn out, would be cheated of their inheritance.

Her father, Jules Boissière, [180] (born 1857) was the illegitimate son of John Nicholas Boissière and a woman of colour, and had been included in the will of his wealthy father. [181] Both Jules and his sister Eliza had been

178 Ernest Laborde notes that Onemia was helped by friends or relatives who came to her rescue. She kept in contact with certain nuns and priests from Trinidad after she went to St. Vincent in 1923 through a Fr. Charles Vashter.

179 Conversations with Flora Gittens.

180 Eliza's other coloured Boissière relatives were well off; some were rich, they knew her. "Eliza had been 'élevée en chapeau' ('brought up in a hat'), she did not tie her head, she did not have bad hair." Andrea McCarthy née Boissière. Interview for Pocock's book *Out of the Shadows of the Past.*

181 John Nicholas Boissière lived at Rookery Nook opposite to Champs Elysées great house owned by his half brother Dr. Jean Valleton de Boissière.

taken as children from their mother and had been brought up in the household of their father, John Nicholas, at the Great House in Rookery Nook, Maraval, together with the children of his marriage. John Nicholas Boissière, was of European descent, but of illegitimate birth, and married to a light-complexioned coloured woman, which was unusual for the time. He had been left well off by his father, Henry Boissière. John Nicholas was a successful businessman, he left his family well endowed upon his death, and made various arrangements for the future of both his "reputed" (illegitimate) children Eliza and Jules. He provided for them in his will and arranged an apprenticeship for the young man, Jules, to be trained as a manager at Palmiste Estate, the property of a friend of the family, Sir Norman Lamont.

For various reasons, this legacy was never received by Jules or by Jules' children. What made it worse were Jules' and his sister Eliza's high expectations. The brother and sister had grown up in the household of the Boissières, as cherished members of the family. [182] To have been denied their birthright must have come as a grave disappointment.

Jules Boissière had married Eveline Redford, [183] the daughter of George Redford, an Englishman, and a woman of colour. Eliza Boissière (named for her aunt, Eliza) would have had European grandparents on both her mother's side (George Redford) and her father's (John Nicholas Boissière) and would have known them and been in their company, not in an inferior or servile manner, but as a young lady who was a member of the family.

The women of colour with whom John Nicholas Boissière and George Redford had these children could have been of mixed race of similar

---

182 John Nicholas Boissière expressed particular wishes for his daughter Eliza, providing funds for her care "as long as she remains a part of the household of my wife." In closing he stated that his trustees should look after the interest of both his lawful and reputed issue, ensuring their future maintenance and education.

183 Jules Arnauld Boissière and his wife Eveline, née Redford had, according to Flora Gittens, ten children: Blanche b.1878, d.1970; Eliza b. 1888; Percy (died in Venezuela in jail); Stella d. 1976 issue: Robert, Arnauld, Jeffrey (she grew to adulthood with Blanche); Elma, d. 1974; Daisy (went to Panama); Frank m. Nora Norgrove, U.S.A.; Violet (Dot, ? a son Joseph d. 2008); Hilda; and Ivy.

backgrounds (Eveline Redford's brother's grandson was Olympic runner McDonald Bailey). With this sort of family background, which was very well known to the Williams, their sense of disappointment and a feeling of being cheated of their inheritance is easy to understand.

It was an emotional, financial and social blow. Williams wrote that his father's "three great expectations for money failed him," that he was "disappointed in his hopes of a legacy," (Williams 2006, 26) a blow that according to Flora Gittens was felt by her brothers Eric and Mervyn especially. They had been victims of clever conspirators who had cheated them of their legacy twice. [184]

In the case of Williams' mother, this may have been perpetrated by one of Trinidad's leading French Creole families, the Valleton de Boissières, who played an active role in the affairs of the colony from the end of the 19th century to the 1920s. They produced two members of the colony's Legislative Council. One of them, Dr. Jean de Boissière, served for about 30 years on this body. The other, Col. Arnold de Boissière, held the important portfolio of Protector of Immigrants, and went on to serve as the highest-ranking West Indian officer on the Western Front in the First World War.

Another family member who was ADC to several governors married the daughter of the British Colonial Governor of Trinidad and Tobago, Sir Claud Hollis, G.C.M.G., C.B.E. (1930-1936). This was a significant event: no locally-born person had married a colonial governor or a member of his family since the 1850s when Lord Harris had married a Miss Cummins. The de Boissières also produced commissioned officers (both in the local forces and in the imperial service.)

General Sir Frank Messervy, whose mother was Nadia Myra de Boissière, received the surrender of a Japanese army in Burma towards the end of the second World War. It produced the most significant, and perhaps most influential, socialite of the period, Poleska de Boissière.

---

184 Conspiracies to defraud minors, the naïve, the trusting or the ignorant have always been a common practice. The 19th century historian E.L. Joseph wrote an account of such a case in his novel *Warner Arundel, The Adventures of a Creole.* My own father, as told in the first part of this book, was also a victim of such fraud.

Genealogy of the Valleton de Bossière Family of Maraval
(descent of selected members as mentioned in this book)

Dr. Jean Valleton de Boissière 1733 - 1820, Ecuyer
(Montpellier University) Huguenot, Member of the Council of Five Hundred during the French Revolution, was appointed Mayor of the town of Bergerac during the Napoleonic period.

With **Zuzule**, an African woman, **Joseph and Auguste Boissière**, to whom he gave town properties and mortgages.

Jean Louis François Valleton de Boissière 1777 - 1853 Known in Trinidad as **John Boissière**, became the sole owner of Champs Elysées estate, Maraval, Trinidad in 1820.

m. **Claire Beaulieu of Guadeloupe** 1760 - 1830 (17 years older than her husband, not an aristocrat, possible a "casket girl", a "fille du roi" or a "placée") one son

With coloured woman **Rosalie Rose** of Champs Elysées **Louis and Alphonse. Boissiere** Their father left money and some personal effects for them in his will. Louis' son **Charles** together with his father **Louis** and his cousins **Auguste and Joseph** who were brothers and their cousin **Jules** were thought of as "brothers".

William Henry Boissière 1799 - 1865

m. 1827 **Louise Emile Roget de Belloquet** 1807 - 1834

John Henry Joseph Boissière 1830 - 1906 (Edinburgh University), Later known as **Dr. Jean Valleton de Boissière**

m. **Whilemina Poleska Roget de Belloquet**

m. **Maraquita Garcia**

With **Rosette Arnaud**, a European woman, while in their teens, **John Nicholas Boissiere** 1816 - 1886 who lived at Rookery Nook, opposite to Champs Elyées
He had with a woman of colour
Jules Arnauld Boissiere (He lived at Rookery Nook together with his sister **Eliza Boissière** 1860 - 1893 died at Rookery Nook.)
Jules Arnauld m. **Evalina Redford,** daughter
Eliza Boissiere m.**Thomas Henry Williams,** son among others
Dr. Eric Eustace Williams

m. **Marie Aurilie Soully,** a woman of colour, they had ten children, among them

Dr. Jean Francois de Valleton 1861 - 1942 Count de Boissière (Edinburgh University)

Armand de Boissière 1879 - 1937 Solicitor m. **Maud Hutchinson,** son **Ralph de Boissiere** 1907 - 2007 Author

Jeanne Claire de Boissière m. **Joseph Pocock** son **Michael Pocock** (Alstons executive, hon. secretary of DLP), **Anthony & John**

Arnauld John Valleton m. **Prunella Hollis,** daughter of Governor, of T&T Sir Claud Hollis

Col. William Henry Arnauld de Boissière, 1872 - 1947,

Note: Professor Ryan, in his "Eric Williams the Myth and the Man" (p.13) writes that Jules Boissière was the son "Monsieur Jean Nicholas de Boissière, the French-creole baron of Champs Elysées, Maraval." This is an error on his part. John Nicholas Boissière was the illegitimate son of Henry Boissière and half-brother of Dr. Jean Valleton de Boissière, who was the husband of Wilhelmina Poleska de Boissière. They lived at Champs Elysées, Maraval. John Nicholas Boissière and his family, which included Jules and his sister Eliza, his illegitimate children, lived opposite to them on Maraval Road at Rookery Nook. The Valleton de Boissières did not hold the title of Baron; as untitled nobility they were described as Écuyer.

Genealogy of the Comissiong/Smith/Hunt/Williams family

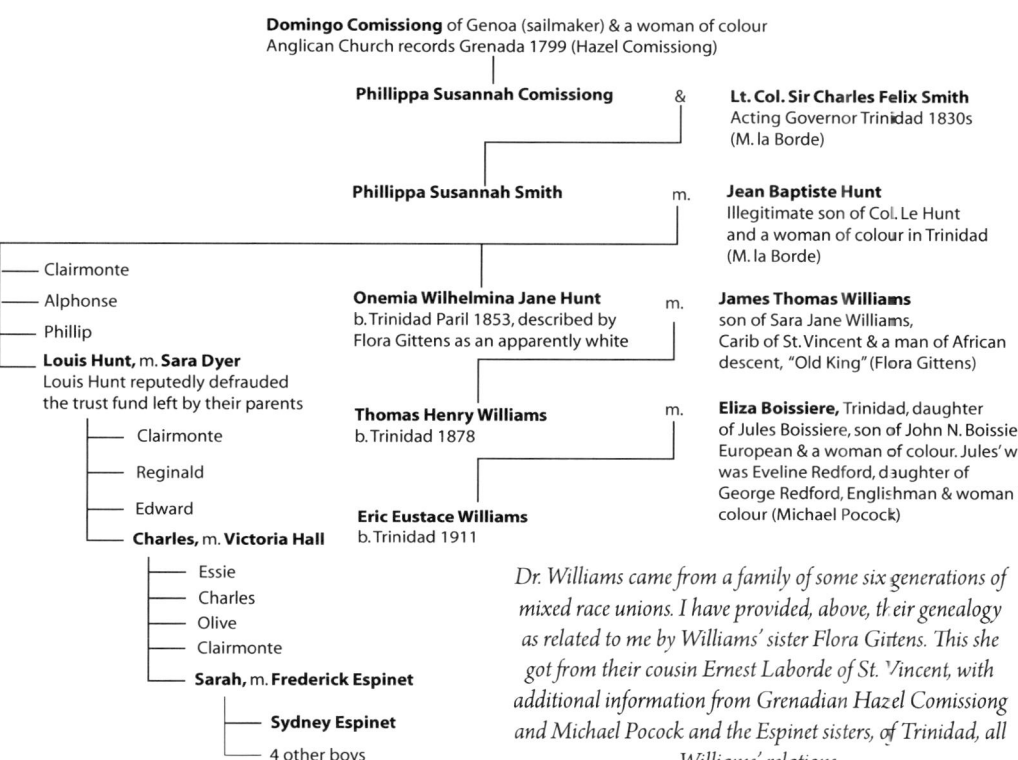

Domingo Comissiong of Genoa (sailmaker) & a woman of colour
Anglican Church records Grenada 1799 (Hazel Comissiong)

Phillippa Susannah Comissiong   &   **Lt. Col. Sir Charles Felix Smith**
Acting Governor Trinidad 1830s
(M. la Borde)

Phillippa Susannah Smith   m.   **Jean Baptiste Hunt**
Illegitimate son of Col. Le Hunt
and a woman of colour in Trinidad
(M. la Borde)

— Clairmonte
— Alphonse
— Phillip
— **Louis Hunt,** m. **Sara Dyer**
Louis Hunt reputedly defrauded
the trust fund left by their parents

Onemia Wilhelmina Jane Hunt   m.   **James Thomas Williams**
b. Trinidad Paril 1853, described by   son of Sara Jane Williams,
Flora Gittens as an apparently white   Carib of St. Vincent & a man of African
descent, "Old King" (Flora Gittens)

— Clairmonte
— Reginald
— Edward
— **Charles,** m. **Victoria Hall**

Thomas Henry Williams   m.   **Eliza Boissiere,** Trinidad, daughter
b. Trinidad 1878   of Jules Boissiere, son of John N. Boissiere,
European & a woman of colour. Jules' wife
was Eveline Redford, daughter of
George Redford, Englishman & woman of
colour (Michael Pocock)

Eric Eustace Williams
b. Trinidad 1911

— Essie
— Charles
— Olive
— Clairmonte
— **Sarah,** m. **Frederick Espinet**

— **Sydney Espinet**
— 4 other boys

*Dr. Williams came from a family of some six generations of
mixed race unions. I have provided, above, their genealogy
as related to me by Williams' sister Flora Gittens. This she
got from their cousin Ernest Laborde of St. Vincent, with
additional information from Grenadian Hazel Comissiong
and Michael Pocock and the Espinet sisters, of Trinidad, all
Williams' relations.*

All this was in the newspapers at the time. [185]

They owned some 350 acres of land in Maraval, the Champs Elysées estate, acquired in 1820 from the de Gannes de la Chancellerie family of Grenada.

Jean de Boissière (also known as John Boissière), founder of the family in Trinidad, was an importer of slaves and a money lender in the 1790s. Lending money to plantation owners, he would often have to foreclose on their estates when they could not repay their mortgages. He would then acquire the slaves, who were more often than not more valuable than the land, particularly after the abolition of the slave trade in 1807 and sell

---

185 Members of the British Royal family, the Princesses of Teck, the Prince of Wales and other visiting notables, such as President 'Teddy' Roosevelt and Colonel Charles Lindberg were entertained by Poleska de Boissière at Champs Elysées.

Poleska de Boissière, née Roget de Belloquet, was the wife of Jean Valleton de Boissière, doctor of medicine, member of the Legislative Council and owner of Champs Elysées estate in Maraval, Trinidad. He was the half brother of John Nicholas Boissière, of Rookery Nook, who was the father of Jules Boissière. The coachman is cricketer Lebrun Constantine, father of Sir Learie Constantine, made Baron of Maraval in the 1960s. (Pocock)

them at a profit. The de Boissières were, without a doubt, one of the masters or "Massas," as they would have been called, of slavery days.

For the Williams', to be treated in such a manner by French Creoles like the de Boissières, especially while some of them still carried the name, was a scandal, and very galling, leaving bitter feelings for generations. Williams' grandfather, Jules Boissière's, illegitimate birth, and exclusion from the legacy may have even implied in the minds of some people doubts as to his paternity.

According to Flora Gittens, the family had waited for a time after the death of John Nicholas Boissière, knowing that the executor of his estate was his half-brother Dr. Jean Valleton de Boissière. Then he too passed away, with no news regarding their inheritance. After a long time they realised that nothing was being done on their behalf. They were later to understand that no lawyer would challenge "La Châtellaine," Poleska de Boissière, now the executrix of the estate, as she was perceived as a person of great influence in the colony.[186] In a letter to me in 1978, Flora wrote: " . . . Jules Boissière was the illegitimate child, was never considered by the family [the de Boissières] and as a result apparently couldn't care less about his ancestors."

Eric Williams was eleven years old when his father's mother, Onemia died. He does not mention her in his autobiography. Neither does he mention his grandfather, James Williams. Were these omissions due to Williams' subconsciously blaming them for the fact that the family had become dark-complexioned and impoverished as a result of Onemia's marriage? "The daily problem of making ends meet dogged the family as a whole and determined the fate and fortune of individual members," Eric Williams wrote in *Inward Hunger*. By not mentioning his grandparents' fate, it could be argued that he deprived himself of catharsis for his own anguish.

In addition to the poverty, the shame that came with being victims of the "cult of the will" may have had severe psychological effects on the Williams family. Ken Boodhoo describes their secluded life: "Because Eliza Williams was generally unsociable and unfriendly, she discouraged her daughters from inviting their friends to the home." She did not want people to know that she cooked in her bedroom. Boodhoo recounts,

> "Eliza Williams was tough, aloof, imperious, and a firm disciplinarian. She was very demanding of her children, and was firmly in command of her family. Henry Williams was also firm, but possessed a warmer personality. Eliza viewed herself as a French Creole [she would have known that lifestyle as a young lady, who as a member of her grandfather's household at Rookery Nook would have seen first hand, and met French Creoles who still lived in the 'old style,' before it was diluted by 'modern times'] and believed that she was superior to those around her. As one daughter recalled, "she had the French embedded in her. She had the French style. She had the many French ways. She thought

---

186 The de Boissière family were prominent but cash poor (Pocock). They would have had to sell property to find the money to meet the obligations of the will of John Nicholas Boissière. This, apparently, they were reluctant to do.

that she was an aristocrat. [187] She believed that she was better than others. We called her Madame (behind her back.) She was very proud." The girls were not permitted to walk home from school with other children. The reason was that Eliza "did not want to hear complaints from others about us. . . ." (2002, 26–39)

I contend that the Williams' sense of deprivation may have been exacerbated by a perceived loss of status. The family may have excluded themselves from polite society due to their poverty and a sense of shame. They felt that they could no longer share in the glamour and prestige of their other coloured relations, or the de Boissières of Rookery Nook for example, with whom their grandfather Jules had lived and had grown up with. Other coloured members of the de Boissière family had become very well off. Some had been left small fortunes in the wills of their white fathers (*see Appendix II for clarification on the use of the particle "de" in this family*).

The Williams' were now, in their own minds, twice over the victims of the "cult of the will," "tarred by the same brush," "Massa" no longer turned his countenance upon them.

An ironical twist compounded Eliza's sense of loss of status. In the late 20th century, the older coloured members of the Boissière family thought Jules was one of "five brothers" and as such an equal and accepted, recognised coloured son of the founder of the family, Jean de Boissière. This being the case, Eliza felt herself especially deprived: all the other "brothers"

---

187 She was descended from an 'ancient' aristocratic French family, *noblesse d' épée,* that had been ennobled in the mid-14th century. African genes, and the happen-chance of illegitimate descent in a previous generation, would not have barred her from that status, being as she was of light complexion, had she lived in Europe, was educated, had some money and was 'known' in certain circles. According to heraldry expert, A.C. Fox-Davies, (1909, pp. 509-511) the mark for illegitimacy, *bend sinister,* is a "difference" not a dishonour, and ". . . *was not invented or instituted, nor were these marks enforced, as punishments or a disgrace."* These prejudices are local, New World contrivances made up by the white colonists to maintain ideas of superiority, 'an aristocracy of skin' as Williams himself describes it, so as to maintain exclusivity and control populations. Her cousins, her father's half-brothers grandchildren, also coloured, with illegitimacy in their past, married into the French upper class while living in Europe, are presently listed in the directories and the armorial of the nobility of France.

The "Boissière House" on Queen's Park West was built by Charles Boissière in 1904. He was the son of Eugene Boissière who was thought to be one of the "five brothers," sons of the founder of the family. Jules Boissière was also supposed to be one of them. (Gerald Watterson)

had benefited from the wills of their antecedents. However, as I later discovered, the "five brothers" had in fact been cousins, but had been remembered as brothers because they had been friends in their youth, and/or had been recognised by their fathers as Boissières, as distinct from other "outside" offspring of the family. [188] Jules then, was a recognised coloured Boissière, who allegedly had been deprived of his inheritance by Madame Poleska de Boissière, the leading socialite of the era.

The Williams, poor as they had become, felt that they could no longer receive their friends and relatives in the same manner that they would be received by them. They may have feared ridicule. They moved constantly, every few years; it might have been difficult for relatives to remember where they lived last. Despite being poor, they never lived "Behind the Bridge" or in East Port-of-Spain, or east of Dundonald Street. Except for a

188   The myth of the "five brothers" was given to me by Muriel Donawa née Boissière and Andrea McCarthy, née Boissière, both of 12 Queen's Park West, Port of Spain. I interviewed them during research for Michael Pocock's book *Out of the Shadows of the Past*. The "brothers", in fact cousins, were Eugene, Auguste, Charles, Jules and Louis Boissière.

short period in 1912 when they lived on Oxford Street, they mostly lived
in Newtown and Woodbrook. Williams writes in *Inward Hunger*:

> "The housing problem was first in the list of evils which afflicted the
> family. We disputed our way all over Port-of-Spain, seeking living space
> at low rentals. In my first twenty one years in Trinidad we changed
> houses eight times, and it is possible to identify members of the family
> not only by name or by sex or by age but also by the house in which
> each was born. The descending family fortunes were reflected in the
> descent from water closet to cesspit and in one bad case the bailiff ap-
> peared. ... The ordeal of removal, the horror of the cesspit, the dread of
> eviction were only the external aspects of the increasing gravity of our
> housing problem." [189]

What was also of considerable consequence was the manner in which
Eliza and Thomas Williams handled their misfortune. Eric was the first
in a family of twelve children. His father, sad and disappointed, was determined that his son would succeed through education. Eliza, cold and
imperious, believed that she was superior to those around her. There was
an extremely rigid family discipline, and a church that sought to shape
and dominate the family's life. I would agree with Boodhoo that Eric Williams was a product of his heredity and environment; birth order, family
dynamics, the colonial condition, class and colour.

---

189 Flora Gittens also related these frequent moves. Eric was born at 16 Dundonald St.
in 1911, not at Oxford St. as he claimed. (Ryan 2009, p.787, Notes). They then lived
in Diego Martin for a short time; then they moved to Oxford St., (Mrs Foyer at No.
45?) then to 76 Picton St. where Mervyn, b. 1912, Camilla b. 1914, Angela b.1915,
Camilla died there. Then they moved to Carlos St., where Flora b. 1917, John b. 1920,
Eileen b. 1922. Theresa b. 1928, Anthony b. 1930. Then they moved to 52 Woodford
St., where Lucille b. 1931. Eric at Q.R.C. Won scholarship 1934, Go'vt Training College. Left for England. Family moved to 45 Murray St. Eric returned in 1944; he did
not live with them, he lived at Francis St. & Perigord Lane, Maraval (de Boissière
lands) Worked at Caribbean Commission, at Rookery Nook (site of the house in
which his grandfather, Jules Boissière, grew up), married, he lived at Laburnum Ave.,
Diego Martin. Fired from the Commission, he lived at the Moyou's at Sackville St.
next to the hat factory,1953. Lived at 2 Cipriani B'lvd. In 1953, at Lady Chancellor
Rd. (PNM formed) In the 1960s, Cornelio St., Crow's Nest, Mary St., Saint Clair, La
Fantasy Rd., St. Anns, Prime Minister's Residence, d. 1981.

As a man who had a knowledge of history and who knew his family history well, Williams would have felt this perceived loss of caste keenly, especially as he would have met young people of his own age and background, but of different circumstances, and he may have developed the mulatto's or "red man's" complex: the so called 'chip on the shoulder," a sense of racial inferiority; social as well as other inhibitions; and maybe he developed a pathologically suspicious and cynical attitude with regard to Europeans, and even perhaps a strong animosity, a rage, against the French Creole community, the colonial establishment of his day, along with a distrust of the legal system that had not supported the family's attempt at redress.

Thin-skinned and suspicious, he was easily offended, and saw race behind every perceived slight, perhaps at times quite rightly. Maybe he was like a white man looking out of a dark-skinned face; a white, upper class, 19th century, educated man, with the closely guarded sense of honour of an aristocrat? But, without a handle on the social graces. A "black French Creole," somehow painfully fallen from grace.

Was Williams and his immediate family actually affected by all this loss? It has been suggested that social change does not occur without change in personality. Withdrawal of status respect and loss of status, for example, result in personality transformation over several generations.

> "This change, in turn, is said to be based on a deep-going change in the home environment. The withdrawal of status respect means for those undergoing it anxiety, embitteredness and dissonance. For the formerly looked-up-to person is no longer esteemed in a society that he himself regards highly, and whose traditional structure of values he has internalised. In the second, third or fourth generation, a pronounced lack of norms becomes evident." [190]

The Williams family seems to me to be a well defined example of the change in personality that the loss of social status creates; two genera-

---

190 Hagen, E.E., "On the Theory of Social Change. How Economic Growth Begins", Homewood, Ill., 1982. As quoted in: Kunczik, Michael: *Communication and Social Change*, 1993 p. 131.

tions after Dr. Williams' two ancestors, on both sides of his family, had been cheated out of their inheritance. Hagen reasons that after some generations, the deprived men retreat into apathy, [191] and the women, as a reaction to the perceived failure of their men, "will react attentively to any achievement and show of initiative on the part of their sons." Hagen argues "that a certain combination and intensity of these attitudes of mothers and the weakness of the fathers creates an almost ideal environment for the development of a type of anxiety-driven creativity. Such persons provide themselves with security, in that they are traditional and authoritarian in most of their ways of behaving, while at the same time being in quite specific aspects daring and creative." (1993, 131)

I would contend here that Eric Williams' outstanding academic and political ambition and (inward) hunger were fueled by the "anxiety-driven creativity" that Hagen postulates. This may also provide an insight into why Williams did not create a Marxist-type revolution, even though he was heavily influenced by James, Padmore et.al. The Williams family had the "traditional structure of values internalised." Because of their loss of social status two generations before, his parents, even though personally weak (his father never succeeded professionally; his mother was an alcoholic), still encouraged their son to value and achieve academic excellence and to make good on the family's loss. On the other hand, extrapolating from Hagen's analysis, Eric Williams was "daring and creative" in propagating his brand of politics, which in combination with his academic achievements served to distance him from the loss of status that his family had experienced and from the less than desirable role models that his parents were. He pursued power to compensate for his sense of deprivation. Deosaran sums this up: "Williams had power and competence. He knew this. And he enjoyed putting both on full display. The vices of his power were usually tempered by the virtues of his reputed competence. Such were the foundations of his political personality." (1981, 29)

---

191 Williams' father, from the descriptions given of him in *Inward Hunger*, seems to have lost all ambition.

Williams did re-write history, attempting to banish for-ever several previously held ideas about race and class. He was a brilliant scholar and consummate politician, whose political personality had been created by a historic melodrama. He could live in the present but had a consciousness that was founded two centuries in the past.

By becoming an historian, a university professor and a prime minister, Dr. Williams became the inheritor of all the hopes and dreams of genera- tions of Creole people of virtually all backgrounds; their entire colonial experience made flesh. He was the messianic legacy of those who, like himself, bore the mental scars of the British colonial experience in the Caribbean. He transferred his family's shame and disappointments to sig- nificant sections of the population while politicising them.

Dr. Eric Williams became the perfect propagandist of post-World War II colonial *angst*. He "invented" his version of black nationalism along the lines of the shamed, deprived and victimised child, what social scientists would describe as "Frantz Fanon's use of Freud's theory to explain the emergence and implications of inferiority in colonially oppressed peo- ples." [192] His brand of black nationalism appeared to some to have only one purpose, and that was to pass on a patrimony, a legacy, to those whom he thought should be the "true inheritors" of the colonial experience, to those who had been the victims of a conspiracy, a lie that had been told to an entire people in exile (i.e. the black subjects of the British Empire). To others it appeared to contain elements 'of revenge.' The Afro-Creole masses would inherit what he and his family could not. He may possibly have seen his personal history as the country's destiny. He utilised politi- cal control to compensate the Afro-Creole population for the inheritance that they had long been denied. This was the basis of Williams' interpre- tation of the ideal welfare state, and would later form an integral part of

---

192 Deosaran 1981, 176. In a personal communication with the author, Deosaran adds: "I have always held the view that the real treatment of Williams is not so much his history scholarship but the psychology of the man himself, his motivations, his clever use of black nationalism, his perpetual quest for compensation for perceived deprivations of which, in his own account, there were many." (Email May 2009)

the political culture of the PNM and of the entire country over the next 50 years. [193]

This perceived deprivation of status and fortune may have caused Williams the Historian to have empathised more with the objectives of the Caribbean revolutionaries of the late 18th and early 19th centuries than with those of the 20th. If this is the case, he may be perceived as a natural successor to Vincent Ogé, the Free Mulatto leader of Saint Domingue; Toussaint L'Ouverture, the liberator of Saint Domingue; Julien Fédon, the Free Mulatto Republican revolutionary of Grenada; or even perhaps Fr. Francis de Ridder and Jean Baptiste Philippe, the Free Mulatto petitioners of Trinidad: all of whom had been looking to right the wrongs experienced by the Afro-French Creoles, both slave and free.

In so doing, perhaps Williams was more interested in securing a legacy for the "true inheritors" (a term used by Williams to describe the Afro-Creole masses) than being a contemporary Third World revolutionary like Fidel Castro, Maurice Bishop or Forbes Burnham, whose objective was to change the system in its entirety.

193 Williams' critics have described this as the "Give me Give me" mentality of his constituents, a perpetual state of various notions of entitlement expressed by helplessness.

The dry river, or the Rio Santa Anna, running along the foothills of Laventille marked the eastern perimeter of the town of Port-of-Spain up to the turn of the 19th century. The forested hillside with its springs and deep gullies, limestone caves and an abundance of game provided a safe haven for runaway slaves; later 'freed Africans' would make it their home, giving it the name Freetown, or Yarraba Ville, it would become the bed rock of the Afro-Creole culture, and be loyal to the PNM for generations (M.J. Cazabon, courtesy, Belmont Harris Trust and Geoffrey MacLean.)

FORMULATION OF THE POLITICAL PERSONALITY
4

Dr. Williams does not appear to have been interested in Marxism[194] for the purpose of world revolution, or to have participated in the left-wing activities that surrounded him as a student in England in the late 1930s. It appears possible that he may have held at times, when it suited him, a morally relativistic world view; "that there were no longer any absolutes: of time and space, of good and evil, of knowledge, above all of value" (Johnson 1991, 4) understanding that fundamental changes were taking

---

194 At Howard University, Williams was thought of as being "on the Left" and as a member of the "Marxist clique." Ryan 2009, 29.

place in the world. The age of deference to social rank, for example, was passing away in the aftermath of the First World War. He might have accepted that the time of individual accountability was being radically challenged by the influence of such thinkers as Einstein, Marx and Freud, And that society could be judged collectively.

The notion that he could re-write history with an eye to the future was empowering. Williams had selected most of what he needed from his mentor, C.L.R. James, and proceeded to reach within himself to tap into his own rage, his painful memories, his sense of frustration, injustice, deprivation, and victimhood, in order to focus on his new narrative. This narrative would express the psychology of confrontation, and a political style reflecting elements of revenge: Which is contemptible to prudence and justice. "The Messiah was conqueror and victim at one and the same time. Conqueror of a political opportunity and victim of his own overwhelming power urge." (Deosaran 1981, 13)

Williams may have deconstructed the justice and humanity theory of the abolition of the slave trade as misleading because this notion did not fit in with the anti-colonial, Pan-African, Pan-Caribbean intellectual and emotional climate in which he moved in London in the late 1930s. These ideas (anti-colonial, Pan-African, Pan-Caribbean) were made vivid by his historical research and academic work, and were supported by his and others' empirical research which brought to light the enormity of suffering experienced by the slaves. This was perceived, especially, when understood against the callous nature of the economics of greed, the selfishness of class, and the hedonism of Great Britain that had defeated France in the Seven Years' War, becoming the dominant European power in North America and India. Although many of its American colonies were soon lost in the American Revolutionary War, which led to the establishment of the United States of America. The West Indian colonies were now a side-show, India was the future. Williams' scholarship allowed him to live, in his mind, in the 18th century.

The reason for the abolition of the slave trade had to be found in something more concrete, more human than ideals such as 'humanity and justice.' The idea that a major advancement of Western civilisation, representing a shift in its moral values, had been actually achieved by the ending of the slave trade, for whatever reasons, would have been an intolerable notion, ludicrous, given the cynical climate of the times and the acrid atmosphere of these discourses. Political expediency in the pursuit of world power, to which could be added hypocrisy, greed and a conspiracy to deceive, was the obvious reason. The people in the colonies had been made helpless victims.

Williams craved empowerment, he hungered for it. "Williams then, in accordance with the theory of compensatory striving, turned to power expecting to overcome such low estimates [of himself]," writes Deosaran, applying the theories of American political scientist Harold Lasswell to the question why Williams would have sought political power. (1981, 21)

To gain power, Dr. Williams promoted a form of nationalistic idealism that became popular in the colonies after World War II. With these ideals, he could form a political party that would be "a rally, a convention of all and for all, a mobilisation of all the forces in the community, cutting across race and religion, class and colour, with emphasis on united action by all the people in a common cause," as he would put it in his *People's Charter*. (Ryan 1988, xvii) He would popularise his own experience of being a victim in order to gain the trust of the masses.

Williams was in fact pushing at an open door. The British Empire, and later the Commonwealth had for some time established that all its colonies were to be prepared for Independence, and handed it when ready. The British White Paper of June 1948 stated: "The central purpose of British colonial policy ... is to guide the colonial territories to responsible self-government within the Commonwealth in conditions that ensure to the people concerned both a fair standard of living and freedom from oppression in any quarter."

The creation of trust and the conversion of trust into power are crucial elements in politics.[195] This is a two-way process: Dr. Williams could only

---

195 I am borrowing this notion from Baigent, Leigh and Lincoln *The Messianic Legacy*, who applied the concept of trust to the creation of religious power. It does in my view not systemically differ from the mechanisms of political power. Baigent et al. write: "The conferring of trust is not a passive process. We tend ... to speak of 'an act of

get deep-felt release from his personal anguish through the "continuing stream of empowering responses" (Lasswell: Deosaran), which he in turn had to continuously provoke by aggressively pursuing the investing of popular "mass trust" in his person. This is of course a Sisyphean struggle whose futility is ironically echoed in the title of his autobiography, *Inward Hunger:* a yearning that can never be satisfied.

Books are often the cornerstones upon which political movements are founded. Who knows how many movements have been launched in this way, from the various *"Volumes of the Sacred Law,"* to Marx's *Das Kapital* and Hitler's *Mein Kampf.* Williams translated the basic ideas of his doctoral thesis as expressed in his book *Capitalism and Slavery* into politics. *The People's Charter,* presented in 1956, was the blueprint for implementing his historical narrative. In it, specific ideas were discussed with regard to remodelling society along the lines of his reinterpretation of history, e.g. West Indianisation and "the cultivation of the spirit of Bandung [196] on the sugar plantations of Trinidad." These publications were underpinned by a series of seven public lectures at Woodford Square from June 1955 to the formal launch of the PNM on 24th January, 1956. In July 1955, Williams added the spin "University of Woodford Square" to his public lectures on topics ranging from his personal grievances to economic problems and constitutional reform in Trinidad and Tobago; the historical background to race relations in the Caribbean; chattel slavery; party politics in Trinidad and Tobago and the Federation of the West Indies. (Williams 2006,

---

trust,' and this, precisely, is what conferring trust entails, an act. Conferring trust is an active, not a passive process. Something is actively given by one party and received by another. There is an intrinsic, inescapable correlation between trust and power. It is as if trust, in the very process of being conferred, undergoes the equivalent of a chemical change. In consequence, what begins as trust when it leaves the donor becomes converted into power in the hands of the recipient. If one actively trusts an individual, one is giving that individual a degree of power over oneself." (p. 169f)

196 The Afro-Asian conference held in Bandung, Indonesia in 1955 brought together leaders from the newly independent former colonies. They positioned themselves as non-aligned either to the West or to the Soviet Union and were described as 'Third World' leaders. "Some of those present were subsequently to plot to murder each other; others to end their lives in gaol, disgrace or exile." (Johnson, 1991, 477)

131ff) In these discourses Williams would, at times, appear to be addressing all black people in the Anglophone Caribbean, and not only a Trinidadian audience. He may have been well aware of the diversity of origins
in his listeners, and the extent to which many of them could empathise
with what he was saying, particularly with regard to the various kinds of
oppression and lack of opportunity, not generally known, or experienced,
in more wealthy, educated, and liberal Trinidad and Tobago.

In the 1950s, Williams was among a relatively small, world political
elite, who became the professional politicians, 'the vote manipulators' of
the Third World. They acquired the ideology, the techniques and, above
all, the vernacular of Western politics in the immediate post-war period of
decolonisation. They spoke to the Colonial Office in a language that was
shared by successive British governments, both Labour and Conserva-
tive. The so-called "people" were a huge walk-on crowd.

Deosaran writes that in his impassioned discourses, Williams was able
to guide the sense of "alienation of his listeners onto a political state similar to his own," thereby facilitating "the ability of the masses to identify
with the leader" and establishing his credentials as a charismatic person.
(1981, 16) All this is reminiscent of the indoctrination techniques of the
French revolutionary societies that were used on Vincent Ogé. As British historian Bryan Edwards, wrote in 1796; *"... it is not surprising that the
efforts of this society should have operated powerfully on the minds of those who
were taught to consider their personal wrongs as the cause of the Nation, and
driven some of them into the wildest excesses of fanaticism and fury."*

This was based on the notion that the emergence of a new nation
from the morass of colonialism and underdevelopment required leadership by charismatic personalities. This idea was also implicit in Lenin-
ism, which endowed "vanguard elites" (and their guiding spirit) with
quasi-sacral insights into the historical process. For many Williams
personified a messianic quality, in that he was not just a political leader,
but a spiritual leader too. The nation incarnated the spiritual yearnings
of a people, and he incarnated the nation. As such, he was perceived as
the "Father of the Nation." Dr. Williams' actions created a personality cult around himself, upon which a nationalistic ethos would even-

tually form.[197]   Out of this *hubris* emerged a political culture: One that would become entrenched in Williams' constituency, one that identified with him, one that in its collective memory had a shared understanding of the nature of colonial opprobrium, deprivation, prejudice and injustice. Having identified with the masses, and established empathy, he would now unmask the real reasons behind emancipation, and expose the conspiracy of colonialism. He asserted that it was based on the exploitation of a people purposely kept uneducated about their history. He would lead them out of ignorance. (Ryan 1988, xvii ff) *The People's Charter* demanded, amongst other things, immediate self-government in internal affairs and reform of local government. The creation of a welfare state was also a basic premise of the *Charter*. It stated that the "provision of social services as a matter of right and not of grace is a fundamental feature of progress in the modern world."

Williams cautioned labour that capital was nothing to be afraid of, and by the same token that capital must be responsive to the legitimate democratic and nationalistic aspirations of the worker. He sought to assuage some of the fears that had developed about his plans for education because of his outspoken hostility to the denominational schools. The *Charter's* statement of fundamental economic principles varied little from the ideas articulated earlier in his *Economic Problems of Trinidad and Tobago*, but it did say that within the movement there were people of "broadly socialist views." [198]

---

197 Economist and U.W.I. Lecturer Lloyd Best described this as "Doctor Politics"

198 Williams may have been referring to, amongst others, Margaret Wyke. Margaret Wyke, a person of colour, was born in the USA. She came to Trinidad in 1946. She was Asst. Secretary of Patrick Solomon's Caribbean Socialist Party and a member of The Co-operative Commonwealth Federation (CCF), a Canadian political party founded in 1932 by a number of socialist and labour groups and the League for Social Reconstruction. In 1944, it became the first socialist government in North America (based in Saskatchewan). Wyke was a member of the PNM General Council, Central Executive and Legislative Group. In 1960, she was a Director of PNM Publishing Co. Ltd., which was run by CLR James. She was a member of the West Indian Federal Senate. She received the OBE in 1963. (Smith, Lloyd: *Who, What & Why*, 1965, p. 844)

The *Charter* was followed at Independence in 1962 by his *History of the People of Trinidad and Tobago,* which has been described as the "iconic text" of the Afro-Creole narrative. (Brereton 2007, 4) Largely polemic in style, it condemned British influence. As a history of "the People," it makes almost no mention of the European colonial pioneers and their descendants, and their important role in the development of Trinidad and Tobago over 150 years. Apart from commenting on the efforts of Philippe Roume de Saint Laurent to implement the Cedula of 1783, Williams refers once to a member of the de Verteuil family and at another time to C. Léotaud. He remarks favourably on A.A. Cipriani's efforts on behalf of the "man in the street" and references Dr. Jean de Boissière (a relative of his mother Eliza), a late 19th century legislator, famous for his lack of contribution to the sittings of the Legislative Council, three times. (In *Columbus to Castro* de Boissière is referenced twice and A.A. Cipriani once.)

In this "iconic text," Dr. Williams may have originated racist attitudes and the scapegoating[199] of present day Trinidadians of European and in particular French descent. He virtually wrote this segment of the population out of his *History*, while in his public declarations "projecting onto them the blame for the evils of the plantation system." (Ryan 2009, 117) Williams, the messianic "Father of the Nation," now consigned the European-descended citizens of the new nation of Trinidad and Tobago to an exile from history. The impact of this omission, and the apportioning of inherited guilt was immediate, and cumulatively immeasurable.

His treatment of East Indians in his *History* also exiles half of the island's population from his historical narrative. The chapter "Contribution of the Indians" deals chiefly with Indian immigration and says nothing about the remarkable contribution that the Indian presence made to the financial, social, religious and cultural development of Trinidad and Tobago's civic institutions and that the presence of the East Indians, for example, distinguishes Trinidad and Tobago (with the exception of Guyana) from other

---

199 A scapegoat is a person who is blamed for the wrongdoings, mistkes and faults of others, generally as a way of distracting attention from the real causes and particularly for reasons of expediency.

West Indian territories. As I have shown, the roots of these prejudices go back to 19th century realities and have no relevance in these times, and Williams, as a middle class, coloured person, might have internalised the prejudices and stereotyping of Indians by people of his generation.

Summing up, far from being celebrated as "iconic", in *History of the People of Trinidad and Tobago* Williams assumes a position which, as a scholar on a national platform, in my view he should have avoided.

It begs the question: if the Williams narrative continues to inform Trinidad and Tobago's political culture, what will be the fate of these population segments, and who will be the next target of scapegoating and social and political marginalisation? The Syrian/Lebanese community? The newly arrived middle class?

Williams appears to have taken for granted the very many benefits of life in British colonial Trinidad and Tobago in the opening decades of the 20th century. The British Empire was liberal, compared to the Russian, Belgian, French, Dutch, and German Empires, but Williams expresses little respect for the historical process that had been evolving in British-ruled Trinidad and Tobago since the 1820s with regard to civil rights and the evolution of democratic institutions. [200] "Colonialism, of course, could not produce political equality; what it could, and at its *best* did provide was equality before the law. But the process of transfer, by making the vote the yardstick of progress, would leave the law to take care of itself." (Johnson 1991, 510) Williams described all ethnic groups in Trinidad and Tobago as "victims of the same subordination, all have been tarred by the same brush of political inferiority." To be "tarred by the same brush" [201] inferred that everyone had something to be ashamed of, be guilty of, or perhaps to hide. Was this so with everyone in the colony? Or was this peculiar only to some?

---

200 J.B. Philippe's *A Free Mulatto* was an important civil rights document. The evolution of legislative reform, and the exercise of the franchise, although limited, was crucial.

201 An 18th century term used in sheep farming, meaning all having had the same faults or bad qualities. The term was transferred to likeness in human beings in the early 1800s. "Touch of the tar brush" implies having African blood in European-appearing people.

Williams, like most of his Third World colleagues, was to spend the rest of his life exploiting the very flexible notion of democracy. A great many ex-colonial peoples, on gaining Independence, thought that they were being given justice, in truth all they got was the right to elect politicians. At the end of the day, to a great many people democracy matters less than the rule of law: the first is the form, the second is the substance. Narratives and interpretations of history change, they come and go, but an independent judiciary and a free press must, for all time, be maintained.

A vast quantity of the people of Trinidad and Tobago, from various ethnic backgrounds and walks of life would, over time, benefit materially and psychologically from what Williams would describe as the 'PNM revolution'. These were well placed to benefit from the evolving Williams narrative. But as the colonial period drew to a close, there was also a large quantity of people from various ethnic backgrounds who did not see themselves primarily as *victims of colonial oppression*, but on the contrary, as responsible and honest, perhaps even as *victors* of the system. They had taken advantage of all opportunities that the British colonial system offered. They were living and enjoying what I identified earlier as an Afro-French Creole subculture, one that served to create their identity in that it was *subversive* to the oppressive British colonial system. Perhaps because of its subversiveness, Williams, once in power and with perhaps a personal grudge against it, created a narrative that was to weaken the perception that the Afro-French Creole subculture was a positive force in the national fabric of Trinidad and Tobago. Many of its members would in time begin to feel themselves victims of the charismatic leader who thought of himself as a victim of the colonial experience.

THE NEUROSIS MANIFESTS
5

As has been outlined in the previous chapter, Williams' political personality had been shaped to a considerable degree by deep feelings of deprivation. This was as a result of how his family had been treated by those perceived by the Williams' as having power over their quality of life and place in colonial society.

Humiliating disappointments had blighted the future of his father in the form of stolen and unhonoured inheritances by the middle class, coloured, "*café au lait*" Smith-Hunt extended family. On his mother's side, there were the people who had adjudicated over his grandfather's will: members of the European-descended de Boissière family, prominent in both government circles and in the French Creole minority during the first decades of the 20th century. All of this had happened against the backdrop of the colonial society of the time, which would have accommodated these wrongs. It was exacerbated when Williams ventured into the "real world" where he experienced racial prejudice, snobbery and lack of opportunity at Oxford University and at the Caribbean Commission in Port-of-Spain. In all instances, he perceived race prejudice as the source of these slights. [202]

He wrote to Norman Manley in the early 1950s, recounting his humiliations:

> "I was denied a fellowship at Oxford, I have always been convinced it was on racial grounds … Taylor did not want me in Mona ….. Macpherson tried to get me out of the Commission in 1945 because of the *Negro in the Caribbean* … Now de Vriendt does not want me. What am I to do, cut sugar cane? They threatened to fail my doctor's thesis because

202 Williams may have seen Reginald Coupland, Professor of Imperial History at Oxford, as a prime example of the apologists for the British Colonial system. See *Capitalism and Slavery*, (1964) pages 45, 178, 188, 211. Coupland may have seemed Massa personified. Williams wrote of Coupland: "… men who have sacrificed scholarship to sentimentality and, like the scholastics of old, placed faith before reason and evidence."

they did not like my view; the British never ceased attacking me for *Capitalism and Slavery* ... Local representatives are always opposing my views ... This impertinent persecution ... I am sick to death of it all ... If they do not want to deal with me as a research worker, perhaps they prefer to deal with me as a legislator." (Deosaran 1981, 22)

Feeling persecuted, Williams became threatening. He would seize power in compensation for his distress, and take control of his destiny by entering Trinidad and Tobago's political arena. He would legislate "Massa" out of existence.

Psychologists see striving for power as a way of compensating for perceived inadequacies. Deosaran remarks: "While power striving is an attempt to heal a psychological wound, it goes on to open up new wounds which propel the individual into searching for further power, or at least a sense of having further power." (1981, 12)

 In the 1956 elections, Williams' party, the PNM, just managed to get into government. Kenneth Lalla comments on the 1961 elections and quotes Dr. Selwyn Ryan: "As a forerunner to the 1961 general elections, the PNM government announced its intention not only to re-draw the electoral boundaries, but also to compile a new voters' registration and to introduce voting machines." (1995, 225)

The Democratic Labour Party's (DLP) reaction to these proposals was to point out that their new voting arrangements were calculated to curtail the voting strength of the Indians, which had been demonstrated as being significant against the PNM in the 1958 federal elections. They further argued that the replacement of the ballot box by voting machines was also designed to frustrate illiterate Indians. Did the PNM manipulate the distribution of the voting population on a racial and class basis so as to give more seats to the PNM? On this issue, Dr. Selwyn Ryan commented:

"The PNM took no chances even in Port-of-Spain, where the boundaries were redrafted, to make sure that all potential DLP areas, i.e. the upper class and upper middle-class residential areas, (where a great many Europeans, French Creoles and other well-off people, some black and coloured middle class, as well as Chinese, Syrians etc. resided) were attached to working class areas where the PNM had been consistently strong. The DLP was not given an outside chance to gain a seat in the capital city as they had done in the 1958 and 1959 municipal elections. In the countryside, there was strong evidence to substantiate the DLP claim that the PNM had herded as many Indian voters as was possible into constituencies which they could not possibly win, and had extracted from such areas large blocks of Negro voters who were then recombined into the other constituencies." (1995, 225)

Having put this electoral apparatus that would secure the PNM's victory at the polls into place through the re-drafting of the electoral boundaries, Williams in the 1961 election campaign was abruptly challenged by having to face an emotionally highly charged subject, the appearance in the election race, significant opponents whom he would dub "Massa."

This occurred rather suddenly when two individuals appeared on the election scene: the *Trinidad Guardian* announced that Sir Gerald Wight had declared his support for the Democratic Labour Party (DLP) and that Michael Rogers Pocock had been named honorary secretary of the Party of Political Progress Groups (POPPG). Williams had to deal with this, his oldest *bête noire,* and exorcise from his own psyche what these men symbolised for him.

Sir Gerald Wight was a political opponent supported by the business community and the *Trinidad Guardian*. [203] He would have personified "Massa" for Williams. (Deosaran 1981, 117) Many felt that Wight had been the target of Williams' acrimonious and invective-filled speech in Woodford Square in December 1960 when the announcement appeared.

This was followed by another, perhaps even more vehement speech in Woodford Square on March 22, 1961, filled with *"fanaticism and fury"* described as "extraordinary, . . . with unusual vehemence, even for him". (Palmer 2006, 28) In this speech, Williams made an all out racial attack on the European-descended minority and attacked the DLP. In this diatribe, Williams was able to link his anger and hate of the class that Wight

---

203 The *Trinidad Guardian* was founded in 1917 by George Huggins, Albert Cipriani, L.A.P. O'Reilly, Edward Pitts, T. Geddes Grant, Sir Norman Lamont, and H.A. Wight. In 1958 the *Guardian* was acquired by Baron Thompson of Fleet. In 1974 the paper was bought by the McEnearney-Alstons Group of companies.

and Pocock represented to the Indian community who formed the majority in the DLP.

Colin Palmer quotes Williams as saying, "Massa still has his stooges, who prefer to crawl on their bellies to Massa ... that they are as much the stooges of Massa of the 20th century as the house slaves were of Massa's eighteenth century counterpart." (ibid) Williams, as I observed earlier, immersed in the 18th century, would add later, "The period of Massa's ascendency, the period of Massa's domination over workers who had no rights under the law, the period of Massa's enforcement of

Dr. Williams in full flight, addressing a large crowd of followers in Woodford Square in the 1960s (T'dad. Express)

a barbarous code of industrial relations long after it was repudiated by the conscience of the civilised world, lasted in our society for almost 300 years ..." (ibid) And "...this pack of benighted idiots, this band of obscurantists politicians, this unholy alliance of egregious [outstandingly bad, shocking] individualists who have nothing constructive to say." [204] Directing his attack to his Indian opponents who he had described as "recalcitrant" (unco-operative to authority or discipline?) he accused the DLP, a political party whose membership was mainly comprised of Trinidadians of Indian descent, "of deliberately being the stooge of the Massas who still exist in our society. I accuse the DLP of deliberately trying to keep back social progress. I accuse the DLP of wanting to bring back Massa Day... I say Massa Day Done."

Gerald Wight was a modern-minded English Creole businessman, born in Port-of-Spain in 1898. He had been educated at Queen's Royal

204 Cudjoe, *Eric E Williams Speaks,* p. 239, in Palmer 2006, p 23.

College and Charterhouse School, England. He was a decorated World War I fighter pilot and an all-round sportsman. These attributes were highly regarded at the time and a great many public figures, and sporting personalities for example, cricketers Jeffery Stollmeyer and Gerry Gomez, were idolised by the general population, notwithstanding their ethnicity.

Wight was the president of the Alstons Group of Companies, and arguably the most powerful "local man" in the colony. [205] George Alston and Co. had been founded in 1881 by George and Louis Alston, sons of James Alston,[206] a Scottish merchant of San Fernando, who had arrived in Trinidad in1835, and a woman of partly African descent.

Because of Wight's general popularity, his decision to return to politics and to become a leading figure in the DLP, despite his evident illness, (Wight suffered from pulmonary emphysema and had resigned from the Legislative Council because of ill health soon after his election, but was persuaded to return to politics by his daughter, Ann, niece of Sir Harold Robinson.) was, despite Williams' electoral arrangements, an upsetting prospect. His return was in truth an important boost to the DLP. Wight brought considerable credibility to the party. He was able to command the respect of black and mixed-race people and attract the support of a cross-section of the working class as well as voters of East Indian de-

---

205 Wight could be credited with spearheading the island's manufacturing sector by establishing the firms Trinidad Clay Products (later ABEL), the Caribbean Development Company (brewers of Carib beer) and Tugs and Lighters (slipways, docks and ship repair yards) Geo. Alston and Co. employed a large cross section of the population in their substantial commission agency, shipping, insurance, import and export and distribution businesses. Among them were hundreds of waterfront workers, the majority of whom lived in East Port-of-Spain and Laventille, men who formed an integral part of the Port-of-Spain East constituency.

206 George and Louis Alston married the daughters of Dr. Robert Knaggs, of English descent, the sisters of Hon. Samuel Knaggs C.M.G. Samuel Knaggs held several important posts in Trinidad's colonial service. He was Acting Auditor General in 1897 and 1901, Receiver General in 1900, Chief Commissioner of Port-of-Spain 1899 to 1903, and acting Governor from 1903 to 1906. The Alston/Knaggs family could be seen as the most influential mixed (black and English), extended family in colonial Trinidad and Tobago in the period before the Second World War.

scent because of his connections to Sir
Harold Robinson's family. [207]

Wight had been a nominated member of the colony's Legislative Council
from 1941 to 1946. In 1945, Wight had
formed the Progressive Democratic Party
(PDP) with a programme for agricultural
advancement, a prosperous peasantry, assistance for local industry and removal of
trade restrictions. The PDP was the forerunner of the Party of Political Groups
(PPG), which contested the 1950 elections. Wight had won a seat, becoming
the first Deputy Speaker under the new
constitution. The PPG would merge with
the POPPG, which was led by veteran
politician Albert Gomes. Gomes was of

Lieut-Col. George R. G. Alston O.B.E.
M.C. son of the founder of Alstons Ltd.
(Wight)

Portuguese descent and decidedly "a man of the people" who had had a
long political career representing the interest of the black working class. [208]
This party was a somewhat disorganised collection of independent political personalities, and would be successfully positioned by Williams as representing business interests, French Creoles and the Catholic Church,[209]

207 Sir Harold, whose mother was said to be of East Indian descent, was managing direc-
      tor of Woodford Lodge Estates Ltd. and president of the Sugar Manufactures Asso-
      ciation; director of the Citrus Growers Association of Trinidad; director of B.W.I.A.
      and most likely the colony's leading spokesman in the agricultural sector.

208 Roy Joseph, another politician of Syrian descent at the time, and Albert Gomes
      would not have been seen as "Massa" by Eric Williams. Both the Portuguese and
      Syrian/Lebanese minorities were not generally perceived as members of the ruling
      class, as the British or French Creoles were, and were not "socially white".

209 In 1956 Roman Catholics numbered 235,500, 120 churches; Church of England
      165,000, 105 churches; Presbyterians 22,000; Methodist 16,000, 32 churches; Sev-
      enth Day Adventists 20,755; Moravian 9,000; Church of the Nazarene 2,000, 9
      churches; Church of God 1,200; Christian Science 2,000; African Episcopal 25,000;
      Jewish Community 5,000; Hindus 151,000; Mohammedans 60,000; other 10,900.

Sir Gerald Wight was the leading business personality of the day. Perceived as a liberal, he had the potential of crossing over into several segments of the society. (Wight)

all of whom would be portrayed by him as egregious enemies of black people.

In 1957, the POPPG, the Trinidad Labour Party (TLP), which represented some aspects of the Labour movement, and the PDP, which had been created in 1953 by Badase Maraj, also a veteran politician, merged to form the DLP. This party commanded the mass support of the Hindus and generally Indian rural agricultural workers. [210]

Alongside Wight, the other man who would have fed, perhaps even more voraciously directly into Williams' neurosis as a "Massa" was the honorary secretary of the POPPG,[211] Michael Pocock. Youthful and idealistic, he brought a fresh impetus to the party. [212] Pocock was an Al-

---

(Smith *Who, What and Why,* 1955-56)

210 It seems inconceivable today that Williams could portray modern 20th century people who were agriculturalists, cane farmers, workers, and in business as living replicas of 18th century slave masters, and that this would be believed by the black masses, to the extent that the agriculturists and business people of today are still perceived as agents of an antique enemy, and that attempts by people to form political movements that are not obviously Indo or Afro based can build no "grass root" support and are doomed to fail.

211 Party of Political Progress Groups, founded 1947 as Political Progress Group and in 1953 re-named Party of Political Progress Group. Approximate membership in 1956, 1,800. President, Dr. A.G.. Francis; vice-president and chairman, L.Randall Duprey; honorary secretary, M.R. Pocock; party secretary; A.F. Raymond.

212 Interviews with Michael Pocock (in1987) former honorary secretary of the POPPG; John Sellier, former director of Alstons Ltd.; and Gregory Wight, grandson of Sir Gerald Wight. The Robinsons, and by association the Wights, could have been seen as the most influential family of mixed East Indian and English descent in the colony in the period after the Second World War.

stons executive and highly visible. He appeared regularly on the DLP hustings at various venues together with Wight in 1960/61. Pocock was a link between the business interest that helped to finance the DLP and the party executive. In conversations with the author in 1987, Pocock recalls writing speeches for some party members, and helping to organise publicity and strategy during this election campaign.

Michael Rogers Pocock was the honorary secretary of the POPPG and a senior executive of Alstons Ltd. as well as a close associate of Sir Gerald Wight. He was Williams' cousin on his mother's side. (Pocock)

Pocock was a third cousin of Eric Williams. His mother Jeanne was born a de Boissière, one of Eric Williams' mother's relatives, and also a manager of Alstons. Poleska de Boissière, Jeanne's grandmother, was the person who had reputedly prevented Jules Boissière, Williams' grandfather, from inheriting a legacy of $4,000. One could therefore well understand the emotions Michael Pocock's appearance in the election campaign, together with Sir Gerald Wight, must have evoked in Williams.

He may have felt angry, and that he must rid himself of these people once and for all.

Even though he had once described Wight as "a liberal-minded businessman," Williams may have perceived him suddenly as a serious long-term political contender, perhaps because he thought of Albert Gomes as a spent force. Hitherto, Williams had thought of the DLP and their leaders Badase Sagan Maraj and later Dr. Rudranath Capildeo with little political respect or otherwise, as "benighted idiots," "recalcitrant" and "nincompoops." In my view, he was expressing the dislike and deep-seated prejudices felt by most Afro-Creoles towards Indians. With Wight's and Pocock's sudden appearance, however, Williams may have sensed a much

Sir Harold Robinson was the leading agriculturist of the 1940s and 50s.
(Camps-Campins)

more acute threat, that of Wight rallying Gomes' old support base and splitting the black vote.

Williams reacted in keeping with his neurosis. He launched an all out racist attack on "Massa." "Massa Day Done" speeches became a necessity for Williams to maintain his self esteem and to assume the role of a powerful aggressor.

There had been earlier manifestations of this neurotic behaviour and the valve of temporary well-being that it achieved for Williams. For example, in 1956, a vitriolic attack against the Indian community in a speech at Woodford Square is described by Winston Mahabir, at the time a fellow PNM founder member. Arriving at Williams' residence after the speech, Mahabir (a medical doctor) describes Williams as "the conqueror, in an exuberant, gloating, hypomanic mood of triumph. He had obviously gained exquisite emotional satisfaction from his diatribe against the Indians." (1978,79) Already at this early stage in Williams' political career, Mahabir is able to identify the need for a scapegoat in Williams — in this case, people in reaction to that particular speech recommended to Mahabir to leave the PNM, stating "that I would then become yet another scapegoat[213] for Williams' fury with further deterioration in race relations in the country." (ibid)

In the case of Wight and the DLP, Williams characterised them as "French Creoles" (which Wight was not), apportioning to them the inherited guilt of slave masters, "Massas" (which Williams' own ancestors

---

213 A medical definition of scapegoating is: "Process in which the mechanisms of projection or displacement are utilised in focusing feelings of aggression, hostility, frustration, etc., upon another individual or group; the amount of blame being unwarranted."

actually were). He knew very well that in truth, the Alstons, Wight, Pocock and Robinson, like a great many other people, represented the island's racial diversity and miscegenation. The Alstons (Wight's and Pocock's employers) were coloured people. Wight was of English descent, whose parents or grandparents had come to the island after the emancipation of the slaves. Wight's brother-in-law, Sir Harold Robinson, was said to be of East Indian and Barbadian heritage, and Pocock had a French Creole mother, a de Boissière, and an English father.

Because Williams was trusted as an authority, a repository of truth, and was an excellent public speaker, only a few realised that he was speaking metaphorically when he labeled these men as "Massas." There were many who understood that what he was really accomplishing was the scapegoating of an ethnic minority, while dealing agonisingly with the worst of his personal *bête noirs*. [214]

Another alarming example of Williams' tendency to take on personal vendettas against his relatives and mix them up in his politics was his attack on the press, where he described the fourth estate as "venal" (susceptible to bribery) and accused it of pursuing a vendetta against his newly-formed political party. [215] During this period, the *Trinidad Guardian* was literally "the press," representing legitimacy and credibility. This attack against the press, although brief, was alarming for the public, as in other former colonies totalitarian regimes were muzzling the press.

A third individual who could have triggered Williams' neurotic behaviour was the editor of the *Trinidad Guardian* during this period, Charles Sydney Espinet, [216] whose mother was a member of the coloured Hunt

---

214 It should be noted that Williams was speaking 125 years after the emancipation of the slaves and 154 years after the abolition of the slave trade in the British Empire.

215 In April of 1960, Williams burnt in a bonfire in Woodford Square what he described as the seven deadly sins: the existing constitution of Trinidad & Tobago & the West Indies, the 1941 Anglo-American Bases Agreement [that would effectively remove American forces stationed here], the Report of the 1956 Capital Site Commission recommending against Trinidad, the Telephone Ordinance, the Democratic Labour Party's manifesto and the *Trinidad Guardian*.

216 Charles Sydney Espinet joined the *Trinidad Guardian* in 1931, became news editor in 1956. Editor of the *Trinidad Guardian* 1961-1965. Was a director of the Trinidad

Frederick Hubert and Sarah Eugenia Espinet (née Hunt) with their sons (left-right)
Cedric, Vernon, Charles Sydney, Kenrick and Wilfred. (Espinet)

family, and as such a relative of Williams. In discussing this period with Espinet's daughters, they recalled a mutual friend, Andrew Carr, bringing Williams to "Verdant Vale," their Diego Martin home. The meeting, as they remember it, was unpleasant, and perhaps disappointing for their father. Williams appeared to be "irritated" with their father, they supposed because of his questions. Of Espinet's attempts to be supportive of Williams they said, "… Eric was vex with our father, from before [the elections of 1956]." The meeting did not go well. They recalled the relationship between their grandmother, Sarah Espinet[217] née Hunt and the Williams family.

Thomas Williams, Williams' father, was Sarah Espinet's second cousin, she was the granddaughter of Louis Hunt. Louis' sister, Onemia Williams, née Hunt was Williams' father's mother. Louis Hunt was the person who

---

Publishing Co. Ltd. He had studied journalism in the U.K. in he early 1950s.
217 Williams' great uncle Louis Hunt had married Sarah Dyer of Montserrat. Their son Charles married Victoria Hall, also of Montserrat. Their daughter Sarah married Frederick Espinet, of Trinidad; their son was Charles Sydney Espinet.

*Sarah Espinet née Hunt, left, and Olive Willoughby née Hunt, right, were the
daughters of Charles Hunt and his wife Victoria Hall, relatives of the Williams' who maintained contact with them in the 1930s and 40s (Espinet)*

had induced Onemia to sign away her rights to properties left to them in
trust by their parents Jean Baptiste Hunt and Phillippa Susanna Hunt née
Smith. The Espinet sisters remember that their grandmother would go to
the Williams' when they lived at Murray Street in the late 1930s and1940s.
They also recalled that their great aunt, Priscilla Foyer (Sarah Espinet née
Hunt's aunt), lived at 45 Oxford Street in Port-of-Spain in 1913, and supposed that that was where Eliza and Thomas Henry Williams may have
stayed in the period after Eric had been born at Dundonald Street. They
recalled that their parents were puzzled by Williams' attitude. They, the
daughters, had at the time no knowledge of the family's contentious past.
However, it may be confidently assumed that Williams had that knowledge, being older than they, and coming from the aggrieved side. His
parents' feelings when receiving Sarah Espinet's charitable visits, while
knowing that her grandfather may have defrauded them of an inheritance,
perhaps twice, may only be imagined. Now faced with the need to meet
Sarah's son, the editor of the island's leading newspaper, Williams could
have had some very mixed emotions.

The appearance of people side-by-side in the election campaign who
symbolised Williams' social insecurities and inhibitions, prompted anxi-

ety and bitter words spoken in anger in Williams, indicating pathological changes associated with a neurosis. A scapegoat needed to be found, and Williams created one in the form of "Massa", which he defined as being synonymous with 20th century business interest the European-descended minority and the coloured middle class on the whole. This was the scapegoat constructed by Williams to divert all opposition against the PNM. In a series of public speeches, Williams clearly identified the local European-descended community, "business big-shot families" as he called them, and in particular the French Creoles, as "Massa", inferring that these 20th century Trinidadians were the inheritors of the guilt of 18th century slave owners (to whom in fact they may or may not have been related). He announced that the merchant families (in fact mostly of Scottish descent and not necessarily former slave owners) and the French Creoles (who worked mostly in the civil service, in the private sector and in agriculture and were generally not business big shots), were determined to push Trinidad and Tobago back into slavery, and suggested that he would like to send some of them to Cuba "for Castro to do a little purging."[218] He would declare "if I started to use history as the murderous ruthless weapon that it could become in my hands, boy I am sorry for them." (Ryan 2009, 287f) He evoked the image of the French Creoles (and the DLP) having their "blasted hands at your throats" or trying to get them back there." He even gave listeners the permission to "cut their throats if you wish" (ibid.), reminding them that violence was nothing new to Trinidad and Tobago. (Perhaps he meant Grenada.) The East Indian DLP supporters, mostly

---

218 The "purges" carried out in Cuba at the time had meant the death of hundreds, perhaps thousands of people (in such a closed society no one actually knows how many people were "purged"). The "purges" undertaken by Lenin and Stalin in the Soviet Union not long before had involved the deaths of tens of millions. People in Trinidad and Tobago were aware of what the word "purge" meant.

In making quite separate segments of the European-descended residents all "French Creoles" and belonging to a class, Williams was acting well in keeping with Joseph Stalin's criteria in his launching of class war in Russia, in which millions died.

Today, even in academia, certainly in "calypso truth", Syrians, mixed race people, French Creoles, British, American, any ordinary white-appearing person is often referred to as a "French Creole". History has shown that such stereotyping could have terrible results.

cane farmers, also came in for harsh criticism in supporting "Massa" and for being "the shoe-shine boys for the planters and merchants in Port-of-Spain" who wished to "return to the old practices whereby troops and scabs were used to break strikes." (Ryan 2009, 289ff.)

"Massa Day Done" not only dealt with the failures of British colonialism but also evoked both the horrors of slavery and the terror of totalitarianism. Elements of the population, black, white, and Indian, reacted in fear. Some of the whites felt personally threatened as being made personally culpable for the atrocities of slavery (especially the French Creoles). There was a public outcry; not surprisingly, because it was by no means certain that the belligerent metaphors that Williams used were not going to be taken literally and provoke state-authorised misappropriation of property and ultimately bloodshed.

To many this was appalling, bearing in mind what was taking place in other former colonies. Not just the European-descended population and the coloured, mixed-race people were frightened, but also black people from various walks of life, to whom such language was abhorrent.

Strong criticism came from several quarters. The respected clergyman Canon Max Farquhar remarked that it was time for Williams to assume a more responsible role and project the image "of a sober and responsible statesman." (Ryan 2009, 291)

Rudranath Capildeo stated that Williams had re-directed frustrations, which would normally at election time be focused on the British colonial government and the local administration, to minority elements within the population who were made the acceptable targets of blame. He said "Woodford Square had become a shrine of hate where minorities were offered up for sacrifice." (ibid)

Albert Gomes in an article in the *Trinidad Guardian* of 19 November 1961 writes that "thousands of people in Trinidad and Tobago who desired the same change that he did, disagreed entirely with both the methods by which he introduced such changes and the venomous character he imparted to the actual changes." According to Gomes, these people did not want "to establish the status quo ante but to retrieve some of the order and the goodwill and the ordinary decency without which, no matter the ostensible gains, progress was not worthwhile." (Ryan 2009, 294ff)

Elections 1956: Tremendous joy, jubilation and celebration were evident on the smiling faces of this crowd, as the streets of Port-of-Spain took on a carnival euphoria. A sense of victory and a promise of freedom filled the hearts of tens of thousands as the results of the election came in. (T'dad. Express)

Over the next few weeks Williams, concerned that he might have alienated voters, was at pains to explain what he had meant by those speeches. Publishing a commentary in the PNM weekly, *The Nation*, he all but admitted that he had committed a 'gaff' overreacted to the people he had seen on the DLP's election platform, and began to obfuscate his outburst:

"On 4 December 1960 the *Trinidad Guardian* announced that Sir Gerald Wight had joined the Democratic Labour Party. The announcement was presented in such a way as to suggest that this was a feather in the cap of the Democratic Labour Party (DLP), and therefore the citizens of Trinidad and Tobago should follow the lead of Sir Gerald Wight. Consequently, in my address here in the University on 22 December, in which I reported to the people the outcome of the Chaguaramas discussions in Tobago, I poured scorn on the *Guardian* reminding them that our population of today was far too alert and sophisticated to fall for any such claptrap.

I told the *Guardian* emphatically: Massa Day Done. What was Massa Day, the Massa Day that is done? Who is Massa? Massa was more often than not an absentee European planter exploiting West Indian resources, both human and economic. I had particularly referred in my address in the University be-

fore Christmas to a book well known to students of West Indian history written by an absentee English landlord who visited his plantations in Jamaica for
the first time around 1815." [219]

Williams explained that "Massa was generally white . . . not all whites
were Massa, at the same time not all Massas were white." Enunciating that
"Massa is not a racial term. Massa is the symbol of a bygone age. Massa Day is a social phenomenon: Massa Day Done connotes a political
awakening and a social revolution," he qualified it by saying that Massa
was the absentee European planter, employing unfree labour, growing
sugar and nothing but sugar" (Williams 1942, 264f), indicating perhaps a distinction between a local French Creole cocoa planter and an
absentee landlord of more than one hundred and forty five years before.
"Massa" he said, was a metaphor for those whom he had exposed in
his thesis, who had conspired to lie to the people about the reasons for
abolishing slavery.

The damage, however, had been done. To many people today who
were not yet born in 1961, Williams' words would remain as statements
of truth that stereotyped both the European and Indian elements in the
society. No amount of explaining away and recanting would obliterate
this notion. Stereotypes had been established, scapegoats named. *Alea
iacta est*; the die was cast by "the father of the nation" in which the political culture of Trinidad and Tobago would be formed and in the future be
manipulated. The post-colonial narrative, the Williams narrative, having
being constructed, it was now politicised.

I would also postulate in line with the theories posited by Hagen and
Kunczik that behind all his ranting against "Massa" was the profound
yearning of the deprived person combined with an above-average high
regard for this segment of society "whose traditional structure of values
he had internalised" but which had utterly eluded him.

"The DLP," (Wight, Robinson and Pocock? Surely not the Indians?)
Williams claimed ". . . wanted to stop the revolution and restore the old

---

219 Massa Day Done (Public Lecture at Woodford Square, 22 March 1961)
  Callaloo - Volume 20, Number 4, Fall 1997, pp. 725-730

order with its social practices that have kept you and me where we have been with all our *frustrations and inhibitions*. But if there is one thing I am going to do in this election, it is to mobilise the whole force of national decency to defeat once and for all the DLP and their reactionary tendencies." (emphasis mine)

The frustrations and inhibitions: "Here perhaps is the 'smoking gun' that links Williams, the 'frustrated black French Creole', to his political and social war against the white French Creoles, who had refused to treat him and his immediate family as part of the kin." (Ryan 2009, 289f) These remarks may also demonstrate his psychological link to the Grenadian Free Coloured Republican revolutionaries of the 1790s. Williams positioned himself firmly in the tradition of the 18th century free coloured revolutionaries, fighting for political awakening and social revolution against the backdrop of 18th century societal conditions; and not against those of the latter half of the 20th. This notion of Williams acting in the tradition of the mulatto revolutionaries also seemed to advance the theory that Afro-Creoles alone were the "true inheritors" of the post-colonial legacy, and that the non-Afro-Creole ethnic groups should "suppress their cultures" in the pursuit of his ideal of nationalism. This was a fairly exclusive view; and to me echoes what I would surmise to have been the mindset of Julien Fédon, Joachim Phillip, Stanislas Besson and the other Grenadian revolutionaries: so convinced were they of their cultural and political righteousness that their instinct of compassion and inclusiveness got suppressed, and they resorted to murder and violation of another ethnic minority.

In those speeches and in the 1961 election campaign, Eric Williams fought hard to expiate, to exorcise, the burden, the curse of previous generations of his family, the opprobrium of deprivation and victimhood, imposed by "Massa." Few realised that this probably lay at the core of Williams' political personality.

In his attempt to vanquish the "Massas" and to expiate his own feelings of deprivation, Williams had overshot his goal and given the average moderate person, of whatever background, a solid reason to oppose and to even dislike him. Williams had provoked a dissonance between himself

and the society which "he regarded highly, and whose traditional structure of values he had internalised," (ref. Hagen/Kunczik), and in order to
re-establish consonance he made a series of moves to the political right
in the months that followed. This included the firing of his old teacher
C.L.R. James from his position in the PNM as well as negotiations with
the American and the British governments.

In addressing a society that was certainly ill-paid but largely not dis-
inherited and dispossessed by the 1960s, who were basically educated
(mostly primary school) and firmly set on a path to Independence and
progress, he established a political culture that generalised his own neurotic character and projected it onto his constituency:

> "Hold up your heads high, all of you, the disinherited and dispossessed,
> brought here in the lowest states of degradation to work on a sugar plan-
> tation or cocoa estate for Massa." [This was said in 1961, almost 125 years
> after the emancipation of the slaves.] "All of you, don't hang your heads
> in shame. You are today taking over this country from the Massa's hand.
> . . . In the last five years I have symbolised, as the head of the Govern-
> ment, the determination of the PNM and the majority of the people of
> the country never to allow Massa to have the privileges that he has had in
> the fifty or a hundred years before." (Ryan 2009, 193)

Williams was to be haunted by the idea that "Massa" had not been per-
manently exorcised. Gordon Rohlehr points out in his essay *Apocalypso
and the Soca Fires of 1990* (1992, 324):

> "Williams never forgot that the old money was alive, and as late as the
> late seventies he was still talking about the POPPG as being a threat to
> what the PNM stood for, though the POPPG as a formal unit had dis-
> integrated in the fifties, and the conglomeration of business, class and
> ethnic interest represented by that party had long formed other and
> more complex alignments in Independent Trinidad and Tobago."

"Dr. Williams would be seriously troubled by an apparent irrational
fear of conspirators and of conspiracies throughout his life," as Professor
Ken Boodhoo notes in his book *The Elusive Eric Williams* (174). Boodhoo
remarks that Winston Mahabir, a colleague of Williams, had catalogued
Williams' suspicious nature, which included misconceived threats to his
leadership from Patrick Solomon, his fear of being poisoned, of a Chinese

conspiracy and of radiation from the U.S. naval base at Chaguaramas. Williams also feared that his former teacher and mentor, C.L.R. James, was hatching a conspiracy against him, which might well have been the case, as they parted company somewhat acrimoniously in the 1960s after the "Massa Day Done" outburst. (ibid)

Williams' apologists today point out that there was a great difference between his rhetoric and his actions. This is entirely true. His rhetoric, however, was of that time; and his actions were to unfold over time.

The polemics of race, over time, would inform the political culture of the future and contribute to the polarisation of the society. The polemics of guilt and victimhood would contribute to the apparent collapse of civic and moral responsibility, particularly in public life, and instill ideas of undeserved entitlement in the general population. The ongoing erosion of the instinct for compassion and of the principles concerning the distinction between right and wrong or good or bad behaviour has produced a cheapening of human life in Trinidad and Tobago. This is apparent in the weary acceptance of murder, averaging at times three or four a day over the last several years.

It has been suggested that Williams' "style persistently reflected elements of revenge ..." said Deosaran in 1981, [220] and added in a personal communication to me in 2009: "A large part of our individual irresponsibility and amoral culture has seeped into the minds of even our young population, so that the future will be occupied with the Williams syndrome for quite some time." With these politics of victimhood [221] and guilt, Williams was eminently successful. What is of interest is the extent to which Williams' political culture that may have emerged from his 19th

---

220 Gordon Rohlehr notes in his essay *My Strangled City:* "The meticulous citation of facts and figures was a necessary defense against the accusation which is still being made about *Capitalism and Slavery,* that Williams as a black man was simply trying to write history as revenge" (*History as Absurdity,* p. 22)

221 The politics of victimhood is perpetuated by keeping a very large segment of the overall population deprived of their basic needs; water, sanitation, health care, justice, security, a knowledge of its history, geography and social science, a useful education. They are made to believe that they are dependent on the government for jobs, handouts, patronage, and entitlements. They are abandoned in the slums of the East/ West corridor to be manipulated by racial impulses at elections.

H.R.H The Princess Royal, and the Right Honourable Dr. Eric Williams take time out
during the Independence celebrations at Governor General's House in 1962, overlooked
by H.R.H's niece, Her Majesty, Queen Elizabeth II . (Photo, George Peters)

century socialisation still lives (and sings) in Trinidad and Tobago of today. In 1985 calypsonian Chalkdust (Dr. Hollis Urban Lester Liverpool, a
teacher who holds to this day various positions in the public administration of culture) sang *Grandfather's Backpay,* in which he gave:

> "a local face and a name (to the ruling class which has passed down its
> wealth and its attitude of arrogance to succeeding generations of ex-
> ploiters): "it is them French Creoles!" The family names that Chalkdust
> lists as French Creole are both well-known French Creole names and

names of English and Scottish Protestants. French Creoles in *Grand-father's Backpay* includes cocoa and citrus farmers, merchants and proprietors, all united by an instinct to exploit the faithful but landless black worker-victim. (. . .) He becomes the harbinger of the new era, one that has been fraught with the identification and the slaughter of scapegoats." [222]

In 1992, Chalkdust in his song *Trinidad ent change* picked up another of Williams' paranoias, contending that the old POPPG was now the NAR, and that racist attitudes were perfectly acceptable as long as they were directed at white people. Chalkdust went on to identify "dem French Creoles' as the perpetual enemies of black people. [223] As Rohlehr says:

> "Chalkdust must be viewed as a major enforcer of the Eric Williams-engendered notion that the PNM as a party of black people were still being threatened by the POPPG, a party of French Creoles, big businessmen, the old mulatto and off white upper middle class whose return to power, authority and visibility under the NAR was most bitterly resented by the new black Yuppie professionals." [224]

This is the working example of the Williams syndrome, and why we, as a people, must refute and condemn racism, especially when it comes under the guise of the "calypso truth."

---

222 Rohlehr, Gordon *The Shape of That Hurt* p. 319 f
223 ibid. p. 320
224 ibid. p. 324

THE AFRO-FRENCH CREOLE NARRATIVE
6

The genesis of the Afro-French Creole narrative in Trinidad commences with the Cedula of Population of 1783, [225] and was to continue with the work of J.B. Philippe's *Free Mulatto* (1824), in the history writings of E.L. Joseph, including his novel *Warner Arundell, The Adventures of a Creole* (1838), L.A.A. de Verteuil's *Trinidad* (London, 1858), J.J. Thomas' *Creole Grammar* (Port-of-Spain 1869) and *Froudacity* (London, 1889), P.G.L. Borde's *The History of Trinidad under the Spanish Government* in two volumes (Paris, 1876 and 1882), and I. Bodu's *Trinidadiana* (1890). There were also newspapers written in French and various other literary forms; for example, the works of poetry by Sylvester (Sylvio) Devenish and Léon de Gannes, the more recent writings of Derek Walcott, and many other poets; the work of historians and other academics at the UWI; as well as oral traditions, the carnival arts, folklore and folk traditions, and both early and recent calypso forms.

Michael Pocock's *Out of the Shadows of the Past* relates the history of the Great House, Champs Elysées, and Ralph de Boissière has written several novels, including *Call of the Rainbow, Crown Jewel* and *Rum and Coca-Cola*, an important account of the between-the-wars period in Trinidad. Adrian Camps-Campins' historical cards and paintings contribute to the maintenance of this rich and colourful narrative. C.L.R. James, Dr. Eric Williams, Sir Vidia Naipaul, Michael Anthony and Fr. Anthony de Verteuil have written histories as well as other significant work of local and Caribbean importance.

---

225 Roume of course did not write the Cedula of Population of 1783, it proceeded from the Court of Charles III, but Carl Campbell, author of *Cedulants and Capitulants*, writes, "Of the highest importance was the last clause of the Cedula, which set aside all previous laws and regulations that obstructed the implementation of its articles. If taken seriously, and the Cedula must be taken seriously as the outcome of a deliberate plan—it amounted to a new constitution for Trinidad" (p.91). It was its first, in truth. Its terms of reference, apart from that of the First People and the Spanish period, formed the basis, the ground zero, for all future narratives..

This expressive Afro-French Creole narrative has been held in commonality, shared as experience and maintained in custom and usage for well over two hundred years. It is today available for the purpose of helping to define "the natives of this place" and may be harnessed for the purpose of building an understanding of the past, for the purpose of casting a more usable future.

To better appreciate Trinidad's history, it should be noted that the 18th/19th century Afro-French Creole historical narrative, which was overlaid by the British colonial narrative, especially after the emancipation of the slaves, should not be separated into a French Creole narrative and an Afro-Creole narrative, but should be treated as one field with different viewpoints, sharing a common ideal of *being native to Trinidad and Tobago*. Its contributors over the centuries are products of the 19th and 20th century experience. They all propagate patriotism, at times with somewhat different perspectives, due to different personal experiences.

Williams' act of appearing to exile certain groups from history served to inculcate an idea that there were some in the overall population who were not to be included amongst "the people" of Trinidad and Tobago. Professor Brereton separates — like Williams — the Afro-Creole narrative of Trinidad into a French Creole narrative an Afro-Creole narrative and an Indian narrative amongst others. In her paper *Contesting the Past: Narratives of Trinidad and Tobago History,* in discussing the French Creole narrative, in the sense that this is what she believes the French Creoles of today think of themselves, remarks:

> "... if it (the French Creole narrative) continues at all, it is a story of
> local whites being pushed to the margins of the nation, no longer even
> an economic elite (overtaken by Syrian/Lebanese, Chinese, and East
> Indian entrepreneurs), without political clout, without any cultural
> status, national recognition through special public holidays or Arrival
> Days, or memorials to the pioneers. Perhaps it is, in fact, the end of the
> [French Creole] narrative: the disappearance of the French Creoles as
> a distinct group, the psychic if not physical eradication of local whites
> in the national fabric. These themes are powerfully conveyed in a
> 2003 video on the French Creoles of Trinidad, evocatively titled "C'est

Quitte" (it's over), [produced by Alex de Verteuil], a nostalgic lament
for a disappearing elite."

C'est Quitte was a film contributed to by members of the extended de
Verteuil family to recall and reminisce about life on the family's cocoa
estate in Grand Couva. It served to capture the memories of a generation who had grown up in the 1940s while 19th century traditions were
still maintained. According to the film's producer, Alex de Verteuil, the
title *C'est Quitte* was chosen because it was his father's drinking toast, and
that of many of his friends.[226] What was toasted was the end of the bottle;
and not, as Professor Brereton surmises, what French Creoles say about
themselves today; it is not a nostalgic lament for a disappearing elite. It
was produced by Elizabeth Cadiz Topp, as a contribution to the retention
of the French culture in Trinidad. (There is, in fact, a companion to it, *The
Blue Devils of Paramin,* the latter being a French patois speaking district in
the Northern Range.)

It is of interest to note that one of the main contributors to the film,
Topp's brother, Stephen Cadiz, chairman of a national pressure group,
the Keith Noel 136 Committee, was able to bring some 20,000 people
onto the streets of Port-of-Spain to protest the alarming murder rate in
Trinidad & Tobago in the first years of the new millennium (when the
documentary was produced). This very large crowd performed a dramat-
ic enactment of mourning for the deaths of the hundreds of people who
had been murdered in the recent past, on Abercromby St. before the Parliament in Port-of-Spain. This group, organised by Cadiz, his friends and
relations, was also able to get in excess of 120,000 signatures, drawn from
all types of people, also in protest of the escalating murder rate, which was
presented to the President of the Republic of Trinidad and Tobago. This
is an indication that Trinidadians of European descent today participate
actively in and shape Trinidad and Tobago society, and are supported by
tens of thousands of Afro and Indo-Trinidadians as well as people from all
sorts of backgrounds. It is of interest to note that the PNM government

226 In Ramabai Espinet's *Nowarian Blues,* published in *Trinidad Noir, "c'est quitte"* is re-
    ferred to as "...old fashioned rum cocktails" (p. 99).

of the day did not participate in the demonstration on the grounds that they took objection to the name of the protest, because it was called "The Death March." Trinidadians of European heritage, or those who appear that way, are far from seeing themselves as a "disappearing elite" or even further from experiencing "psychic if not physical eradication [227] of local whites in the national fabric."

Be that as it may, European-descended, or those appearing that way, Trinidadians all, were made scapegoats for injustices of the past by the politics of the Williams narrative. The notion of inherited guilt is, however, fundamentally wrong, morally unjustified and distinctly unscientific. Collective guilt is a basic fallacy of Marxism, which denies the individual of importance, only seeing him or her as a member of a class. It also seeks to condone racism, and to convey the notion that it alright to alienate Indians and hate white people in general, and French Creoles in particular.

When politicising the idea of inherited guilt in the 1960s, Williams as an Afro-French Creole himself had obviously forgotten that his own forebears, his father's people, had been slave owners.

Scapegoating is often more devastating when applied to minority groups, as they are less able to defend themselves. I would like to draw the parallel that Williams' scapegoating of the European-descended Trinidadians is in principle not dissimilar to that which was applied to the Jews of Europe, by the medieval Christians, in their propagating the belief that the Jews had murdered Jesus Christ and that those Jews who lived amongst them, more than a thousand years later, had collectively inherited this guilt. This misguided belief in inherited guilt has been responsible, over the centuries, for the murder of millions. The specific reasons put forward by Williams were different, and the outcome thankfully not murderous for the European-descended Trinidadians. But the underlying immorality of the argument for inherited guilt expressed in nationalistic politics is and remains the same, especially in the hands of powerful historians and politicians, calypsonians and academics. These are the roots of some of the racial divisions that bedevil our lives to this day.

---

227 An interesting choice of words; eradication means to destroy completely, to put an end to, from the Latin eradicat, torn up by the roots.

By the time Independence was granted in 1962, Williams had deconstructed the British interpretation of history, the colonial narrative that had obtained for more than one hundred and fifty years. He exploited the authority invested by the public in the university-trained historian, harnessing that authority in the service of politics and corrupting the scientific methodology of history for the popularisation of "nationalist" politics. [228] This was, to a degree, understandable as a political expedient in view of the absence of an external foe. Independence was granted without bloodshed.

But if his narrative came out of a personal affliction, why then were quite similar narratives constructed all over the ex-colonial world in the period after the last World War? While there are probably many reasons, I would suggest this one as perhaps the most salient: a common ideology expressed in terms of moral relativism that was fostered in a colonial environment that was based on a flawed and misguided ideology of the racial superiority of the European race.

The Williams' narrative should not be treated in isolation, but rather should be seen in the context of other similar narratives. Some of these shared origins dating from before the Second World War or even earlier. As previously discussed, C.L.R. James in 1934 was a member of an entrist [229] Trotskyist group inside the British Independent Labour Party. Together with a coterie of Pan-Caribbean and Pan-African intellectuals and academics, some of whom were Marxists, they were operating out of London in the 1930s, ironically in the same period when mass murder and enslavement were taking place in the Soviet Union under Stalin. (Between 1929-36, 10 million men, women and children met unnatural

228 Williams' dismissal of the European population from Trinidad and Tobago's history by hardly mentioning them in his published *History of the People of Trinidad and Tobago* is an example of this. His theory as put forward in his doctoral thesis, and published in *Capitalism and Slavery,* has been challenged and disproved by scholars who disagree. See Drescher, Seymour, & Anstey, Roger.

229 Entryism (or entrism or enterism) is a political tactic by which an organisation or state encourages its members or agents to infiltrate another organisation in an attempt to gain recruits, or take over entirely.

deaths.) [230] Recent historians have suggested a likely total of around 20 million deaths, citing much higher victim totals from executions, Gulags, deportations and other causes.) James was not alone, as there were other similar Trotskyite/Marxist cells in London, Paris, Geneva, Berlin and New York, where idealistic young men and women were hard at work seeking change in the order of things.

James' circle included Kwame Nkrumah, Eric Williams and Jomo Kenyatta, among others, some of whom would become leaders of independent states, as well as some who would become historians, academics, trade unionists, politicians, writers and publishers by the 1960s. James and others of a similar political view point would have exposed these young people to Trotsky's version of moral relativism, a subjectively defined code of ethics and contempt for objective or universal moral truths, a personal identification (of the leader) with history and a view that "history was above all moral restraints." [231] Moral criteria became secondary to criteria of political efficacy. James' influence and the influence of other communist ideologues would touch more than one generation of African and Caribbean scholars, intellectuals, teachers and future leaders.

Trotskyite/Marxist ideology, endorsed by European intellectuals, would shape public consciousness and opinion. A generation of anti-colonialists, the 'Bandung generation,' who had acquired the ideology and the techniques of Western politics, understood how to create "political nations" within their own countries. From these minority activist, cells would emerge, national movements, political parties that would become personality cults based on patronage and sometimes terror, at all times manipulating the democratic process so as to create totalitarian states.

It should be remembered that Williams was principally a nationalist (some argue that he was a populist) and not a communist. Neither were some of the other Third World leaders who came to power during this period. But the dialectic of communism, the manipulation of

230 Johnson 1991, 272
231 ibid. p. 263

emerging black consciousness, and the philosophy of moral relativism tended, in this period of decolonisation, to facilitate their personal and political goals.

The politicising of Trinidad and Tobago by the PNM in the post-Independence period for the purpose of institutionalising a nationalistic identity eroded not only the British colonial influences, but also served to diminish the status of the century and a half-old Afro-French Creole culture. By placing the local European-descended French Creoles and those who supported that culture in terms of religion (Catholicism), an agricultural lifestyle and an independent denominational education, in opprobrium, an ambivalence, a sense of mixed feelings about each other, and a dissonance, a decrease of racial harmony, has emerged within the society on the whole. Bearing in mind the significance of the long-established Afro-French Creole culture, that was in several ways united, if only against British colonialism (its art forms, calypso and steelbands, perhaps even patois, for example, were perceived as subversive by the British), this has engendered, collectively, deep psychological divisions whose repercussions are yet to be recognised or reconciled. These changes, however, did not go unrecorded even at their incipient stage. V.S. Naipaul, in his recollections of the 1960s Independence movement, remarks "It was as though, with the colonial past, all the colonial landscape was being trampled over and undone; as though, with that past, the very idea of regulation had been rejected; as though, after the sacrament of the square, the energy of revolt had become a thing on its own, eating away at the land." (1994, 38)

Placed against the unprecedented emigration of families of mostly Afro-Creole backgrounds, some of whom were seeking an education and better opportunities, while others, perhaps disillusioned, did not want to continue living here under the PNM regime, and the large quantity of immigrants who have continued to arrive from the other islands, from the 1960s and 70s and beyond, Trinidad has experienced a demographic dislocation, from which it may never recover, and one that no other island in the Caribbean has had.

Founded on the philosophy of moral relativism, the political culture
that came into being in Trinidad and Tobago has been, at times, described
as "tribal" by some social scientists. The divisiveness of the British colonial
system has continued under the several governments with tribal type divisions. [232] Tribal divisions emphasise not what people have in common,
but what divides them. These divisions ignore the universal and shared
aspects of human experience and derive their energy and impetus from
social insecurity and racial prejudice, resulting in the willful creation of
the scapegoat.

Just eight years after Independence, and fourteen after the launch of
the People's National Movement, a new generation was coming to the
view that Williams' revolution, the PNM's revolution, was obviously not
their revolution at all, but his. The new generation sensed its irrelevance to
them as black people. The Black Power uprising of 1970 brought tens of
thousands of black people onto the street almost every day, over a period
of several weeks in April of that year, while elements of the T&T Regiment mutinied.

In 1970, the younger generation of intellectuals mounted its challenge
to the Williams' narrative in an book entitled Is *Massa Day Ded?* These
young people may have perceived the somewhat personal link between
Williams' exposé of British hypocrisy as discussed in his book *Capitalism
and Slavery*, and his "Massa Day Done" politics of the early 1960s followed
by *History of the People of Trinidad and Tobago*. Gordon Rohlehr, writing in
Tapia, an intellectual forum that also published regularly, remarked:

> "These days (1970) it is difficult to view without scepticism anything
> Dr. Williams has to say either as politician or as historian. His last two
> history books have been the objects of quite astringent criticism from
> professional historians at UWI. Dr. K.O. Laurence, for example, views
> Dr. Williams' *History of the People of Trinidad and Tobago* as an "excel-

---

232 Interestingly, Professor Brereton in her paper *Contesting the Past* bases her approach
of systematic classification of the historical narratives of Trinidad and Tobago also
on the same ethnically-based segmentation (with the exception of Tobago, which is
regionally based). This indicates the pervasiveness of the Williams narrative in local
academia.

lent manifesto of a subjected people," but criticises the author for a tendency to overstate his case, and to omit a number of things which would significantly modify his conclusions. Dr. Laurence mentions in particular Dr. Williams' failure to credit the contribution of Albert Gomes; [233] to assess the work of the abolitionists; to treat the system of apprenticeship, the effect of World War II and the American occupation of the islands; to consider the Moyne report; [234] or to see the long struggle for self-government as a continuous and unbroken process. [235] He sees Williams' treatment of the post 1956 era as "frankly partisan" and ends with an implicit rejection of his methodology. *"However, it is obviously desirable that the books which will dictate the view of their own history which the people of the Caribbean will possess for the next generation should be written as histories, not as nationalist manifestoes. Otherwise it will be necessary for later generations to unlearn much of the "history" which the first generation learned."(. . .)* Dr. Laurence then goes on to define the problems (implicit in *History of the People of Trinidad and Tobago*) as an imperfect marriage between the historian and the politician: *Dr. Williams, of course, is both politician and historian, and if it be said that it is the politician who gives the book its punch, it is certainly the historian who gives it its authority. That authority needs frequently to be challenged, for the nationalist's politician has from time to time led the historian to swerve dangerously. But the book is a great achievement.'* One wonders whether the last statement is not defeated by all that precedes it." [236]

"Elsa Goveia's review of *British Historians and The West Indies,* first published in *Caribbean Quarterly* and since republished in John La Rose's

---

233 An important political and cultural figure from the 1930s to the 1960s.

234 An important yardstick for change in colonial administration.

235 This is the most significant criticism, as it points out Williams' rejection of the French Creole and Afro French narratives as important to nation building. In fact, these narratives started with the Cedula of 1783 (which may be seen as T&T's first Constitution, Campbell 1989, 91) and continued with the work of J.B. Phillipe & de Ridder, petitioners for civil rights, on through to the end of the 19-century reformists' movements.

236 Rohlehr: *History as Absurdity,* in: *My Strangled City and Other Essays,* pp. 18ff. Rohlehr quotes: Laurence, K.O., *Colonialism in Trinidad and Tobago* in: *Caribbean Quarterly,* Vol. IX, No.3 [Sept. 1963] p. 53

New Beacon Reviews, Collection One (1968), is in its calm way a devastating piece of criticism. Goveia thinks that Dr. Williams has misnamed his book, and is able to show that he does not examine the work of seven or eight major British historians who wrote extensively about the West Indies. She mentions the "combination of omissions and hasty dogmatism which mars his present work," and concludes: *"Whether in education or history, good intentions are not enough, and the road to hell is paved with authoritative half-truths. No one is ever educated or liberated from the past by being taught how easy it is to substitute new shibboleths for old."* She finds the book "disappointing and even somewhat irresponsible," and sees it as "just not good enough for the people or for the students of the West Indies who are likely to read it." Later, she suggests that Dr. Williams write essays on the contemporary West Indian scene, "which his experience as historian and politician could render valuable." [237] (emphasis not the author's)

The point of these critiques is to show that not all thinkers, writers and intellectuals had bought into Williams' narrative as naïvely and as readily as his constituency had. Professional historians saw the weaknesses of these books and could see how a troubled personality like Williams, on becoming a trained historian, could use his knowledge and skills and link them to the political yearnings of people in such a way that power was gained for his own purposes. These critics were all black, brown and coloured: perhaps they were not victims of the colonial experience in the same sense as Williams was.

His books, *Capitalism and Slavery* and the *History of the People of Trinidad and Tobago,* plus his *Negro in the Caribbean;* his autobiography *Inward Hunger,* and his work on West Indian history, *Columbus to Castro,* his significant writings such as the *People's Charter,* and a great many other papers and speeches; all comprise the Williams' narrative, representing a formidable body of work principally dealing with historic deprivation and social injustice. All together, they tended to express a flawed ideology that informed the politics of inherited victimhood and guilt, which over

---

237 ibid. Rohlehr quotes Goveia, Elsa *New Shibboleths for Old,* in: *New Beacon Reviews* No. 1 (1968) p. 37 (John La Rose, editor)

time would take the form of the emasculating politics of entitlement and patronage, through which his principal constituency would be bound in perpetuity to the plantation of the PNM.

Williams took the country to Independence in 1962 and after the Black Power uprising in 1970 to republican status. He was Prime Minister of Trinidad and Tobago from 1962 to 1981, the longest-serving Prime Minister in the British Commonwealth, having been successively Chief Minister, Premier and Prime Minister for a quarter of a century.

Over the next twenty to thirty years, a certain "coarsening of the society" (Ryan) was experienced by the different sections of society, depending on what they were accustomed to. In my view, this coarsening ultimately stems from Williams' idea (which was accepted, and carried forward by his successors) that the people of Trinidad and Tobago were still victims, and therefore could not be held individually accountable for their actions and that they were entitled to unearned benefits. This led to the collapse of civic and moral responsibility and expressed itself in the breakdown of civil society and the institutions that serve it, as we experience today.

The victors of the colonial experience (especially the urban, secondary school-educated middle and lower middle classes, very much a part of the Williams constituency) were adversely affected by this "coarsening of society." This group had sought refinement through education, the inculcation of moral values, the acquiring of the social graces, appreciation of cultural forms such as music and art, and had developed a beneficial attachment to religion.

Over time, the pursuits and habits of these families and individuals were perceived as colonial, some would say "Afro-Saxon," old-fashioned, and not "what Independence was about." As discussed, a considerable number of people from the black and coloured middle class left Trinidad in this period; it was the beginning of the brain drain that was really a cultural drain. Their emigration marked the point in time when Trinidad started to lose its Afro-French Creole soul. With the steady influx of small islanders who were mostly rural and primary school-educated, Trinidad would, except for the existence of its Indian population (about

50%), acquire a more Caribbean reality. [238] By far the most tragic result of this coarsening of the society has been the ongoing and climbing murder rate, mostly experienced with the deaths of young men in seemingly abandoned black urban communities, bringing fear and heart-breaking tragedy and dislocation to families.

One of Williams' most important and lasting achievements was that he did not destroy the "old money," the family-owned, import-export (commission agency) trading businesses that had been founded and built by 19th century English and Scottish merchants. He did, however, cause the demise of the large department stores, also owned mostly by Scottish merchant families on Frederick Street. This was achieved by causing them to pay retroactive severance pay to their past employees, which resulted in the erosion of the working capital of those companies. Their closure in the 1960s and 70s was to change the nature of downtown Port-of-Spain.

The private sector had developed with the old trading firms, which had worked in tandem with the cocoa economy and the mostly foreign-owned sugar interest with its links to foreign-controlled insurance companies and banks. From early in the 19th century this sector had been the basis of the colony's economy, although the oil industry would soon assume dominance.

Williams saved some of the old firms from foreign take-over bids and introduced the Alien Landholdings Act to protect the local private sector. He also brought into existence an Industrial Court and passed acts and statutes that appeared to be specifically anti-trade union and obviously pro-capitalist. Williams, unlike Forbes Burnham or Fidel Castro, did not want the merchants to leave. They were important to the country's economy. However, he disapproved of their way of doing business, of exporting capital and of their links to the British and Canadian banks. He accused them of being racially prejudiced in their employment practices, of form-

238 The small island immigrants, politicised by the PNM as "true inheritors," soon saw themselves as Trinidadians, and tended to view the East Indian segment, about 50% of the population, as alien, perhaps even as foreign. This was so despite the fact that many Trinidadians of East Indian descent had been in Trinidad for some five or six generations, and were in truth the real Trinidadians!

ing monopolistic cartels with interlocking directorships and of practising an incestuous oligarchic hold on opportunity.

Nonetheless, he wanted them, and the businesses they ran, to stay on as the non-oil sector; important in an oil-based economy that generates wealth but not much employment. It became increasingly clear that his "Massa day done" diatribes had been his attempt to exorcise his own demons, but that they had served as rhetorical exhortations that excited the gullible and those inclined towards anti-white and anti-Indian racism.

From the early1960s, a new generation of business leaders emerged. They were drawn almost entirely from the old moneyed establishment. Some of them were decorated veterans of the Second World War. They had opted to stay and work in Trinidad as opposed to taking their money and migrating. Their business model tended to evolve away from the traditional commission agency, and export of local produce, as the agricultural economy stagnated, although sales and distribution would continue to be central to their operations. Following in the wake of Sir Gerald Wight of Alstons Ltd., who had pioneered local modern manufacturing in 1940s, they would over time become more involved in manufacturing and the service industries. The leading figures were Ralph Gibson of McEnearney-Alstons, Sydney Knox of Neal & Massy, and Thomas Gatcliffe of Angostura. These were among the founders of the modern conglomerates, who in the wake of the collapse of the Federation of the West Indies worked towards and were partly responsible for the creation of CARIFTA. [239]

Several of the older family firms, if only in name, were to survive as a result of conglomerate take over. Retaining the names of old firms maintained a sense of continuity, contributing to feelings of security and permanence in the face of frightening changes taking place in Trinidad and Tobago and the world beyond.

Continuity in business also perpetuated international business contacts and goodwill. The growing conglomerates provided increased employment, improved working conditions and gave training and scholarships

---

239 See unpublished manuscript of the History of Neal & Massy by Alice Besson, UWI
    Library, St Augustine.

to their employees. All this contributed to the retention of the country's middle class, which served to keep the intellectual capital from migrating completely. This vibrant new private sector also served to raise standards in terms of quality, competitiveness, productivity, value and service that are necessary in the free enterprise system.

It is very unfortunate that the island's agricultural sector that was once the mainstay of its economy, with sugar, cocoa, and coffee, together with its vibrant livestock sector, was made to fail, and be eventually left to die, a political expediency perhaps, as the adherents of these occupations were perceived as opposers to the new narrative. [240]

The Williams era also saw a new cadre of business people emerge, mostly from the long-established, Indo-Trinidadian population, but increasingly from the Syrian-Lebanese community. These would bring a refreshing vibrancy, in fact, creativity to the country's business world. At the same time, a much larger state sector emerged, powered by the petrochemical industry with personnel drawn mostly from the class of black, mixed race and Indian professionals, who, in the main, do not all necessarily subscribe to the Williams narrative, or the political and economic model that was created to maintain it.

The power and status that some historians/apologists claim was enjoyed by "Knox and Gatcliffe" was negligible when compared to their contribution in terms of maintaining "quality of life" in Trinidad and Tobago. The firms, which they ran as public companies, gave thousands of families

---

240 In 1955 there were 409 agricultural credit societies with 16,000 peasant membership, assets $300,000 and working capital of $1,067,140. Sugar Estates canes acreage 36,000. Farmers' canes acreage 44,000; number of farmers 111,000. Citrus acreage planted 13,000, 432,000 crates of citrus handled in 1954. Bananas 45,546 stems exported in 1953, Rice; 18,000 acres devoted to rice production in 1953, 288 mills produced 12,000 tons of rice. Coconuts, 40,000 acres under cultivation, 21,400 tons of copra valued $1,840,509, 1953. Cocoa 120,000 acres under cultivation produced 200,000 cwt., in 1954. Forest production reserves in 1953 were 49,000 acres; protection reserves, 194,900 acres; Teak plantation 7,000 acres. Timber production for 1954 all woods, 5,607,000, ft. Life stock population; 1954, cattle, 37,900, water buffaloes, 3,000, goats, 39,000, sheep, 5,000, swine, 35,000, horses, 2,400, mules,2,800, donkeys, 6,000, poultry, 1,134,244. *Who, What and Why 1955-56.*

a sense of security for some 50 to 60 years. Their overall endeavour and that of many others in the private sector helped to maintain and improve the standard of living enjoyed by a wide cross-section of the population. Their vision of the ideals of progress, patriotism and duty served to sustain confidence and hope in the future from the 1960s to the present day.

This—and not *C'est Quitte*—may well be the defining narrative of the European-descended people of Trinidad and Tobago. They are the sons and daughters of the pioneers.

CONCLUSION:
THE WILLIAMS LEGACY
7

What is the legacy that we, the people of Trinidad and Tobago, have received from the Williams' narrative? His reinterpretation of history.

I have suggested in this study that to some considerable extent the politicising of victimhood and guilt, and the acceptance in the society of scapegoating certain of its members, as well as the engendering of a sense of alienation experienced by some members of the Indo-Trinidadian population, have all served to erode ethnic harmony, respect for law and order, and notions of moral and civic responsibility, in the collective mind of contemporary society. The Williams narrative has contributed to a feeling that everything is outside of the law and up for grabs or reinterpretation. Many civil institutions (the police service, the administration of justice, the education system) have lost considerable credibility and are hardly capable of conveying meaning or confidence in civil society. This loss of understanding of what is right and wrong is apparent in the continuous introduction of scapegoats in our public discourse.

I will give this example: the calypsonians' scapegoating in the aftermath of the 1990 attempted coup. In July of that year, a party of Muslim extremists fired Police Headquarters in Port-of-Spain and took hostages in the television station and the parliament. This occurred against the background of an economic downturn, brought about by the very poor handling of what remained of the significant economic windfalls in the oil industry from 1973, first by Williams and later, his successor George Chambers.

Throughout the 1980s, the nation suffered dramatically increased job losses, the failure of old firms, rampant inflation, the introduction of IMF' strictures and alarming evidence of increased poverty and homelessness. In 1986 the whole population, fearful of deprivation, voted in the National Alliance for Reconstruction (NAR) by a landslide victory of 33 seats to 3 seats. Was this "Massa's" return? However, the NAR, a disparate group of politicians, was not "Massa." The party was comprised almost entirely of those who had attempted to challenge the Williams' narrative and had failed. Despite their competence in some areas, they were to fall apart along the old fault lines of race and envy. The aftermath of the attempted coup was replete with the expected recriminations and an interesting interpretation of scapegoating. Rohlehr describes it:

> "In Trinidad, the true cause of many people's cynical and bitter mockery of the humiliated parliamentarians lay in the NAR's mission, a mission particularly dear to [prime minister A.N.R.] Robinson and [attorney general Selwyn] Richardson to unearth matters that the ancient regime (the PNM) had worked so hard to bury.

> "For in so doing, Robinson and Richardson were unmasking not only the PNM, but an entire culture that had grown out of its thirty years in office; a society, too, whose social and cultural mechanisms are all attuned to the task of evading moral responsibility, side stepping moral commitment and, when these strategies fail, to dispel fact and the magnitude of corruption, by out-staring guilt.

> "The spontaneity and intensity with which so many Calypsonians sang figuratively to mangle and disembowel the already battered NAR parliamentarians, clinches my contention that the nation had become caught up in a ritual of classical scapegoating at its most archetypal. In such scapegoating, guilt is transferred to the accuser, who then becomes the monstrous double of the very people he is accusing. He is then run out of town and beaten or stoned to death in a frenzy of communal rage." [241]

The question now, some sixty-five years after the first publication of *Capitalism and Slavery* in 1944 and the declaration of the demise of "Massa" in 1961, is whether the Williams' narrative, as expressed in his political personality and eventually the political culture it engendered, was a successful "recasting of history to produce a usable past?" Did the Williams narrative provide a process of identity-formation and give us a usable past, one that we could use in the service of the future? I think not, as it tended to reflect individual preoccupations and Williams' attempt to define his

---

241 Rohlehr: *Apocalypso and the Soca Fires of 1990,* in *The Shape of that Hurt* p. 343

own identity. Was it a narrative that has produced a political culture that successfully evades both moral and civic responsibility and commitment to the rule of law? I believe that it is.

Did it have any lasting relevance at all in a multi-ethnic society like Trinidad and its neighbouring island Tobago, which has had a different historical experience from Trinidad's? And is the political culture created by it of use to us today? On both counts, I think not.

This study, as indicated in the introduction to the first part, came out of a discussion with a local historian about the manner in which the post-colonial narrative of Trinidad and Tobago had treated the European settlers in this country. In truth it is a very long answer to her question, "Do you want to make them heroes?" The answer to that is I would indeed like to make them heroes, beginning with Philippe Rose Roume de St. Laurent, particularly bearing in mind the words of Michel Chevalier (1806–1879), French statesman, economist and free market liberal, who is quoted on the front cover of P.G.L. Borde's *The History of the Island of Trinidad under the Spanish Government* (first part):

> "He who views the events of the past with the eyes of his time is very much exposed to a chance of error. Many a time, it is a panorama in which the objects are dim, because one is placed beyond the point of view.

I have shown in the first part (François Besson) through analysis of the historical traces of an extended French Creole family from the mid-18th century that the French Creole and Afro Creole narratives may be combined into one category. I will suggest that this colonial narrative should be fleshed out into a continuum of a Western narrative that has lasted from before Spanish colonisation to today's globalised world, with Trinidad and Tobago forming presently a part of the United States of America-dominated political and cultural domain.

That Western, or New World narrative that began before Spanish colonisation is far from over. It has experienced various European, including British, imperial interventions, which have come and gone. This Western narrative is presently undergoing what may appear as paradigm-altering changes with, for example, the election of the Southern hemisphere's first indigenous head of state, Evo Morales, in Bolivia, the emergence of a left wing, perhaps radical, government in Venezuela under Hugo Chavez, the longevity of the communist regime in Cuba under the Castro brothers, and the election of the first mixed-race president in the USA, which, even as an idea, would not have been entertained a decade ago.

This New World narrative was, and still is, the main force that shapes how conceptions of the past are put into the service of needs of the present, which are going to shape the future.

Trinidad and Tobago is undoubtedly experiencing social and political changes that seem to indicate that the model that was introduced at Independence with the Eric Williams narrative, has run its course. To portray the European settlers who ventured out into the New World in the 17th century as villains and 'unheroic' because it suited the nationalistic anti-colonial politics of the 1950s, and to continue it today in history teaching, is wrong and only contributes to racial and societal discord.

In the second part (Eric Williams), I have explored the personality and personal background of the framer of the present-day historical narrative of Trinidad and Tobago as enshrined in its governmental agencies, many of its institutions, and the official public discourse of the constituents of its main party, the People's National Movement. As this part attempted to show, the Williams narrative was born out of the misfortunes of an extended family and lived out in the neurosis of an academic, who sought and found in the nationalist politics of the 1950s a method of dealing with his own psychological problems. Perhaps he was convinced that men are imprisoned by their own history "in circumstances existing already, given and transmitted from the past" (Marx) and that history is destiny—which in my view is a fallacy. Perhaps he took the position that moral or ethical propositions do not reflect objective and/or universal moral truths.

The purpose of this study, from inception to even more intensely its conclusion, is my belief that it could contribute to solving Trinidad and Tobago's social malaise of today. I seek to expose and as much as possible give empirical proof for the fact that what we are suffering from is a syndrome that Eric Williams has infected us with. This syndrome is one of feeling like a perpetual victim, and of needing a scapegoat in order to compensate for low self esteem. It led to what Professor Gordon Rohlehr defined almost two decades ago as

> "a society . . . whose social and cultural mechanisms are all attuned to the task of evading moral responsibility, side stepping moral commitment and, when these strategies fail, to dispel fact and the magnitude of corruption, by out-staring guilt." (1992, 343)

Nobody wants to be part of such a morally lacking society. But having been indoctrinated, it is difficult for each and every one of us to define when this amoral process began, to leave victimhood behind us, and to expurgate the scapegoat from our discourse, our feelings and our thinking. The politics of inherited victimhood and inherited guilt have become subversive of this country's civility, ethnic harmony, democracy and perhaps eventually, its rule of law.

How can we, as a people, cure ourselves from the Eric Williams syndrome? It is my view that first we must attempt to diagnose its causes. These causes, we might discover, stem from particular "historical conjunctures" when for various reasons shifts in moral values in the Western world took place. An example for such a historical conjuncture is the abolition of the slave trade in 1807, which, for whatever reasons given or causes explained, brought to an end the officially sanctioned buying, transporting and selling of human beings in the British Empire. This was followed in 1834 by the granting of freedom to those still enslaved, thus putting into place a British colonial narrative. One hundred and fifty years after the abolition of the slave trade, another shift in moral values was indicated when Dr. Williams' deconstruction of the British-sponsored colonial narrative had taken root, and was accepted by the public in general in the 1960s. [242]

Notably, history is now offering the opportunity for us to take advantage of yet another shift in moral values.

---

242 Another history-making shift in moral values occurred with the liberating revolutions of 1989 that brought about the fall of communism across Central and Eastern Europe, ending in the overthrow of Soviet-style communist states within the space of a few months. The Soviet Union was dissolved by the end of 1991.

During the period of researching and writing this study, Barack Obama emerged on the world stage and was elected president of the United States. In his book, *The Audacity of Hope*, one reads of his own personal struggle to come to terms with himself in his youth, where he writes (2008, 38):

> "... the role of victim was too readily embraced as a means of shedding responsibility, or asserting entitlement, or claiming moral superiority over those not so victimised." [243]

This observation, which appeared to challenge politicised victimhood in the Western world, was remarkable not so much for its occurrence, but for its profile on the world stage.

"Eureka!" I wanted to exclaim. Obama's words addressed the "elephant in the living room"—showing that if one takes history to be destiny, the resulting narrative would scarcely "place a part of the past in the service of conceptions and needs of the present" in the words of Barry Schwartz. Wasn't this, the election of a "black" man to the Presidency of the United States of America, an investment of trust made by a majority of persons who are "white," a major paradigm shift, in terms of moral values in the Western world's historical narrative? Was it as significant to the collective consciousness of the United States, the Caribbean, in fact the Western hemisphere, as the shift in moral values that proclaimed the slave trade over in the United Kingdom and its colonies two hundred and two years ago? Could Obama, notwithstanding his "success" or not, as a President, be the harbinger of a new, New World, Western narrative, one that will finally mean that Trinidadians, in fact West Indians can now leave the post-colonial Williams narrative of inherited victimhood and inherited guilt behind? I hope that my work will contribute to this process.

---

243 Williams' political personality appears to hanker after the creation of these sentiments of victimisation, that would eventually become, some people claim, the political culture of Trinidad and Tobago. One cannot help but wonder that if Williams
was the instigator of the post-Independence, third world narrative of inherited victimhood and inherited guilt, and if President Barack Obama as the writer of a new
World narrative that finally leaves the colonial, Williams narrative, behind.

Finis.

APPENDIX I

SOME WILLS OF THE COMISSIONG, LOREILHE & DE BOISSIÈRE FAMILIES

These wills indicate the extent to which some families were committed to bequeathing to their descendants, legitimate and illegitimate, various forms of inheritance. Some members of these families had, during the 18th and19th century, lived in *plaçage*, with African or coloured women and had fathered children, others had fathered children out of wedlock with European women. These offspring, both white and coloured, were not only to be remembered in the wills of their parents but were, at times, brought up in the homes of their fathers with their fathers' wives and children.

 The wills tell a story of remembrance, recognition and gratitude over several generations, and may serve to indicate something of the surprise and disappointment felt by Jules Boissière, his wife Evalina and their children when they realised that they were not to receive the inheritance left for them in their father's will.

We will show the basic content of the will of Domingo Comissiong, 1799, (spelt with one 'm' in Grenada and the Leeward islands, with two in Trinidad,) it pays particular care not to let his fortune get out of the hands of his children.

The will of Michael Loreilhe, a relative of the founder of the de Boissière family in Trinidad, shows his concern for the future of his coloured offspring. And that of Jean Valleton de Boissière born Bergerac, France, 1777, died Trinidad 1853, founder of this branch of the family in Trinidad, demonstrates the care taken by him, a former money lender and slave trader,[123] to ensure that his past associates in "the trade" do not cause

---

123 Michael Pocock writes in <u>Out of the Shadows of the Past</u>: "The only item in the Wilberforce Museum in Kingston upon Hull concerning slavery in Trinidad is a promissory note dated 18 March, 1805 in favour of Mr. Boissière and Mr. Pietry 'for the sum of seven hundred round dollars, twenty seven joes in an accepted order from Mr.

upsets in the lives of his descendents. The will of the founder's legitimate son, with his wife Claire, née Beaulieau, Henri, who was baptised, William Henry Boissière, (but was always known as Henri) b. 1799, Trinidad, d. France, 1865, contain bequests to his father's illegitimate children, his two half-sisters. Henri does not, however, bequeath anything to his two half-brothers, Joseph Numa and Auguste Louis Boisseire, as both these men, sons of the African woman Zuzule with whom his father had lived in *plaçage* for several decades, had been educated in France, and had been given town properties and some sort of start-up in business in the 1840s. All the children of Jean de Boissière and Zuzule had been born in slavery.

Henri makes it plain in his will that he has left his estate to his legitimate son Dr. Jean Valleton de Boissière, but makes it equally plain that he leaves a quantity of his possessions to his illegitimate son John Nicholas Boissière, b. 1816, France, d. Trinidad, 1886. He had fathered John Nicholas and a daughter, Rosette, possible twins, at a young age,16 perhaps, with his future wife's aunt, (who appears to have gone to France to have them.) They had been brought up by Henri in his household and John Nicholas was considered to be Henri's "favourite son." (Pocock 229) John Nicholas was educated in Switzerland and was established in business in Port-of-Spain. Henri, who appoints John Nicholas as executor of his will, also includes in his will two other sons of his, Louis and Alphonse. Their mother is named, she is Rosalie Rose of Champs Elysées. Baptismal and Marriage records show that the sons of Henri, the half brothers John Nicholas Boissière and Dr. Jean Valleton de Boissière witnessed each others weddings and were godfathers' to each others children, and in the case of John Nicholas Boissière, his half brother Dr. Jean de Boissière is the executor of his estate. They were not only half brothers, they were also cousins.

John Nicholas Boissière in turn, in his will, clearly provides for his legal issue as well, but also makes particular reference to his reputed children, Jules Arnold, b. 1857, d. ? and Eliza Boissière, who had been brought up

---

Rigby and the balance (sic) in sugar...' The security was two new male Negro slaves from the cargo of the ship "Agnes." The slaves were mortgaged by Antoinette St. Louis, who placed her mark 'pour Marth San Mary.' The loan was repaid in 'compte courant', the receipt being signed on behalf of Jean Boissière & Co. by John Smith on 30 July 1806.

in his household. John Nicholas had married a woman of colour, Marie Aurelie Soully. A family tradition tells that his father, Henri, made a gift of a large parcel of land opposite to his own home, Champs Elysées. Because John Nicholas had married a woman of colour and with her had several children, in addition to taking in his two illegitimate coloured offspring, local wags quipped, "One crow is a crow, several crows makes a rookery" referring to the colloquialism of a crow being a black person. John Nicholas's response was to call his estate "Rookery Nook."

The will of Louis Boissière, nephew of the founder, is of interest. Evidently a man of means, he distributed his fortune amongst his workers and friends, he does not appear to have had a coloured concubine or any illegitimate children.

Also contained in this appendix are the wills of some of the grandchildren of Jean de Boissière (also known as John Boissière) through his *plaçage* with the African woman, Zuzule. They are; Joseph Numa, b. 1820, d. 1870, and Auguste Louis Boissière, b. 1822, d. ? As mentioned, they had both been educated in France. This branch of the extended coloured family received from their father, and passed on to their children, cash and town properties. Joseph Numa's son Eugene was able to set up a successful business, Eugene Boissière & Co. in Port-of-Spain, Joseph Numa's brother, Auguste Louis, also went into business in Port-of-Spain but was not as successful. The knowledge of these various inheritances in the overall de Boissière family may have been common to all its members.

The Will of Domingo Comissiong dated 28th May 1799 reads:

In the name of God Amen I Domingo Comissiong of the Town of St. George in the island of Grenada Sail maker being very sick and weak of body, but of sound and disposing mind memory and understanding thanks be given unto God calling unto mind the mortality of my body and knowing that it is appointed for all men once to die. Do make and ordain this my last will and testament that is to say principally and first of all I give and recommend my soul into the hand of Almighty God that gave it and my body I recommend to the earth to be buried in decent

Christian burial at the discretion of my executors and as touching such worldly estate wherewith it has pleased God to bless me in this life I give and dispose of the same in the following manner and form.

Imprimis I give and bequeath unto my son Joseph Thomas Comissiong and my daughters Fanny Cinderilla Comissiong and also Margaret Comissiong the mother of said children all my estate of property both real and personal. Share and share alike to them and their heirs forever, to wit my houses lands messuages tenements and slaves my wharf and the new buildings lately erected and by them freely to be possessed and enjoyed. It is my will and desire that nothing of my property shall be sold, but kept in good repair. (Domingo Comissiong's sail making loft existed "in good repair" well into the 20th century in St. George's Grenada.)

Item. I will and desire that Nancy Comissiong mulatto woman belonging to the Honorable Thomas Bridgewater who I believe to be my daughter may be purchased if possible emancipated set free and released from all slavery and servitude whatsoever.

It is my will and desire and I do hereby declare that if the above mentioned Margaret Comissiong enter into the state of matrimony she shall have no part right or title to any thing I die possessed of but shall give up all possession and right whatsoever and in lieu of which one shilling sterling shall be presented to her.

To any of my parents or relations who may send or come here to make or claim of upon any thing I die possessed of I give and bequeath unto any other or all of them one shilling sterling. I do hereby constitute nominate and appoint my worthy friends Thomas Trail now residing in Petty Martinique Thomas Redhead Joseph Colhoun and Elizabeth Watts of the town of St. George in the island aforesaid my true and lawful executors to this my last will and testament and I do hereby utterly disallow revoke and dis annul all and every other former Testaments wills legacies bequests and executors by me in any wise before named wills whereof I have hereunto set my hand and seal the fourteenth day of March in the year of our Lord One thousand seven hundred and ninety seven. He signed with his mark, X.

This is the will of Michael Loreilhe a French planter, he was also a cousin of Jean de Boissière. (Also known as John Boissière) Michael Loreilhe died at an early age on his estate at Marabella South Trinidad in 1800.

"In the name of God the Father, the Son and the Holy Spirit etc.

1st.   I commend my soul to God, etc., etc.

2nd.   I declare that I am the proprietor of the estate Marabella and its appurtenances in partnership with Mr. Thomas Smith (which property has been valued at £36,000 Stg.) and the estate called Union in partnership with Governor Picton, also in the estate in Grenada called Thelsaide, formerly planted in coffee, but at present abandoned, also a parcel of land (in Grenada) consisting of 90 acres situated in the same quarter used as a garden for the Negroes of the Corinth estate.

I declare that it is my wish that this parcel of land be given to the Proprietor of Corinth Estate in exchange and for the balance of my total debt realising the impossibility of adjusting otherwise having lost my books and papers at the time of the Revolt. (Fédon's uprising)

3rd.   I wish also that the Negro called Sampson and the two Negresses called Jeannette and Marguerite be given to Messrs. Alysen (or Alefssan) directing that, for all that, the said agents should sell the said slaves to the owner of best repute in the Island or give them the opportunity of choosing their own Master.

4th.   I declare that I have two Natural children by the Mulatress Luce living at present in my house, the boy was baptised in Grenada by the Minister of the Parish on the 3rd April, 1792 under the name of Charles Barclay and the girl was born in this island on the 26th November last and baptised under the name of Marie-Anne.

5th.   I declare that I give to my Mulatress, Eliza, her liberty and my wish is that she enjoy all that is possible after my decease; I give to her and bequeath fifty *portuguesas* which are to be paid to her by my testamentary Executors (whom I will name hereafter) as soon as the state of my affairs will permit.

6th.   I give and bequeath to my Mulatress Magdelaine, a Negro named Jean Francis at present employed on Union estate which Negro I have deliberately not included in my various partnerships because he belongs to my nephew.

7th.   I declare to give to the Widow Dognon, widow of the deceased lawyer Dognon in the Island of Grenada, the sum of six thousand silver pounds of the Islands which amount I received in Grenada to repay to him (or her?) in Marseilles which the outbreak of war has prevented me from doing.

8th.   I give and bequeath to the Mulatress Luce the sum of five hundred portugesas payable in three equal installments upon the sale of Union estate.

9th.   I give and bequeath to my son Charles Barclay the sum of one thousand portuguesas which sum is to be paid to him on his majority and which is to be guaranteed by all my properties bearing interest at the rate of six percent for his upkeep and education.

10th. I gave and bequeath to the girl Mulatress, Marie-Anne, his sister, the sum of three hundred *portuguesas* which sum is to be paid to her at her majority and which is to be guaranteed by all my properties bearing at interest at the rate of six percent for her upkeep and education.

11th. I appoint for Tutor to my above mentioned children M. Salvador Dominici, my neighbour and friend, entrusting him to undertake this task.

12th. I give and bequeath to the child to be born in two or three weeks to the wife of Lieutenant Colonel Balfour commanding the 57th Regiment the sum of £300 Stg. payable a year after my death on the demand of its mother.

13th. I give and bequeath to Governor Picton a cask of Madeira wine and a cask of Rum which are at present in my store with his mark.

14th. I give and bequeath to the Mulatress Luce, all my clothes and household furniture which have been declared to belong to me by the District police.

15th. I appoint my testamentary Executors Mr. Robert Prentis and M. La Sourd Mardither giving to each of them personally the sum of five hundred *portuguesas*, entreating them to accept this trust which I give to them full of sorrow. They have the power to act together or separately, but I assert that I have chosen them in the firm belief that there are no others who are able to put my affairs in order which are truly in confusion. No account is make up for Union estate, everything is in two notebooks which I consider can be put in order in a few days. I beg my Executors to examine my papers with care and by this means draw up an account. In general they will find my papers in a safe place waiting to be found. They are not to destroy any document after they have examined it in case they have to be re-examined. My friend Prentis has knowledge of many Chattels which I have in Port of Spain in various places.

16th. I declare to have sold to Messrs. Peschier the Coppers and Mill for one hundred and fifty *portuguesas* payable at the next crop. I have received on account nine *portuguesas* from the mother of these Gentlemen.

17th. I commend to Governor Picton my Mulatto children to obtain for them everything which is possible following the satisfactory sale of Union. (Estate)

18th. I the undersigned bequeath as my residual heir and legatee my brother Zacharie Loreilhe, residing at present at Bergerac in France. Done and signed at my Marabella estate, island of Trinidad, the 12th day of September 1800.
Michael Loreilhe. Witnesses: J.J. Derneyere (or Demeyere), Alexandre Williams, Doctor Polustre, John Delly (or Relly), James Gamayan (or Gabayan), N. Le Sucur

The will of Jean de Boissière, (also known as John Boissière) native of Bergerac, France. He was the son of the late Jean Valleton de Boissière, Doctor of Medicine, and Esther, née Sargenton. Year, 1854, No. 9.
In his will he states that he was born, and has lived, and wishes to die in the Protestant religion. He states; "I will that all my debts be paid in the most

accurate manner possible and I request my Testamentary Executors and my son in particular to fulfill all the engagements I may have contracted previous to my decease: but I caution them to be upon their guard as to any notes of hand payable to order, particularly those of very old dates, knowing that when I was in business some remained outstanding which had been paid in settlement of account or otherwise in the course of business and which had never been called in owing to neglect or because they had been lost or misplaced.

There is one amongst others in triplicate for the sum of £1,288.6.9 currency in the year 1806 made by Boissière and Chanaud & Co. to the order of Capt. Baker which I have paid to Masdiren (?) & Simpson who were the holders thereof and which they were unable to return to me after having received the amount thereof because they had mislaid or lost the same."

He goes on to refer to other such arrangements, mentioning the sums involved and cautioning against being called upon to pay out on old I.O.U.s. He then goes on to describe his relationship with François Chanaud (A relative of the senior branch of his family) as being one of mutual trust, stating that he did in truth owe some 5 or 6 thousand pounds to him, but, that the firm had lost more than that amount. He goes on explain the circumstances of another transaction; "…..Jean Pictry from the effects consequent upon the sale of a cargo of Negroes for which the said Jean Pictry had an interest of one third, the said Pictry having taken for his own private account a quantity of Negroes for which he had not paid before his death and besides which cargo had been purchased by Boissière and Chanaud and Jean Pictry in "solidum" the one for the other, the successors of Pictry being insolvent I was compelled to pay the portion of the said Pictry for the balance, £2,700, besides that several debts arising out of the cargo of Negroes . . ." He leaves to his aunt Celeste Sargenton an annuity "at the rate of £15 per month payable to her on the first of every month, with the condition that "…if I come to purchase a house in which I give her residence this annuity would be diminished of £3 per month and I declare also that it is because on the first of August next she will have no domestic slave to serve her that I leave to her such a large sum in order that she may hire a servant."

In closing he states: "I leave to my beloved son Henri as the heir of all I possess at my death and so with the blessings of God and mine he may enjoy the same and make good use thereof, charging him to pay exactly the sums which I may owe and the legacy that I bequeath in this testament." He names his son Henri Boissière and his brother Eli Boissière to act jointly as executors of his estate.

The will of Henri Boissière, native of Trinidad, legitimate son of Jean de Boissière. Year, 1865, No. 63.

"In the name of God etc. . . . I leave to Esther, a natural daughter of my father, now wife of William Munso, $500. To La Cocadie, also a natural daughter of my father, $500. To Madeleine Mazely, the sum of $400. To Claire, my servant, the sum of $150. To Edward Stewart, my butler, the sum of $100, provided he is with me at the time of my death. (Henri Boissière died in Bergerac, France). To John (Jean François Boissière), my Godson, the son of John Nicholas Boissière, I leave $500. (Jean François went to France and claimed the courtesy title of count). To Mrs. St. Luce Vincent, $400. I make a gift to Rosette Boissière, (possibly John Nicholas' twin sister), $400, which she now has for me in case she decides to pay me before my death. I give my phaeton carriage, my bay horse called Captain and harnesses to John Nicholas Boissière. I give my bed head and all bed clothes, linens etc. to Alphonse (one of his sons with Rosalie Rose of the Champs Elysées estate). I give to Louis (another son of Rosalie Rose) my gold watch and chain. I give all my wearing apparel to Louis and Alphonse in equal share. I give and bequeath the seal on which the arms of my family are inscribed, to my legitimate son Dr. Jean Valleton de Boissière. I give my land, my sugar estate house, Champs Elysées, to Jean Valleton de Boissière and to his sisters Nadia Claire de Boissière and Louise Armande de Boissière. It is my will that the cemetery lot in which my father Jean Valleton de Boissière is buried, shall stand as it is and contain only him and me. I nominate John Nicholas Boissière and Auguste Bogen of Port of Spain as joint executors." (his illegitimate son and the husband of Henri's niece Poleska, who subsequently marries his legitimate son Dr. John. At the time of Henri's death, Dr. John served in the Crimean Wars and in India, at the time of the Mutiny, as an army surgeon).

The will of John Nicholas Boissière, native of Trinidad, illegitimate son of Henri Boissière. Year, 1886, No. 138.

"In the name of God etc. . . . I nominate my wife Marie Aurélie and the honourable Dr. Jean Valleton de Boissière of Champs Elysées, my half-brother, as executors and trustees of my will, and the descendants, survivors, guardians of above. As guardians of the persons and estates of my lawful infant children during their respective minorities." He leaves his silver plate, linen, furniture, books, horses, carriages, wine cellar and the other household effects to his wife. He gives all money, securities, stock in trade, to his wife for her use and all his real estate as well. He does not leave her the properties on 25 Queen and 26 Henry Street, which is described in their marriage settlement of the 12th July 1860. He goes on to say that his property may be sold by the trustees of his will as they see fit. His legacy is to be paid after his debts are settled. "$2000 to be applied to the purpose which I have already made known to my wife. £200 to my half-brother Dr. Jean Valleton de Boissière. £100 to my friend Arnold Lamy. £100 to Ms. Rosette Boissière (possibly his twin sister). £100 to my godchild, the son of my half-brother Dr. Jean Valleton de Boissière. £50 to the treasurer for the time being of the asylum established by Archbishop Spacchiapietra to be applied to the said benefit. £50 to the treasurer of the Daily Meal Society. To my son or reputed son Jules Arnold Boissière the sum of $4000, and to my daughter or reputed daughter, Marie Eliza Boissière, on her marriage or if she should die unmarried, to whomsoever she should appoint, the sum of $5000, and so long as she should reside and form part of the household of my wife, the sum of $200 being interest on the sum of $5000 at the rate of 8% per annum from the day of my death to be paid yearly." He points out that his "trustees should look after the interest of both his lawful and reputed issue, ensuring their future maintenance and education or benefit." 13th June, 1881.

The will of Marie Eliza Boissière, native of Trinidad, sister of Jules Arnold Boissière, illegitimate daughter of John Nicholas Boissière

In her will, Marie Eliza names her half-brother Jean François Boissière as her executor. He resides in London. She gives to the Chapel of the College of the Immaculate Conception $200. She leaves to rest of her real and personal property to Jean François Boissière absolutely. 15th May, 1888

She does not leave anything for her full brother Jules Boissière.

The will of Louis Boissière, merchant of Port of Spain, son of Eli Boissière who was the brother of Jean Valleton de Boissière the founder. Year, 1855, No. 42.

He nominates his first cousin Henri Boissière and John McLeod Graham, merchants of Port of Spain, as executors of his will. To his sister Esther Bonaire, the sum of £750. To the children of his late esteemed friend Mrs. Marie Reine Corslie, the following: to Philippa Corslie, the sum of £250; Julia Corslie, £100; Rosa Corslie £100; Thomas Corslie £300; "to my godson Louis Edmond Corslie £400. I give to Fanny Farquharson £1000 in consideration of her care and attention to me during some severe attacks of illness. I give to my cousins Nadia, Irma, Louise Boissière, the children of my cousin Henri Boissière, the sum of £250 each. To my goddaughter Louisa Philippe, the daughter of St. Luce Philippe (brother of Jean Baptiste Philippe, the petitioner, a coloured man) the sum of £250. To my goddaughter Victorine Savary, the daughter of Charles Louis Savary, the sum of £500. To my clerks Henry Thomas Savary and Charles Thomas Savary the sum of £300 a piece. To my friend, Ms. Caroline Dubois, the sum of £200. To my goddaughter Sophie Flament, the daughter of Joseph Flament Esq., the sum of £100. To my goddaughter Henriette, daughter of Alphonse de Sarres Esq., £100. To my godson John Graham, son of John McLeod Graham, £100. £40 to the rector of the Trinity Church, £50 to the Methodist Minister, £15 to the Presbyterian Church, £30 to the Curé of the Roman Catholic Cathedral, the above to be distributed by the above ministers to the poor and needy of the respective congregations within 12 months. To Esther Bonair, my sister, my property at Cambridge Street (Pembroke Street), to which I am entitled jointly with her, and also to her one fifth part of the property Frederick Street, recently purchased from Ajax Cadette. My property Frederick Street to Philippa, Julia and Rosa Corslie as tenants in common. Whatever remains of the estate, including all my personal belongings, to my father Eli Boissière, now residing in France, for his own use and benefit. 10th May, 1855.

The will of C. Boissière, native of Trinidad, granddaughter of Joseph Numa Bois-
sière who was the illegitimate son of Jean Valleton de Boissière, known as John
Boissière, and the African woman Zuzule (I have removed the first names of per-
sons mentioned so as to protect their privacy) Year, 1938, No. 278.

She appoints C. Boissière, her brother, or his son E., now in the United
States of America, as executors and trustees of her will. She leaves various
sums of several hundred dollars for the church and similar sums for nephews and nieces. To her grand niece P. Boissière she leaves $250, and to
her nephew S. Boissière $1800. To her Godchildren E. Troja, W. Pouchet
and A. de Silva, $100 each. The property at Dundonald Street "to my sis-
ter, R. Negretti and to her children A., I., F. and F. Ferguson as tenants in
common," Gordon Street to her niece M. Boissière. Woodford Street to
her niece E. Boissière. Edward Street, to C. Boissière. Maraval Road to her
nephew A. Paul L'Ange, the son of her sister N., or to his children Mrs. I.
Nieves, née L'Ange, N. L'Ange, V. L'Ange, T. and P. L'Ange. Edward Street to
my nieces I. Hosang and D. Boissière. All other real property etc. to her sister R. Negretti. Real estate at the time of death $31,763.42. Cash $667.84.
Cash at Barclay's Bank $5,900.00. Furniture $405.00. Shares in Queen's
Park Hotel $60.00. Trinidad and Tobago Debentures 120 pounds =
$629.33. Mortgages $3,300.00. Promissory note $200. Rent due and a
stock of 878 ft of cyp (lumber) $200.00.

The will of Henriette Elizabeth Boissière, wife of Louis Boissière, son of Henri
Boissière and Rosalie Rose of Champs Elysées, who had inherited his father's
watch and chain among other things. Year, 1900, No. 41.

"In the name of God etc. . . . to my husband Louis Boissière and to my
son Charles Leon Natividad Boissière as executors of my property. #
Abercromby Street to be sold. To my five children Charles Leon, Louis
Joseph, Amos François, Joseph, Marie Esmé, Vernon Raymond Boissière, the proceeds of the sale of the house to be divided equally. To my
grandchildren Nellie and Olive Boissière $500 each. To Charles, my son,
a special legacy of $500 as a mark of especial appreciation for his constant
and untiring care given to his father in his troubles. I give to my devoted
maid Louisa Ross $100. I give my property, 87 Abercromby Street, to my
daughter Esmé Boissière."

APPENDIX II
THE USE OF THE PARTICLE "DE"

Jean Valleton de Boissière, ecuyer, arrived in Trinidad in the company of an aunt and two younger brothers. As far as can be ascertained they arrived a short time before the Capitulation by the Spanish government to the British forces in February, 1797. He was not yet 20 years of age. "Endowed with a practical turn of mind, and entertaining no false illusions of grandeur he wisely resolved that the safest and most lucrative means of earning a satisfactory return on their money was in the mercantile sphere." (Pocock, 1993, p. 149) He appears to have been in possession of a substantial amount of capital. (Family legend claims that he had a small chest of gold coins) With in a year or so he had set himself up as a money lender and at some later stage was a slave trader in business with one Chanand.

As these occupations were not in keeping with his family's noble status he dropped the particle 'de' from his name, according to Lionel M. Fraser, 1897 in the Centenary Catalogue, "for a reason which shows that he was a man of great practical common sense. He saw that so long as he was engaged in commerce of any kind, however honourable, (slave trading!) it was absurd to bear a title of nobility.' He also Anglicised his name and was to describe himself as John Boissière. It is of interest that he took the trouble to swear to, and register, his right to the particle 'de' in the presence of a Notary, ensuring that this oath was recorded at the Town Hall of his native city, Bergerac, France as well as in Trinidad.

His sons, legal (Henri,) and illegitimate (Joseph Numa and Auguste Louis) all bore Boissière as their last name. It was his grand son Dr. Jean Valleton de Boissière, son of Henri, who first resumed the use of the particle upon his being commissioned in the British Army. He was followed by his cousin, Dr. Jean François de Valleton de Boissière, the eldest son of John Nicholas Boissière, (Henri's illegitimate son) when he established himself in France and claimed the courtesy title of Count. Since then the descendents of both these branches of the family have used the particle 'de'.

It is of interest to note that the descendents of Joseph Numa Boissière, and Auguste Louis Boissière, illegimate sons of the founder, did not use the particle "de," but some of their sons did. This family, the sons of Jean (John) de Boissière, ecuyer, and the African woman Zuzule, a product of their *plaçage,* who were born in slavery, became the most wealthy of the extended family. The descendents of the legitimate son of the founder of the family in Trinidad, Henri Boissière, were able to keep in the hands of their family the estate and Great House Champs Elysées for more than one hundred years. From their midst came legislators, soldiers and social figures, from his illegitmate son John Nicholas Boissière came the writer Ralph de Boissière, and the most significant personage in recent Trinidad history, Dr. Eric Williams.

Appendix III
SOME WILLS OF THE BESSON FAMILY

The earliest wills of the Bessons in Trinidad are at this time unavailable. The ones that hold our interest are the will of Eli François Besson de Beaumanoir of 1813, the will of the widow Besson No. 8 of 1831, and the that of Elizabeth Besson No. 16 of 1832.

Letters of Administration for Vincent Besson's estate, Year 1867, No. 50
The Supreme Civil Court of the Island of Trinidad to Andriette Darcueil of the Town of Port of Spain in the said Island widow a daughter and one of the next of kin of Vincent Besson late of the said Island of Trinidad Planter deceased Greeting whereas the said Vincent Besson as is alleged lately died intestate having whilst living and at the time of his death goods chattels or credits in the said Island of Trinidad We being desirous that the said goods chattels and credits may be well and faithfully administered applied and disposed of according to Law do therefore by these presents grant full power and authority to you in whose fidelity we confide to ad-

minister and faithfully dispose of the said goods chattels and credits and to ask demand recover and receive whatever debts and credits which whilst living and at the time of his death did in any way belong to his Estate and to pay whatever debts the said deceased at the time of his death did owe so far as such goods chattels and credits will thereto extend and the Law requires you having been already sworn well and faithfully to administer the same and to make a true and perfect inventory of all and singular the said goods chattels and credits and to exhibit the same into the Registry of the said Court or as before the twenty fourth day of September now next ensuing and also to render a just and true account thereof on or before the twenty fifth day of June which will be in the Year of Our Lord one thousand eight hundred and sixty eight and We do by these presents ordain depute and constitute your administrating of all and singular the goods chattels and credits of the said deceased.

In Witness whereof the honorable William George Knox Chief Justice of the said Island of Trinidad has hereunto set his hand and cause the Seal of the said Court to be hereunto affixed. Dated at the Court House in the Town of Port of Spain in the said Island of Trinidad this twenty fifth day of June in the Year of Our Lord one thousand eight hundred and sixty seven.

The Will of Alexander Besson, Shopkeeper in Arima, Year 1902, No 6

This is the last Will and Testament of me, Alexander Besson of the Village of Dabadie in the Ward of Arima in the Island of Trinidad, Shopkeeper. I revoke all former Wills and Testaments heretofore made by me.

I declare that I am possessed of and entitled to the following properties in the said Island of Trinidad viz:-

(A)   Four quarrees of land at Cabeeterre in the ward of Guanapo, partly planted in cocoa.

(B)   Two lots of land with business premises thereon, viz:-Provision and rum shops in the village of Dabadie.

(C)   One lot of land with dwelling house thereon on the Lopinot Road in the Ward of Tacarigua.

(D)   Six shares in the Trinidad Building and Loan Association valued at One Thousand Five Hundred Dollars ($1.500).

I give devise and bequeath all my above-named properties and shares in the Building and Loan Association of Trinidad to my lawful wife Angelina Besson her heirs and designs subject to the payment of all my just debts, funeral and testamentary expenses. I appoint, nominate and constitute Angelina Besson , my lawful wife, as the sole executrix of this my last will and testament.

In witness whereof I have hereunto set my hand this twentieth day of January in the year of our Lord One Thousand Nine Hundred.

Alexander Besson signed with two Chinese characters, and was witnessed by Sydney Smith as "his mark".

The Will of Eusebia Lazarina Besson, Year 1919, No. 204

This is the last Will and Testament of me Eusebia Lazarina Besson, the wife of Leon Besson, of the Town of Arima in the Island of Trinidad, married woman hereby revoking all wills or testamentary dispositions by me at any time heretofore made and declaring this to be my last will.

I devise and bequeath all real and personal property which I may die seized or to which I may be entitled at the time of my death unto my husband Leon Besson In Trust as regards of the share of the Estate I inherited under my late father's will and subject thereto to apply the profits arising therefrom to the education and maintenance of my infant son Joseph Ambroise Besson during his minority. When he shall have attained twenty one years of age then to assure the said property unto and to the use of my son Joseph Ambroise absolutely.

I appoint my said husband Leon Besson guardian of my son aforesaid and also Executor and Trustee of this will. In witness whereof I have hereunto set my hand in the town of Arima this twenty sixth day of May in the year of our Lord One thousand nine hundred and eighteen.

The Will of Leonide Besson, Year 1869, No. 50

This is the last will and testament of me Leonide Besson of the Town of Port of Spain in the Island of Trinidad Singlewoman revoking as I do hereby revoke all former wills or other testamentary dispositions heretofore made by me.

After payment of all my just debts funeral and testamentary expenses I give grant decree and bequeath all my property both real and personal of whatever value or kind and wheresoever found of which I may die possessed of or entitled to unto my infant children Frederick Louis Latour and Louisa Ultima Latour their heirs executors administrators and assigns absolutely and forever. In the event of either of my said children dying before attaining the age of twenty one years and without bearing lawful issue then and in such case the share of the one so dying shall revert to the survivor of them; but in case both of my said children shall die before attaining the age of twenty one years and without leaving lawful issue then I give grant decree and bequeath all my said property, real and personal, unto Louis Latour of the said Town of Port of Spain, Gentleman, his heirs executors administrators and assigns absolutely and for ever.

I hereby constitute and appoint the said Louis Latour and George Ajax Cadet of the Plantation "Trafalgar" in the Ward of Chaguanas, Planter, the executors of this my will and the guardians of my said infant children during their minority. In witness whereof I have hereunto set my hand at Port of Spain aforesaid this first day of December in the year of our Lord one thousand eight hundred and seventy four.

The Will of Frederick Besson, Freed African, Year 1870, No. 15
(parts of the will are not legible due to photocopying)
In the name of the Father, the Son and the Holy Ghost. Amen.

I, Frederick Besson, a native of Africa, now living in the District of Mayaro in the said Island, Laborer, being of sound and disposing mind and memory, and understanding, do make … ordain this my last will and testament in the manner following:

First and principally I resign my soul to God Almighty and hope for …. Through the mercie of my blessed …. "Jesus Christ". I desire to be … [buried] at the discretion of my executors …. herein after named but without any …. pomp.

As to my temporal Estate I dispose there of as follows: I name and constitute … Elizabeth Nicholson and Mr. Stephen … of the said District of Mayaro to be my Executors. I declare that my property of two quarrees of land being a portion of "Marguerite Estate" situate in the aforesaid District of Mayaro together with all and singular of the buildings, hereditaments [?] and appertenances thereunto attached, belonging and appertaining respectively. I give and bequeath to Elizabeth Nicholson two quarrees of lands as been afore mentioned. The said two quarrees of land to be by her the said Elizabeth Nicholson possessed and for and during the term of her …. Life and after her decease to descend …. Three children together with all and every … or augmentations which the said Elisabeth … son shall have made on the said two quarrees of land which shall be divided in three portions for their three children viz Joseph Besson, Felicianne Besson and Marie Marguerite Besson, and after the death of the said Elizabeth Nicholson whatever I may have or … to be possessed, enjoyed, and dispoed of by the said Joseph Besson, Felicianne Besson and Marie Marguerite Besson and I do hereby revoke and annul all former Wills or Codicils by me and any time heretofore made declaring this to be my last Will and Testament. In witness whereof I have hereunto set my hand and seal in the Quarter of Mayaro this sixth day of December in the year of our Lord one thousand eight hundred and sixty nine.

He signed with his mark, X .

APPENDIX IV
DESCENDANTS OF GERALDINE CARIGE

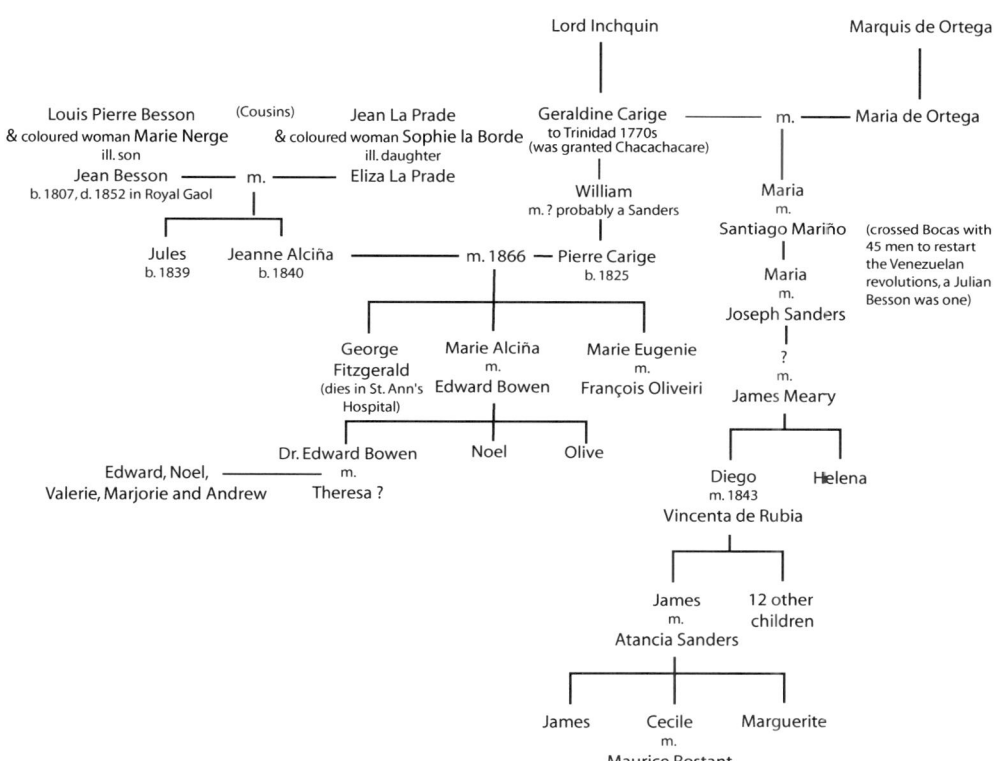

Lord Inchquin

Marquis de Ortega

Louis Pierre Besson
& coloured woman **Marie Nerge**
ill. son

(Cousins)

Jean La Prade
& coloured woman **Sophie la Borde**
ill. daughter

Geraldine Carige
to Trinidad 1770s
(was granted Chacachacare)

m.

Maria de Ortega

Jean Besson
b. 1807, d. 1852 in Royal Gaol

m.

Eliza La Prade

William
m. ? probably a Sanders

Maria
m.
Santiago Mariño

(crossed Bocas with
45 men to restart
the Venezuelan
revolutions, a Julian
Besson was one)

Jules
b. 1839

Jeanne Alciña
b. 1840

m. 1866

Pierre Carige
b. 1825

Maria
m.
Joseph Sanders

George
Fitzgerald
(dies in St. Ann's
Hospital)

Marie Alciña
m.
Edward Bowen

Marie Eugenie
m.
François Oliveiri

?
m.
James Meary

Dr. Edward Bowen
m.
Theresa ?

Noel

Olive

Diego
m. 1843
Vincenta de Rubia

Helena

Edward, Noel,
Valerie, Marjorie and Andrew

James
m.
Atancia Sanders

12 other
children

James

Cecile
m.
Maurice Rostant

Marguerite

BIBLIOGRAPHY

Baigent, Michael; Leigh, Richard and Lincoln, Henry. *The Messianic Legacy*. London: Transworld Publications Ltd., 1987

Besson, Gerard and Brereton, Bridget. *The Book of Trinidad*. Port-of-Spain: Paria Publishing Co. Ltd., 1986

Besson, William W. *The Life and Times of a Trinidad Scholar*. London: Karia Press, 2001.

Bodu, J.M. *Trinidadiana*. Trinidad, 1900

Boodhoo, Ken. *The Elusive Eric Williams*. Port-of-Spain: Prospect Press, 2002

Borde, Pierre Gustave Louis. *The History of the Island of Trinidad Under the Spanish Government*. Port-of-Spain: Paria Publishing Co. Ltd. 1982. First published, Paris 1883

Brereton, Bridget. "Contesting the Past: Narratives of Trinidad and Tobago History". In: *New West Indian Guide*, Vol. 81, No. 3&4, 2007, pp. 169–196

- *History of Modern Trinidad 1783–1962*. Kingston, Port-of-Spain and London: Heinemann, 1981
- *Race Relations in Colonial Trinidad*. Cambridge University Press, 1979

Brizan, George and Brizan, Kwamina. *Grenada Fortitude and the Human Condition*. Port-of-Spain: Republic Bank and CL Financial Limited, 2001

- and Jessamy, Michael. *St. George's – The Prettiest Town in the West Indies*, Grenada: Züblin, 2004

Campbell, Carl. *Cedulants and Capitulants*. Port-of-Spain: Paria Publishing Co. Ltd.,1992

Carmichael, Gertrude. *The History of the East Indian Islands of Trinidad and Tobago*. Port-of-Spain: Columbus Publishers,1961

Coupland, Reginald. "The British Anti-Slavery Movement", London 1933. In Williams, Eric. *Capitalism and Slavery*; and in James, C.L.R.: *Black Jacobins*.

Coleridge, Henry Nelson. *Six months in the West Indies*. London: John Murray 1825.

Cox, Edward. "Fédon's Rebellion 1795-96; Causes and Consequences", in: *The Journal of Negro History*, Vol. LXVII 1982

Craig-James, Susan E. *The Changing Society of Tobago 1838-1938–A Fractured Whole*. Port-of-Spain: Cornerstone Press, 2008

Daniel, Edward W. *West Indian Histories*. London: Thomas Nelson and Sons,1936

de Boissière, Jean Antonio. "The French in Trinidad", in: Land of the Rising Inflection, ca. 1944

Devas, Raymond P. "A History of the Island of Grenada", 1498-1796. In: Cox, Edward.

de Verteuil, Anthony. *To Find Freedom*. Port-of-Spain 1998

- *The Corsicans in Trinidad*. Port-of-Spain 2005
- The *Black Earth of South Naparima*. Port-of-Spain 2009
- *Seven Slaves & Slavery: Trinidad 1777 - 1838*. Port of Spain 1992

Deosaran, Ramesh. *Eric Williams, The Man, His Ideas, And His Politics.* Trinidad: Signum Publishing Company Limited, 1981

Driggs, Seth. *Freemason's Sure Guide*, Port-of-Spain 1819

Durant, Will and Ariel: *The Age of Faith.* New York: Simon & Schuster, 1961

- *The Age of Reason Begins.* New York: Simon & Schuster, 1961
- *The Age of Voltaire.* New York: Simon & Schuster, 1961
- *The Age of Napoleon.* New York: Simon & Schuster, 1961
- *Rousseau and Revolution.* New York: Simon & Schuster, 1961

Edwards, Bryan. *The History, Civil and Commercial of the British Colonies in the West Indies. Vol. III* London, 1807.

Engerman, Stanley and Solow, Barbara. *British Capitalism and Caribbean Slavery: The Legacy of Eric Williams.* Cambridge University Press 2004.

Espinet, Ramabai. *Nowarian Blues.* Published in *Trinidad Noir.* Ed. Lisa Allen-Agostini and Jeanne Mason. New York: Akashic Books, 2008

Fernández, Américo. *Historia del Estado Boliva.* Ciudad Bolívar: Editora Boscán C.A., 1994. In: Parra Pérez, Caracciolo and Mendoza, Cristóbal L.: *Historia de la Primera Republica de Venezuela*

Fox-Davies, Arthur Charles. *A Complete Guide To Heraldry.* New York: Bonanza Books, 1978

Franklin, C.B. *Yearbook of 1916.* Port-of-Spain 1916

Henry, Frances. *He had the Power, Pa Neezer, The Orisha King of Trinidad:* A personal Memoir: Lexicon Trinidad Ltd, 2008.

Fraser, Lionel Mordaunt. *History of Trinidad.* London: Frank Cass & Co Ltd., 1971

Harricharan, J. T. *The Catholic Church in Trinidad 1498 - 1852.* Trinidad: Inprint Caribbean Ltd., 1981

Hearn, Lafcadio. *Two Years in the French West Indies.* United States: Harper Brothers, 1923

Higgins, Donald. *A History of Trinidad Oil.* Port-of-Spain: Trinidad Express Newspapers Ltd., 1996

James C.L.R. *Black Jacobins.* New York: Vintage Books, 1989

Joseph, E.L. *History of Trinidad*, re-published by H.M. Hodley/Columbus Publishers Ltd., originally published 1837

Johnson, Paul, - *Modern Times.* New York: Harper Collins Publishers, 1991
  - *The Birth of the Modern.* New York: Harper Collins Publishers, 1999

Kein, Sybil (ed.). *In Creole.* Baton Rouge: Louisiana State Press, 2000

Kunczik, Michael. *Communication and Social Change.* Bonn : Friedrich-Ebert-Stiftung, 1993

Lalla, Kenneth. "Indian Influence in Constitutional Reform" in: *In Celebration of 150 years of the Indian Contribution to Trinidad and Tobago*, Diane Seukeran (ed.), Trinidad 1995

Leahy, Vincent. *The Catholic Church in Trinidad* Vol. II. Port-of-Spain: St. Dominic Press, 1980
  - *Bishop James Buckley, 1820–1828.* Port-of-Spain: St. Dominic Press, 1980

Lebeau. *De la Condition des Gens de Couleur Libres sous l'Ancien Regime.* Poitiers, 1903. Cited in James, C.L.R.. *The Black Jacobins*

Léotaud, Charles. *Memoirs of an Honourable Gentleman,* Edited by Dillon and Claudette Léotaud, Port-of-Spain 1980.

Mahabir, Winston. *In and out of Politics*. Port-of-Spain: Inprint Caribbean Ltd. 1978

Marryat, Joseph. *Thoughts on the Abolition of the Slave Trade*, London 1813.

Marx, Karl. *A Contribution to the Critique of Political Economy*. 1859 (internet)

Massé, Abbé. *The Diaries of Abbé Massé 1878 - 1883 Vol. IV*. Port-of-Spain, 1988

Mavrogordato, O.J. *Voices in the Street*. Port-of-Spain: Paria Publishing Co. Ltd., 1996

Meacham Gould, Virginia (ed.). "Chained to the rock of Adversity, To be free, black and female in the old South", The University Georgia Press, 1998

Meighoo, Kirk. *Politics in a Half-made Society*. Kingston: Ian Randle Publishers, 2003

Mijares, Augusto. *The Liberator, North American Association of Venezuela*. Caracas 1983

Naipaul, V.S. *The Loss of El Dorado*. London: André Deutsch, 1969
    - *A Way in the World*. London: André Deutsch, 1994

Obama, Barack. *The Audacity of Hope*. Random House Inc., 2008

Palmer, Colin A. *Eric Williams & The Making of the Modern Caribbean*, University of North Carolina Press 2006

Parra Pérez, Caracciolo and Mendoza, Cristóbal L. *Historia de la Primera Republica de Venezuela*. Caracas: Biblioteca Ayacucho, 1992

Pinel, Monsieur. "A Topographical Description of the Island of Grenada surveyed 1763", in: Paterson, Daniel. London: W. Faden, 1780

Pocock, Michael. *Out of the Shadows of the Past*. Hastings, 1993

Revauger, Cécile (ed.). *Lumières, No. 7 Franc-maçonnerie, et politique au siècle des Lumières: Europe-Amériques*. Bordeaux: CIBEL, 2006

Rodriguez, Junios P. *Encyclopedia of Slave Resistance and Rebellion*. 2007

Rohlehr, Gordon. *The Shape of that Hurt*. Port-of-Spain: Longman Trinidad Limited, 1992
    - *My Strangled City*. Port-of-Spain: Longman Trinidad Limited, 1992

Rouse-Jones D. M. *The Colonial Bank Correspondence 1837-1885*. St. Augustine: University of the West Indies Press, 1987

Ryan, Selwyn (ed.). *The Independence Experience*. St. Augustine: Institute of Social and Economic Research, University of the West Indies, 1988
    - *Eric Williams–The Myth and the Man*. St. Augustine: University of the West Indies Press, 2009

Steele, Beverley. *Grenada: A History of its People*. Oxford: Macmillan, 2003

Stewart, Trevor: *William Hutchinson (1732–1814). An 18th Century English Freemason and Ani-Slavery Dramatist*, in: Revauger, Cécile (ed.). *Lumières, No. 7 Franc-maçonnerie, et politique au siècle des Lumières: Europe-Amériques*. Bordeaux: CIBEL, 2006

Tothill, Vincent. *Trinidad's Doctor's Office*. Trinidad: Paria Publishing, 2009

Turnbull, Stephen. *The Book of the Medieval Knight*. London: Arms and Armour Press, 1985

Smith, Lloyd Sydney (ed.). *Who, What, and Why, 1955-56 (The British Caribbean)*. Glasgow: Bell & Bain Ltd. 1955

Williams, Eric. *British Historians and the West Indies*, Port-of-Spain: PNM Publishing Co. Ltd., 1964.
    - *Capitalism and Slavery*. London: Andre Deutsch, 1964
    - *From Columbus to Castro*. London: Andre Deutsch, 1970

- *Inward Hunger.* Princeton: Markus Wiener Publishers, 2006. First published in 1942

- *The Economic Aspect of the Abolition of the British West Indian Slave Trade and Slavery* (internet)

- *The Negro in the Caribbean.* Brooklyn, New York: A&B Books Publishers, 1994

Wood, Donald. *Trinidad in Transition– the Years after Slavery.* Oxford University Press, 1968

Wooding, H.O.B. *A Collection of Addresses.* Trinidad & Tobago: Government Printing Office, 1968

INTERNET REFERENCES:

Brogues, Anthony. *Black Heretics Black Prophets*

Drescher, Seymour. "From Slavery to Freedom: Comparative Studies in the Rise and Fall of Atlantic Slavery". In: Anstey, Roger. *The Atlantic Slave Trade and British Abolition, 1760-1810.* Gregg Revivals; New edition (1993)

Lewis, Gordon K., Maingot, Anthony P. *Main Currents in Caribbean Thought*

Loney, William. R.N. *The West African Squadron*

Loosemore, Jo. *Sailing Against Slavery*

Rodriguez, Junius P. *Encyclopedia of Slave Resistance and Rebellion*

Roget, Jacques Petitjean. *The Superior French Staff of the Island of Grenada in 1782.* After "The Precious Firsts of Grenada", Cahier 15 of CC-HIA 1986 (Rossignol, genealogical forum)

Vendryes, A. *The French Revolution in Grenada.* Translation by David Watson and Ernest Wiltshire (Rossignol, genealogical forum)

The Oxford Dictionary of National Biography

OTHER REFERENCES:

Arima Catholic Church Santa Rosa records of births, marriages and deaths

Arima Town Hall records

Benjamin Franklin Papers, University of Pennsylvania 1705-1788

Besson, Alice: The History of Neal & Massy, unpublished manuscript, UWI Library, St Augustine

Callaloo - Volume 20, Number 4, Fall 1997

Collas, Henri: *Besson–Essai de Monographie.* Mairie de Besson,1968. (unpublished manuscript)

Cathedral of the Immaculate Conception records of births, marriages and deaths

Gallia Regia

Grand Armorial de France

Grenada Handbook 1909

Inventaires et documents publiés par ordre L' Empéreur titres de la Maison Ducal Bourbon. Huilard-Breholles , Book 1. Paris 1807.

L'Armorial du Bourbonnais

L'Armorial General de France 1696

Lee, Simon: Literary Foundations: "CLR James's contribution to initiating Creole discourses and defining Creole Space," unpublished manuscript

Lodge records of Les Frères Unis 251 S.C.

Lodge records of Royal Prince of Wales 867 E.C.

Mavrogordato, Olga. Our Ancestors, unpublished manuscript. 1966, (Rowena Scott.)

McDaniel, Lorna: "Madame Philip-O: Jeanette Free Negro Woman", unpublished manuscript

Odorici: Recherches sur Dinan et ses Environs, 1977

Port-of-Spain Gazette news papers.

Port-of-Spain Town Book, a registry of real estate transactions, 1810-1870

Seemungal, Lionel: Compendium of Masonry in Trinidad & Tobago, Vol. 1: 1794 - 1820 Paper No. 26 (manuscript)

   - Notes on Members of Les Frères Unis [L.U.B: 251 S C] from its transfer to Trinidad in 1794, Paper No. 74. (manuscript)

   - The First Erection and Consecration of Lodge United Brothers No. 251 SC under the Grand Orient of France 1789. (lecture paper)

   - with Acosta, José Angel: The Rose Croix and Higer Degrees in Trinidad (1795-1975), Trinidad Kilwinning Ancient & Accepted Scottish Rite Bodies in Trinidad, 1980

Registre Heralogique de d'Hozier: Registres de dessins de l'Armorial de France de 1696

Registres Paroissiaux de Gosier (Guadeloupe) and the baptismal registry of Pons.

Registrar General's Office in Port-of-Spain, records of births, marriages, deaths and wills

Rev. hist. de l'Ouest, Doc I, 52w

Trinidad Guardian newspapers

Trinidad slave registers, index to claims [T71/939]

INDEX

(p) = picture

1990 attempted coup 248

A

Abbé Armand Massé 129
Abbé Besson 88
Abbé Massé 129
Abbé Peissonier 63
Abbé Raynal 31, 69
Abbey of Cluny 20
Abercromby Street 117
Abolition of the Slave Trade Act 160
African slave woman (p) 72
Alston, Lieut-Col. George R. G. (p) 217
Alstons Group of Companies 216
Angostura 245
Antonmattei, Simon 91
Ariapita 41
Arima 133
Ashwood-Garvey, Amy 144
Aunis 19

B

Balthazar estate 32, 48, 63
Bandung generation 238
Barrie, François la 48
Beauford, Simon de 31
Beauvais, Louis 81
Behson, Hugo and Rotilde 20
Bellevue 33
Bellevue, Domaine de (Tanzac) 50
Bellevue estate 48, 85
   sale for debt 90
Bellevue estate, oil wells 98
Bellevue (p) 25
Belvedere estate (purchased by Fédon) 35, 41
Berio, Jacob 50
Bertram de Clisson 27
Besson
   Adrienette 91
   arms of 16

Charles (son of François) 42
compensation received at abolition (1838) 93
Eli François Xavier 16
François (death in 1826) 91
François Étienne (son of François) 31
François fils 42
François' move to Trinidad 47
island scholarship winners 119
Julien (Immortal 45) 79
Junian 19
Louis Eli (brother of François) 31
Marie Françoise Adelaïde 17, 81
Marie Louise (daughter of François) 31
Oliver de 27
Pierre 16
Pierre (sailing from Marseilles) 54
Property on Marine Square (p) 101
Stanislas 62
Stanislas, son of François? 79
village in France 17
Besson, Adèle 125
Besson, Alexander (native of China) 119
Besson: Chacachacare connection 126
Besson, Charles François 101, 105
Besson, Charles François (death in 1872) 105
Besson, Charles Frederick 102
Besson, Charles Jospeh (death in 1872) 105
Besson, Dr. William (island scholarship winner) 119
Besson, Emmanuel Léon 113, 132
Besson, end of the family's interest in South Trinidad 100
Besson, family businesses by Charles François and by Gerard 101
Besson family grave at Lapeyrouse cemetery 134
Besson family of Toco 104
Besson family, poverty 102
Besson, Frederick 103

Besson, Frederick (native of Africa) 103
Besson, Henri Numa 113
Besson, Herman (high court judge) 119
Besson house at Oxford and St. Vincent
        Streets (p) 118
Besson, Jeanne Alciña 126
Besson, Jean (wars of liberation) 105
Besson, Joseph Ambrosio 135
Besson, Joseph Ambrosio (p) 135
Besson, Joseph Léon 134
Besson, Pierre Besson (wars of liberation) 105
Bessons in Freemasonry: Julien, Pierre Jean,
        Jean, Jean, Charles François, Charles
        Frederick, Pierre Numa 121
Besson Street 50, 102, 131
Besson: Venezuelan connection 125
Besson, Vincent 104
Bettius 20
Black Caribs 188
Black Caribs in St. Vincent (p) 64
Black nationalism 201
Black Power uprising of 1970 240
Blanchard, Marie Louise de 29
Boissière, Eliza (mother of Eric Williams) 189
Boissière, Eliza (mother of Eric Williams) (p)
        183
Boissière, Ella 136
Boissière House (p) 197
Bolívar, Simón 79, 105, 125
Bonaparte, Napoleon 87
Bosanquet & Fatio 35
Boue-John 50
Bourbon L'Archambault 20
Brigands' War 56
Brousse 19
Building and Loan Association 175
Bulam fever 50
Businessmen of African descent 171
Buxton, Thomas 145

C

Cadiz, Stephen 235
Cadiz Topp, Elizabeth 235
Calypsonians 231
Campbell, James 41

Candomblé 58
Canteloupe de Bourdieu family 87
Capildeo, Rudranath 225
Caracas 42
Caribbean Development Company 216
Carige, Gerald 126
Carige, Pierre 126
Carting Sugar (p) 69
Cassar 48
Cedula of Population of 1783 32, 47, 55, 58
    Terms 47
Census of Trinindad 1946 163
Census Trinidad 1783 45
Census Trinidad 1784 53
Census Trinidad 1797 84
C'est Quitte 235, 247
Chacachacare 79
Chacachacare (p) 126
Chacón, Don José María 83, 133
Champs Elysées 41
Champs Elysées (p) 46, 74
Charles François Besson & Company 105
Charles the Great 20
Charras, Bertrand de 35
Chatoyer 188
Chatoyer (p) 64
Christophe, Henri (p) 61
Cipriani, Jules 117
Cipriani, Leon 117
Cipriani, Mikey (p) 115
Clarkson, Thomas 145
Cocoa economy 171
Code Civil de France (Code Napoleon) 87
Cold War 176
Coloured society of the New World 69
    social pressures 71
Comissiong, Domingo 184
Comissiong Family (p) 182
Commodore Swanton 27
Compulsory Manumission clause 90
Congress of Vienna in 1815 160
Conquest of Trinidad by the British 1797 83
Cooperative Bank 175
Cortes, Louis 91
Count de Cerillac 18

Count de Poullain (Joseph Alexander)er) 32
Count D'Estaing 33
Count de Tovar (Francisco Nicolas) 125
Creole society 178
Cumberland House 117
Cumberland House (p) 116
Cummings, Margaret 102
Cutting canes (p) 74

D

Darmanie, Laurencine 113
Darmanie, Rose Celine 42
Darmanie, Rose Laurencine 104
de Boissière 77
de Boissière family 191
de Boissière, Poleska 194, 219
de Boissière, Poleska (p) 194
de Gannes 18, 34
  bankrupcy 35
  Rose 34
  Rose, establishment in Maraval 85
  Simon 34
de l'Isle, Eusibia Lazarine 131, 135
de l'Isle, Henri Paulin Josse 131
de Jacques de la Bastide (p) 110
de la Bastide, Jean Baptiste 113
de Lande, Rose 117
Delpeche, Jean and Jeanne 33
Democratic Labour Party 213
de Poullain, Jules Édouard 87
de Rabot family 87
D'Imbert 32
Drago, Armante 102
Drourad 19
Duc D'Orleans 33
Duquesne estate 35

E

Economic Problems of Trinidad and Tobago
  208
Elections 1956 Crowdshot (p) 226
Enteric fever 135
Esnard
  Marguerite 17, 19

Marianne 17
Espinet, Charles Sydney 222
Espinet Family (p) 222
Espinet (née Hunt), Sarah 222
Espinet, Sarah née Hunt (p) 223

F

Farquhar, Canon Max 225
Faut-Huerne, Henriette 104, 113
Fédon, Julien 40, 151, 228
  French citizens executed by Fédon uprising
    66
  revolution 56
  Slaves 41
  uprising, Prisoners condemned to the gal-
    lows 67
Fédon rebels (p) 61, 63
Fifi family 113
Filles du roi 76
Flavigny 32
Fleury 19
Form for compensation of slave owners (p)
  96
Fouquet 19
François fils, death in 1831 92
Free blacks and people of colour 34, 44, 51,
  165, 185
Free Coloured revolt 56
Freed Africans 165
French and an African presence in Spanish
  Trinidad 51
French colonial pioneers 57
French colonists 51, 83, 164
French forces (p) 43
French planter families 47
French planter interest 32
French planters of Grenada 41

G

Ganteaume de Monteau (p) 106
Ganteaume family (p) 108
Ganteaume, Pierre Alphonse 125
Gatcliffe, Thomas 245
Gellizeau, Pauline 134

Gibson, Ralph 245
Gomes, Albert 217, 225
Gomez, Gerry 216
Gordon Grant & Co 171
Gouyave 41, 63
Goveia, Elsa 241
Green Street 134
Grenada, Map of (p) 21
Grenada's development at the end of the 18th century 45
Grenada, surrender of the French 27
Grenada was formerly returned to the France 33
Grenville 62, 68
Gru Gru Palm (p) 89
Guadeloupe, plan of attack 1759 (p) 39
Guanapo 133
Guapo 48, 84, 92
Guapo, oil wells found 98
Guira, Angelo 91
Guira, François 91

H

Henry Street 50, 84, 104
Hezekiah, Sheelagh 120
History of the People of Trinidad and Tobago 209
Hogshead in boat (p) 80
Home, Ninian 59
Honoré, Rose 105
Hugues, Victor 59
Hunt, Jean Baptiste 185
Hunt, Onemia Wilhelmina Jane 186
Hunt, Sarah 222
Hurricanes 33

I

Immortal 45 79, 121
Immortal 45 (p) 126
Indian indentured workers 168
Indians: stereotyped perceptions 169

J

James, C.L.R. 237

early influences on Williams 143
Firing by Eric Williams 229
James, C.L.R. (p) 154
Joachim, André 136
Joachim, Margaret (wife of Joseph Ambrosio Besson) 136
Johnson, Sir Edgar Gaston 188
Jones, Claudia 144
Jordan Hill estate 101
Julien, Pierre Bartholomew 30

K

Katronice, Geneviève 81
Keith Noel 136 Committee 235
Kenyatta, Jomo 144
Knox, Sydney 245

L

Labastide, Roseilie 117
Laborde, Philippa 181
La Fille de Couleur (p) 73
La Fortunée estate 48, 90
La Fortunée estate, oil wells found 98
Lambert, Fanny 81
Lande d'Aussac, Rose de 113
Landon 19
La Prade
    Elizabeth 32
    Jean Baptiste 29
    Marie 29
la Prade, Elizabeth 104
La Romaine estate 48, 92
La Rouque, Jean Delpèche de 31
Lascarie, Madeleine 31
Lataste estate 35
Latour, Louis 91
Latour, Rose 105
La Valette, Pierre 62
Lefer, Louis (p) 108
Léon, JOseph 131
L'Épine, Rochard 31, 81
Les Frères Unis 105, 124
Les Frères Unis: 19th century membership 127

Limoges (p) 19, 23
l'Isle, Simon Josse 136
Lodge Eastern Star 124, 131
Lodge United Brothers 124
Lodge United Brothers (p) 129
Lord Hailes 120
L'Ouverture, Paul 81
L'Ouverture, Toussaint 55, 81
L'Ouverture, Toussaint (p) 60

M

Malcolm, Anthony 30
Manley, Norman 144, 212
Mansfield, L.C.J. 145
Maraj, Badase 218
Maraval 41
Mariages de la main gauche, 76
Marine Square 50
Mariño, Santiago (p) 126
Martineau, Reine (third wife of François) 51, 91
Marxist/Trotskyite worldview 143
Masonic Diploma (p) 122
Maupeon, René Nicholas de 30
McEnearney-Alstons 245
Milne-Home 120
Molenier 18
Moral relativism 151, 238
Moruga 92
Mossion 19
Mount D'Or estate 87
Mount Qua Qua 66
Mount Tamana (p) 132

N

Naparima 48, 54, 84, 98
Naparima Hill (p) 80
N. Besson & Co. 113
Neal & Massy 245
Negress with child (p) 75
New generation of business leaders 245
New World cults 58
Nkrumah, Kwame 144
Noel 18, 48

Nogues, Charles 41, 62

O

Oath of allegiance to the King of England 32
Obama, Barack 253
O'Brien, Rosa Anna 102
O'Connor brothers and their sister (p) 108
O'Connor, Eliza (p) 109
O'Connor, Philip (p) 108
Ogé, Vincent 58, 149
Ogé, Vincent (p) 61
Old King 188
Olivier 18
Olivier, Benoît 92

P

Padmore, George 144
Papal Bull 128
Papal Bulls issued against Freemasonry 128
Paradise estate 35
Party of Political Groups 217
Party of Political Progress Groups 217
Pére Labat 30
Perseverance estate house (p) 114
Petit Havre, estate 33
Petitions for Abolition 156
Philippe, Joachim 62, 63
Pierre, first Duke of Bourbon 27
Pitch Lake 50
Pitch Lake (p) 52
Pitch Lake Palm (p) 88
Pitt, Prime Minister 149
Plaçage 76, 117, 185
Plenet, Jean Joseph Marie de 87
PNM
    Redrafting of voting boundaries 213
Pocock, Michael 218
Pocock, Michael Rogers (p) 219
Point Salines estate 32, 33, 48
Poitou 17, 19, 34
Pons (p) 16, 24
Port-of-Spain 50
Port-of-Spain, Marine Square (p) 82
Port-of-Spain (p) 49, 103, 163

Professionals of African descent in the 19th
    century 166
Progressive Democratic Party 217
Prudhomme 18

Q

QUARTI CURA 128
Queen's Royal College (p) 143
Queen Street 113

R

Racism
    Examples from the Press 172
Red ant infestation 33
Reform Movement 175
Rennison, Columbe 102
Respectability 179
Retraîte estate 87
Richmond estate 31, 33, 48
Robespierre 61, 149
Robinson, Sir Harold (p) 220
Robles, Marclina 50
Rochard L'Épine family 42
Rochard L'Epine, Thomas Daniel 81
Rochard, Marianne Elizabeth 81
Rohlehr, Gordon 240, 249
Roman Catholicism 57
Roman Catholic men in Freemasonry 121
Rookery Nook (p) 178
Roume, Laurent Philippe 34
Roume, Philippe Rose 32, 34, 81
    (purchasing land in Trinidad) 41
Roume, Philippe Rose (p) 36
Roume, Rosette 82
Roume - spellings Room, Roome, Ruim,
    Rome, Röhm 42
Roux, Joseph 91
Ruim, Marie 42

S

Saint Domingue 55
Saint Joseph Convent girls (p) 184

Saintonge 17, 19
Santería 58
Scapegoating 236
Seven Year War 30
Shango 58
Simon & Hankey 48
Simon, L.A.R. de 30
Slaves 28, 34, 42, 48, 50, 51, 53, 73, 90, 164
    Abolition of slavery in Saint Domingue in
        1793 59
    Abolition of Slave Trade 1807 86
    payments received from the British govern-
        ment by the Bessons 93
    revolt in Grenada 30
    Slave Amelioration Regulations published
        in 1823 89
Smith, Philippa Susannah 181
Smith, Sir Charles 181
Sorzano, Marie Léontine 133
Sorzano Street 134
Sorzano, Thomas 134
Soubise estate 17, 31, 42, 81
Souvigny (p) 23
St. Genis de Saintonge 87
St. George estate 87
St. George's (p) 16, 20, 43
St. Laurent estate 34
St. Martin, church of (p, Besson) 22
Stollmeyer, Jeffery 216
St. Saturnin, church of (p, Tanzac) 26
Sugar Duties Act 100

T

Tanzac 50
Tanzac, village of 19
Tardieu, Honoré 48
The Black Jacobins
    Examination of pages 38-41 153
The People's Charter 208
The Wilderness (p) 130
Thibaudeau 19
Thibaudeau, Antoine 87
Thibaudeau, Elizabeth (wife of Pierre Besson)

16
Third World leaders 238
Treaty of Paris 29
Treaty of Versailles 44
Trievia estate 35
Trinidad Clay Products 216
Trinidad: Map of the Pitch Lake area (p) 52
Trinidad: South-West Peninsula map (p) 98
Trinidad: Whittle map of 1797 (p) 49
Tugs and Lighters 216

U

University of Woodford Square 206

V

Valleton de Boissière, Dr. Jean (p) 179
Valleton de Boissière Family (p) 183
Ventour, Etienne 63
Vettius 20
Victimhood 53
Victors of the colonial experience 243
Voodoo 58
Vouyours, Chatillon de 33

W

Waltham estate 34
Wars of Liberation (Besson involvement) 105
West Indian immigration to Trinidad 166
West Indian Slave Trade 38
Wight, Sir Gerald 214
Wight, Sir Gerald (p) 218
Wilberforce, Abolitionist 149
Wilberforce, William 145
Williams, Eliza
   character 195
Williams, Eric
   And 18th Century revolutionaries 202, 228
   and his father (p) 155
   and Sir Gerald Wight 214
   "anxiety-driven creativity" 200
   as French Creole man 179
   change in personality created by the loss of
      social status 199

compensatory striving 205
Conspiracy theories 148
Doctoral thesis 144
Economic/expediency theory for the aboli-
   tion of the slave trade 61
Effects of his narrative 248
Experiences at Oxford 212
Houses that he lived in 198
Influences in his youth 143
In Woodford Square (p) 215
personality cult 207
politics of victimhood and guilt 230
public lectures at Woodford Square 206
Racial mix in his own person 152
Reasons for abolition of the slave trade 145
"red man's" complex 199
Relationship to James paralleled to Robespi-
   erre/Ogé 149
Treatment of non-creole segments in his
   literature 209
With the Princess Royal (p) 231
Williams, Eric (p)
   Pictures with his relatives 182
Williams family
   aristocratic British officers 181
   as slave-owners 181
   Financial & social setbacks 177
   French nobility 184
   housing problem 198
   loss of inheritance by Jules Boissière 189
   loss of inheritance by Onemia 187
   Williams/Hunt/Smith/Commissiong 180
Williams, James Thomas 187, 188
Williams, Thomas Henry (father of Eric) 189
Williams, Thomas Henry (father of Eric Wil-
   liams) (p) 182
Willoughby, Olive née Hunt (p) 223
Women, slave and free coloured 77
Workingmen's Association 175

LaVergne, TN USA
07 October 2010
199794LV00001B